THE IDEA OF THE MIRACULOUS

Also by T. C. Williams

THE CONCEPT OF THE CATEGORICAL IMPERATIVE
THE UNITY OF KANT'S *CRITIQUE OF PURE REASON*

The Idea of the Miraculous

The Challenge to Science and Religion

T. C. Williams

Professor of Philosophy
The University of Guelph, Ontario

St. Martin's Press   New York

© T. C. Williams, 1990
All rights reserved. For information, write:
Scholarly and Reference Division,
St. Martin's Press, Inc., 175 Fifth Avenue,
New York, N.Y. 10010

First published in the United States of America in 1991

Printed in Great Britain

ISBN 0–312–05774–1

Library of Congress Cataloging-in-Publication Data

Williams, T. C. (Terence Charles)
The idea of the miraculous : the challenge to science and religion
T. C. Williams.
        p.   cm.
Includes bibliographical references and index.
ISBN 0–312–05774–1
1. Miracles. 2. Religion and science— 1946 – I. Title.
BT97.2.W485   1991
211—dc20   90–49486
                                                           CIP

To Nik

Contents

Preface

Despite the fact of its contemporary unfashionableness, the idea of the *miraculous* is pre-eminently such as to bring into relief the competing and seemingly contradictory claims of two main types of thinking. On the one hand – the *religious* outlook with its deep roots in the *spiritual* aspects of human being. On the other – the modern *scientific* endeavour with its foundational base in the conception of *natural necessity*.

Nor is the matter of merely nominal interest. To endorse the idea is necessarily to embrace a radically different reality from that in which such events are impossible or even the thought nonsensical. To this extent, it is an issue which goes to the very heart of the modern dilemma. A world governed exclusively by *natural necessity* remains forever one in which *religion*, and with this, *spirituality* in general, can have only illusory status.

In one sense, of course, this is not to proceed very far. For, it is precisely the *empirical* weakness of the traditional (*religious/theological*) view of the *miraculous*, as set against the demonstrable power of the doctrine of *scientific necessity*, which has led to the fulsomeness of its present-day rejection. At the same time, and as constituting the main thrust of the current concern, there are two further considerations. First, that the idea is open to clear development in a way which connects directly with the modern conception of the *mentalistic/psychical*. Secondly, that the *empirical* pressure arising from this reconstruction is such as to present a vast and inescapable challenge to the parametrical frameworks of both (*materialistic*) *science* and (*Judæo-Christian*) *religion* alike. On this basis, the book with all its far-reaching ramifications, together with such theoretical optimism as it might impart, is offered as a *philosophical* wedge driven between the irreconcilable extremes of the two foregoing arms.

On a personal note, there may be full acknowledgement that the book, in its original conception, arose through my being present at some of the main experiments discussed in Chapter 8.

My thanks are due to my colleagues, Douglas Odegard, Jakob Amstutz and Jay Newman of the Department of Philosophy, University of Guelph, Ontario, for suggestions and encouragement during the writing of the book. So, too, and most especially, to

Judy Martin of the same Department for her expertise, as well as forebearance, over a long period, in the production of the typescript.

Sagres   T. C. Williams
Portugal
March 1989

Acknowledgements

I gratefully acknowledge permission to quote from: John Hasted, *The Metal-Benders* (London: Routledge, Kegan Paul, 1981).

I would also like to thank the Authors and Editors of the following volumes:

H. W. Bartsche, (editor) and R. J. Fuller (translator), *Kerygma and Myth: A Theological Debate* (London: SCM, 1953), 2 vols; David Bohm, *Causality and Chance in Modern Physics* (London: Routledge, Kegan Paul, 1959/84); C. D. Broad, *Religion, Philosophy and Psychical Research: Selected Essays* (London: Routledge, Kegan Paul, 1953); Henri F. Ellenberger, *The Discovery of the Unconscious: The History and Evolution of Dynamic Psychiatry* (New York: Basic Books, 1970); Alan Gauld, *The Founders of Psychical Research* (London: Routledge, Kegan Paul, 1968); R. Lawrence Moore, *In Search of White Crows: Spiritualism, Parapsychology and American Culture* (New York: Oxford University Press, 1977); John A. T. Robinson, *Honest to God* (London: SCM, 1975); John Taylor, *Superminds: An Enquiry into the Paranormal* (London: Macmillan, 1975); L. L. Whyte, *The Unconscious before Freud* (New York: Basic Books, 1960).

Introduction

This book is about *miracles* – though not, it must be added, about the presumed reality of any particular event which might be taken as falling under this heading. Rather, the main concern is with the *idea* of the *miraculous* and with the validity and significance of this idea in a twentieth century world dominated by scientific thinking.

As viewed in this way, an immediate distinction may be drawn between the idea in question (in its modern setting) and that of the merely wondrous or marvellous which is of much greater antiquity and exclusively religious in origin. Though derivative from this latter, the idea of the miraculous is, philosophically speaking, of relatively recent lineage. Involving as it does the idea of the wondrous in its specific relation to that of a strong conception of *nature* as a *system*, that is of *laws of nature* or *natural necessity*, it is, essentially, a product of the philosophy and science of the eighteenth and nineteenth centuries. Its classical formulation remains that of David Hume: 'a miracle may be accurately defined, *a transgression of a law of nature by a particular volition of the Deity, or by the interposition of some invisible agent.*'[1] Following from this, and of most particular interest, is the fact that, as defined in this way, the idea is one which brings into sharp focus the competing and seemingly contradictory claims of two main types of thinking. On the one hand, the *religious* outlook, with its deep roots in the spiritual aspects of man's being. On the other hand, the modern *scientific* endeavour imbued with all the confidence of its spectacular successes over the past four centuries.

With this, too, there is the fact that the issue, as outlined above, is far from being of only theoretical interest. A world which embraces the *miraculous* is necessarily a radically different reality from one where such events are impossible, or even the thought nonsensical. To this extent the question of the viability of the idea is one which goes to the very heart of the dilemma of modern man. More specifically, it brings to the fore the whole question of the *super-natural/normal* with all that this holds for man in a world dominated by empirical and material considerations. As an illustration at a most basic level, it strikes, for instance, at the validity of one of the most prevalent of all human indulgences – that of intercessionary prayer. A world governed exclusively by *natural necessity* remains, as Freud was all too ready to accept, one in which religion, and with this, all man's spiritual aspirations, can have only illusory status.

In what follows, it will be argued that, despite its intellectual unfashionableness at the present time, the idea of the *miraculous*, with all the rich harvest that may be reaped from it, remains open to construction in a way which is not only viable, but which, also, constitutes a vast and continuing challenge to both (*orthodox/ theistic*) *religion* and (*materialistic*) *science* alike. The discussion, though representing a single sustained argument, is offered in two main parts with the conceptual development pursued primarily in Chapters 1–5 and 9–12, and with Chapters 6–8 constituting empirical support for the contingent viability of the former. Should the reader wish, Chapters 6–8 may be omitted and the rest taken as a purely intellectual exercise.

It remains only to mention that the approach, though thoroughly *philosophical* in intent, is, yet, mildly polemical in its starting point. For, in one of its aspects, at least, the argument is motivated by the conviction that certain of the best known *theological* writers of the past half-century have already surrendered far too much to the claims of *science* in the urgency of their efforts to exorcise any vestige of *super-naturalism*/normality from, what they conceive to be, a 'progressive' religious outlook. It is to a development of this point that attention may be turned in opening the main discussion.

A time will come when *philosophy, animal magnetism* [the *psychical*] and *natural science*, that has made unparalleled progress in all its branches, will shed so bright a light on one another that truths will be discovered at which we could not otherwise hope to arrive.

Arthur Schopenhauer (*circa* 1850)

1

The Crisis in Modern Theology

In talking about a crisis in modern theology the reference is, mainly, to Protestant theology – though this is not to underestimate the range of its implications. More specifically, it relates to the so-called 'revolution' in this discipline which saw its inception with the publication, in 1942, of Rudolf Bultmann's manifesto, *New Testament and Mythology*.[1] Other important theological thinkers, most notably, Dietrich Bonhoeffer and Paul Tillich – as too, at a more popular level, (Bishop) John A. T. Robinson – are also intimately bound up with this challenge. More recently, again, the name of (Bishop) David Jenkins may be added to this constantly expanding list. Notwithstanding, and without underestimating, the innovativeness of these writers, the real interest of what they have to say, certainly with regard to the present discussion, still revolves around the claims of Bultmann. To this extent, what follows is centred mainly around the views of this latter with only incidental (though sometimes extensive) reference to other writers associated with his famous stand.

What is common to these thinkers, and what constitutes the crux of their position, is the assumption that Christianity, with all the richness of its association with sacred books, rites, places, objects and actions, with prayer, miracles and the priesthood, is reducible in the last resort to what may be characterized as, 'man and his condition'. In short, and notwithstanding the ambiguity of the theological language in which this idea is expressed – that *religion*, and, with this, the whole idea of the *supernatural*, is reducible to what, in the final analysis, amounts to little more than *anthropological* considerations.

Despite the undoubted impact of the above-mentioned thinkers there is no imputation that they are to be regarded as having anything like a monopoly over current theological thinking. Against them, for good or ill, may be set, at once, the whole living traditions of both the Roman and Greek Churches. Further, there is

1

the clear fact that they are opposed by other great names of the
Protestant faith, such as Karl Barth, who, with unabated zeal, have
continued to maintain a more fundamentalist position. At the same
time, the very strength with which such fundamentalist views are
held raises the possibility of their own self-transformation. For, it
would appear to be an entirely legitimate enterprise to seek
whatever deeper truths that Christianity (or, for that matter, any
other religion) might hold through the methodology of critical
scholarship. It is, of course, this concern which has motivated the
so-called *liberal* theologians over the past century and a half to the
task, amongst other things, of eliminating from the New Testament
message elements which are mythological in character. Bultmann's
'revolution' and its startling consequences are but a culmination of
this approach.

Bultmann's aim is not merely to identify the mythological
elements of the New Testament, but to offer an interpretation of
this (presumed) mythology. With regard to the actual mythology,
it is Bultmann's view that the whole of the New Testament
teaching of man's redemption is presented within the framework
of, what is, demonstrably, the cosmology of late antiquity with its
roots in Jewish Apocalyptic, on the one hand, and the redemption
myths of Gnosticism, on the other. Most specifically, it is, as
Bultmann maintains, a cosmology whose principal features are: (a)
a 'three-storied universe' of heaven, earth and the underworld; (b)
a supersensible realm of God, Satan, angels and demons; (c) the
intervention, for good or evil, of these supernatural powers in the
affairs of men; and (d) the imminent end of the present natural
order. Thus more fully:

> The cosmology of the New Testament is essentially mythical in
> character. The world is viewed as a three-storied structure, with
> the earth in the centre, the heaven above, and the underworld
> beneath. Heaven is the abode of God and of celestial beings – the
> angels. The underworld is hell, the place of torment. Even the
> earth is more than the scene of natural, everyday events, of the
> trivial round and common task. It is the scene of the supernatu-
> ral activity of God and his angels on the one hand, and of Satan
> and his daemons on the other. These supernatural forces inter-
> vene in the course of nature and in all that men think and will
> and do. Miracles are by no means rare. Man is not in control of
> his own life. Evil spirits may take possession of him. Satan may

inspire him with evil thoughts. Alternatively, God may inspire his thought and guide his purposes. He may grant him heavenly visions. He may allow him to hear his word of succour or demand. He may give him the supernatural power of his Spirit. History does not follow a smooth unbroken course; it is set in motion and controlled by these supernatural powers. This aeon is held in bondage by Satan, sin and death ... and hastens towards its end. That end will come very soon, and will take the form of a cosmic catastrophe. It will be inaugurated by the 'woes' of the last time. Then the Judge will come from heaven, the dead will rise, the last judgement will take place, and men will enter into eternal salvation or damnation. (*KM*, pp. 1–2)

This cosmology, Bultmann maintains, is completely antiquated and of no relevance whatsoever for modern man. *'The kerygma'*, as he says, *'is incredible to modern man, for he is convinced that the mythical view of the world is obsolete'* (*KM*, p. 3). As such, it must be excised from the New Testament teaching if the latter is to have any relevance for the future. The whole redemption story is in no way to be taken literally. It is 'a hotch-potch of sacrificial and juridical analogies, which have ceased to be tenable for us today' (*KM*, p. 35). And what remains when this exercise of excision is completed and the gospel re-interpreted? Bultmann's answer is that, in the person and life of Jesus Christ, there is a profound expression of the ultimate, unconditioned significance of human life as such, of 'man's understanding of himself in the world in which he lives' (*KM*, p. 10). More specifically, there is his point that what remains as the core and abiding message of the *kerygma* after all the mythology has been cut away is a clear anticipation of the modern *existentialist* idea of the *'authentic* life', the life which involves 'the abandonment of all self-contrived security' in the interests of man's true dignity and moral development (*KM*, p. 19). In short, as he concludes, the mythological elements of the New Testament 'should be interpreted not cosmologically, but *anthropologically*, or better still, *existentially'* (*KM*, p. 10, my italics).

This conclusion is asserted elsewhere in the most uncompromising terms by Bultmann as where, in replying to a challenge from Barth, he writes: 'I would heartily agree: I *am* trying to substitute anthropology for theology, for I am interpreting theological affirmations as assertions about human life' (*KM*, p. 107). The clear implication from this would appear to be that Bultmann's position reduces, in the last resort, to a thoroughgoing *secularism*. This, however, is what he is curiously reluctant to accept. For, whilst denying any form of supernaturalism, and whilst asserting that the essence of Christianity is that of the modern existentialist message, most particularly, that of Heidegger, he notwithstanding maintains that this message, as expressed through the Bible, is to be regarded as 'the Word of God . . . the work of the Holy Ghost' (*KM*, p. 192). It is, of course, easy enough to understand Bultmann's attachment to such language after a lifetime's work as a professing Christian. The fact is, as one distinguished English theologian, Austin Farrer, comments, that Bultmann 'scarcely pauses to justify the apparent reintroduction of a type of language which it was the whole profession of his argument to discard' (*KM*, p. 213). But within the context of his manifesto it is difficult to see how this can be anything other than merely nominal. The point is one that was early exploited by Bultmann's pupil, Wilhelm Kamlah, who maintained that his master's existentialism entailed a secularism that is logically independent, not only of supernaturalism, but also of any particular historical happening, including that of the historical Jesus. Its most incisive expression, however, is that given by Bonhoeffer in using Bultmann as a stepping stone to the starkness of his own conception of a 'religionless Christianity' – as where he writes from prison in 1944:

> My view . . . today would be, not that Bultmann went 'too far', as most people thought, but that he didn't go far enough. It's not only the 'mythological' concepts, such as miracle, ascension, and so on (which are not in principle separable from the concepts of God, faith, etc.) but 'religious' concepts generally, which are problematic. You can't, as Bultmann supposes, separate God and miracle, but you must be able to interpret and proclaim *both* in a non-religious sense.[2]

For present purposes, therefore, it may be seen that the real interest of Bultmann's manifesto is to be found, not so much in its existentialist interpretation of the Christian message, but in the challenge it represents to *religious* thinking as such. In short, in the fact that in its implications it raises the whole question of the validity of specifically *religious* discourse; and, in particular, that of the meaningfulness of the very concept of *God*.

As a purely philosophical issue the question of the *epistemological* nature of this concept is of long standing. Indeed, it would be true to say that the present-day state of this controversy goes little past that in which it was left two hundred years ago in the opposed positions of Hume and Kant – with Hume, on the one hand, maintaining that this is a concept which is rooted, ultimately, in no more than man's *psychological* disposition; and Kant, on the other, in conscious opposition to Hume, insisting that it has the quite peculiar status of being what he calls an *Idea of Reason*, that is an idea arising from the nature of (human) *rationality* as such. At a more general level, again, it is the presumed meaninglessness of this term which lies at the heart of the atheist creed; and, with this, its strong links with humanism and naturalism. Within the more restricted sphere of debate among theologians themselves, however, the question has become a lively issue only in fairly recent times. Here the influence of Bultmann has been paramount, as, also, the theological sketches which came from Bonhoeffer's pen during the loneliness of his last years in prison. Another is the voluminous writings of Tillich. At the same time, as an influence in crystallising the views of the above writers for the full glare of the public forum, prime place must be given to (John) Robinson's best-selling *Honest to God*.[3] The furore raised by the book, coming as it did from a bishop of the Church of England, is now a matter of history. Suffice it to say that the proclamation it contained was immediately front page news in the English national press. 'Bishops without God', 'Our Image of God must Go', 'Resign? Not me says the Bishop', 'Bishop's book that will shock thousands: God is not a Daddy in the sky' were just some of the headlines that greeted its publication. What Robinson has to say in this connexion may be summarised in amplification of the significance of Bultmann's claims.

Thus, as Robinson proclaims, we are being called in modern times to a revolution in theology, a revolution on the scale of that achieved by Copernicus in the field of natural science. In effect, a veritable 'Copernican revolution' in *theology* (*HG*, p. 27). This involves 'far more than a restating of traditional orthodoxy in modern times (*HG*, p. 7). A much more radical recasting is necessary. Indeed, what is demanded is a recasting in which 'the most fundamental categories of our theology – of God, of the supernatural, and of religion itself – must go into the melting' (*HG*, p. 7). With regard to the former category, first of all, the fact is, as Robinson continues, that Christian thinking has hitherto been dominated by a conception of *God* or *transcendence* which inherently involves *spatial* determinations. That is to say, which involves the idea of a supreme and separate Being – 'a God "out there", a God who "exists" above and beyond the world He made, a God "to" whom we pray and to whom we "go" when we die' (*HG*, p. 14). This kind of thinking, he maintains, is now so thoroughly outmoded that 'we shall eventually be no more able to convince men of the existence of [such] a God ... than persuade them to take seriously the gods of Olympus' (*HG*, p. 43). It is 'an idol' that should be torn down (*HG*, p. 41). It is, as he contends, following Bultmann, part and parcel of the *supernaturalistic* world view; the completely antiquated way of thinking involving the supposition

> that the network of empirical relationships is but a veil for a world of occult realities which lie behind the outward order of things and constitute the truth about man or society or nature, however much the empirical facts may appear to dispute it. (*HG*, pp. 107–8)

It is, of course, the case that 'for the New Testament writers the conviction of the personal character of God as gracious, holy, self-giving love was expressed unquestioningly in the representation of him as *a* Being, a supreme Person.'[4] But to them 'this was the only available projection' (*HGD*, p. 262). Again, to say that Jesus used such language 'is in itself to say no more than he was genuinely a man of the first century' (*HGD*, p. 262). To tie Christianity to this projection, however, is to raise grave fears 'for its ability to *become* a reality for many in our generation' (*HGD*, p. 262). The very scale of the number of people 'who instinctively seem to feel that it is no longer possible to believe in God in the space-age' is ample testimony to this fact (*HG*, p. 13). It 'shows how crudely physical much of this thinking about a God "out there" has been' (*HG*, p. 13). The only question, therefore, is '*how* the Biblical doctrine is to be given expression today, in a non-supranaturalistic world-view' (*HGD*, p. 262). In other words, what is needed for modern man is a new concept of *God/transcendence*.

More specifically, what is needed, as Robinson continues, is Tillich's conception – where *God* is understood not in the spatial terms of physical science, that is as 'a projection "out there", an Other beyond the skies, of whose existence we have to convince ourselves' (*HG*, p. 22), but, instead, in terms which approximate to those of 'depth psychology' (*HG*, p. 45), that is, for instance, as 'the Ground of our very being' (*HG*, p. 22). This latter, as he continues, is 'an alternative (and quite traditional) way of indicating another "projection" (apart from supranaturalism . . .) in which all the great Biblical language about God may be cast' (*HGD*, p. 263). Conceived in these terms, God is not to be regarded as another Being at all – not, that is, as a supernatural agency 'to whom one can turn away from the world and who can be relied upon to intervene from without' (*HG*, p. 47). What is meant by *God*, rather, is 'the ultimate depth of all our being, the creative ground and meaning of all our existence' (*HG*, p. 47); that is – as expressed by Tillich himself – 'the feeling of the inexhaustible mystery of life' (cf. *HG*, p. 55); or, again, more fully:

> The name of this infinite and inexhaustible depth and ground of all being is *God*. That depth is what the word *God* means. And if that word has not much meaning for you, translate it, and speak of the depths of your life, of the source of your being, of your ultimate concern, of what you take seriously without any reservation . . . He who knows about depth knows about God.[5]

In short, as Robinson concludes, what is required for any real understanding of the Christian faith in the modern world – and what Tillich has already provided – is a 'reinterpretation of transcendence in a way which preserves its reality while detaching it from the projection of supranaturalism' (*HG*, p. 56).

It is easy enough to see from the above that the stridency with which Robinson expresses himself is useful enough in bringing to the attention of a wide audience difficulties in the notion of God that are all too easily passed over at an uncritical level. It may well be, too, that what he has to say reflects a justifiable criticism of the tardiness of theologians and of the clergy in general in educating an ever increasingly sophisticated laity to the *philosophical* difficulties of the Christian faith. What is certainly not clear is the validity of the dichotomy which he draws, and which he regards as exclusive, between the two senses of *transcendence*. There is no doubt, of course, that the sense of this term which is stressed by Robinson, and which he takes, most principally, from Tillich, represents a vital aspect of the Judæo-Christian conception of God. The idea of God's 'indwelling' in man, of His 'residing' in the 'depths' of man's 'being', is a very old one. It goes back, as

Robinson fully recognises, to Old Testament times and has been a dominant theme in the writings of mystics and masters of the spiritual life ever since. At the more strictly philosophical level, too, it constitutes an essential feature of the self-avowed 'Copernican' revolution in *philosophy* which Kant proclaimed two hundred years ago in his *Critique of Pure Reason* – in his doctrine of *noumenon* as the unknown and unknowable ground of *being/consciousness*. More to the point for present purposes, however, is Robinson's emphasis on this sense of *transcendence* to the complete exclusion of the other, that is the *theistic*, sense.

Here, once more, it may readily be conceded that his rejection of the crude anthropomorphism which is embraced in a *literal* acceptance of this latter is entirely justified. At the same time, it may well be questioned whether such a literal interpretation – the complete inadequacy of which was fully exposed well before the Christian era by Xenophanes – exhausts the significance of this sense of the term. Any modern treatment of this question must, again, involve reference to Kant and the demonstration of his *Critique* that, by its very nature, talk of God can never be literal but only *metaphorical*. But granted this, it may still be asserted, in opposition to Robinson, that this (*theistic*) sense of *transcendence* is expressive of a fundamental aspect of the Judæo-Christian idea of God which is not covered by the sense emphasized by Robinson. That is, the idea, which necessarily involves spatial analogies, of 'otherness' or 'over-againstness'. Viewed in this way the two senses of *transcendence* need not be taken as being in opposition to each other as Robinson assumes. Rather, they may be, and traditionally have been, understood as being *complementary*; and, despite all the difficulties involved, as both contributing vital aspects to the idea of God instantiated in the Nicean Creed.[6]

Robinson is fully sensitive to the significance of this far-reaching consideration. 'To be asked to give up any idea of a Being "out there" at all', he acknowledges, 'will appear to be an outright denial of God' (*HG*, p. 17). Merely to criticise this sense of *transcendence*, as he goes on, '[appears] to threaten the entire fabric of Christianity' (*HG*, p. 31); while 'to sacrifice it seems at once to take one quite outside [this faith]' (*HG*, p. 40). The fact that, notwithstanding, he takes the line he does is simply the measure of his antagonism to any vestige of supernaturalism. This, however, has certain immediate consequences. There is, first, the fact that, in place of the *supernaturalistic* framework of traditional Christianity, what Robinson offers is, like Bultmann, a more limited and strictly *ethical* underpinning. This leads directly to the further point that, for Robinson, as for Bultmann (and, also, Bonhoeffer and Tillich), the essential and abiding message of the *kerygma* is reduced to no more than a form of what may be characterised as 'moral serious-ness'. The difference between Robinson and Bultmann in this respect lies in nothing more than the nature of the ethical base which is offered in each case. For Bultmann, the ethical 'key' is (Heideggerian) *existentialism*. For Robinson it is, more specifically, *love* – as this is expressed, for instance, in a passage where he refers approvingly to Bonhoeffer's idea of a 'non-religious understanding of God':

> Whether one has 'known' God is tested by one question only, 'How deeply have you loved?' ... Encounter with the Son of Man is spelt out in terms of an entirely 'secular' concern for food, water supplies, housing, hospitals and prisons. (*HG*, p. 61)

To this extent, and accepting the equivocation inherent in Robin-son's theological language, his 'sole concern and contention' is, as he says, 'for the Scriptural revelation of God as dynamic personal love' (*HGD*, p. 262).

This ethical stance, further, provides the basis for the conception of prayer which he offers as a replacement for the traditional Christian idea of intercessionary 'communication' with God. 'Prayer and ethics', for Robinson, 'are simply the inside and outside of the same thing' (*HG*, p. 105); or, again, more fully:

> To open oneself to another *unconditionally* in love *is* to be with him in the presence of God, and that is the heart of intercession. To pray for another is to expose both oneself and him to the common ground of being; it is to see one's concern for him in terms of *ultimate* concern, to let *God* into the relationship. (*HG*, p. 99)

These points, as may be seen, bring into clear focus, once more, the question raised earlier in connexion with Bultmann. In short, the vital issue of how far specifically *religious* thinking is possible in a context where any sense of the *supernatural* is replaced entirely by *ethical*, or, more broadly, *anthropological*, considerations.

Robinson openly faces this difficulty. 'We are here on very

dangerous ground' (*HG*, p. 50); for, as he goes on,

> if statements about God are statements about the 'ultimacy' of personal relationships, then we must agree that in a real sense Feuerbach was right in wanting to translate 'theology' into 'anthropology' ... To say that 'theology is nothing else than anthropology' means that 'the knowledge of God is nothing else than a knowledge of man'. (*HG*, p. 50)

His claim is, however, that his *Tillichian* sense of *transcendence* (in its relation to *love*) saves his outlook from this difficulty and its associated slide into naturalistic/humanistic atheism:

> Theology, as Tillich insists, is about 'that which concerns us ultimately'. A statement is 'theological' not because it relates to a particular Being called 'God', but because it asks *ultimate* questions about the meaning of existence; it asks what, at the level of *theos*, at the level of its deepest mystery, is the reality and significance of our life. A view of the world which affirms this reality and significance in personal categories is *ipso facto* making an affirmation about the *ultimacy* of personal relations: it is saying that *God*, the final truth and reality 'deep down things', *is* love. (*HG*, p. 49)

It is on this basis, and this basis exclusively, that Robinson, as a bishop of the Anglican Church, is able to assert that his own conviction as a Christian remains unimpaired by his rejection of *theism* and its *supernaturalistic* framework – that, as he says, 'the only God who meets my need as a Christian is "the God of Abraham, Isaac and Jacob", the God and Father of our Lord Jesus Christ' (*HGD*, p. 262). Whether such a claim is really sustainable in the light of the philosophical implications of his position may, at this point, be left for the reader to decide. What is certain is that there must be initial sympathy, at least, with the concluding comment of one reviewer of Robinson's book: 'Une religion sans Dieu! Mon Dieu, quelle religion!'[7]

These surveys of the positions of Bultmann and Robinson have been undertaken with the sole purpose of bringing to the fore the central significance of the idea of the *supernatural* for Christian thought, in particular, and, more widely, for religion as such. This does not hide the fact that no real attempt has been made, to this point, to come to grips with the term itself. It is, of course, this – and, with it, the associated idea of the *miraculous* – which forms the main topic of the present discussion. Suffice it to say, for the moment, that, while any attempt to make sense of this idea must involve *some* kind of *two-world* view – that is a projection of *some* form of interaction between the *sensible/physical* world, on the one hand, and a *supersensible/invisible* 'realm', on the other – such an outlook need not necessarily be framed in quite such crude terms as those which have been encountered so far. Indeed, as will be argued, the problem is one which, in a very real sense, is reducible, in the last resort, to the *matter/mind* paradox which lies at the heart of the whole Western tradition in philosophy. To say this, it is hoped, will make it clear beyond doubt that it forms no part of my object to argue for any kind of theological *fundamentalism*. It is conceded, right from the start, that the *liberal* movement in theology has made great gains over the years through the critical appraisal of biblical events. Again, in this connexion, it will be clear that there is no intention to argue for the historical authenticity of any *particular* (putative) miracle. What *is* at issue is simply the culminating stance of theological *liberalism* in its rejection of the very idea of the *supernatural*. Returning, however, to the main discussion, this much will be obvious. That is, that, in so far as Bultmann and Robinson (as, also, Bonhoeffer and Tillich) are right in their complete rejection of *any* form of *supernaturalism*, then a very drastic revision of what is involved in a *religious* outlook is necessary. The consequences of this rejection are, indeed, so far-reaching that the ground on which they are based is worthy of the very closest scrutiny.

It turns out, in fact, to rest purely and simply on the claim that the mere *existence* (or, at least, technological *success*) of modern *science*, of itself, in some way, negates any form of *supernaturalism*. Thus, as Bultmann writes:

Now that the forces and laws of nature have been discovered, we can no longer believe in *spirits, whether good or evil* ... It is impossible to use electric light and the wireless and to avail ourselves of modern medical and surgical discoveries, and at the same time believe in the New Testament world of daemons and spirits. (*KM*, pp. 4–5)

or, again, more loosely, in a number of assorted passages:

All our thinking to-day is shaped for good or ill by modern science (*KM*, p. 3) . . . What matters is the world view which men imbibe from their environment, and it is science which determines that view of the world through the school, the press, the wireless, the cinema, and all the other fruits of technical progress (*KM*, p. 5n.) . . . Modern man *par excellence* is technological man, and for that reason he is doubly enslaved to the modern scientific world, even if in theory he disclaims all interest in and knowledge of it (*KM*, p. 122) . . . Modern men take it for granted that the course of nature and of history, like their own inner life and their practical life, is nowhere interrupted by the intervention of supernatural powers . . . Modern man acknowledges as reality only such phenomena or events as are comprehensible within the framework of the rational order of the universe.[8]

These and similar statements constitute the full extent of Bultmann's case against *supernaturalism*. It would be easy enough in today's climate, half a century after they were written, to take issue with their factual, that is psychological/sociological, accuracy. More important is the fact that they plainly do not succeed in their main intention. For despite the apparent modernity of their appeal to the triumphs of contemporary science and technology there is nothing in them which relates to what is really required in the present connexion – that is, a critical assessment of the *idea* of the *supernatural* in its relation to that of *science*. Instead, the vital conclusion which Bultmann draws from them, that is the complete rejection of *supernaturalism*, rests merely on the assumption of the very point that needs to be proved. More specifically, the presumption that science and supernaturalism *are* intrinsically incompatible – and, hence, that any possibility of the latter is negated simply by the existence and success of the former. To this extent the underlying basis of Bultmann's position is fulsomely, if only obliquely, acknowledged by Robinson in his own frank acceptance of a *secularist* stance; and, with this, of a 'secularised Christianity':

The 'religious', in the technical sense of the religious orders, is the antithesis of the 'secular' (*HG*, p. 84) . . . Secularism rejects a supranaturalistic world-view (*HGC*, p. 256) . . . [My book] is a dialogue between religious man and secular man . . . Indeed . . . [it] . . . was born of the fact that I knew myself to be a man committed without reservation to Christ *and* a man committed, without possibility of return, to modern twentieth-century secular society. It was written out of the belief that both these convictions must be taken with equal seriousness and that they *cannot* be incompatible. (*HGD*, p. 275)

To summarise, therefore, Bultmann's whole 'revolution' in theology (and, with this, Robinson's own position) rests, in the last resort, on what amounts to no more than a wholesale and unargued rejection of *any* form of *supernaturalism*.

It will be the main object in what follows to question the legitimacy of this far-reaching assumption.

2

The Idea of the Miraculous

Enough has been said in Chapter 1 to justify the assessment of Karl Jaspers regarding the far-reaching implications of Bultmann's challenge – that 'Bultmann's views on the demythologization of religion . . . have assumed the proportions of an event touching the very essence of religion.'[1] In the light of what has been said the reason for this is not far to seek and turns on two senses of the term *demythologizing* as used by Bultmann. Thus, in the first place, there is the entirely legitimate sense which constitutes the cornerstone of the *liberal* theological movement and which relates to the continued reappraisal of the biblical narratives through the method of critical scholarship. But, further, and more importantly, there is the sense which involves the outright rejection of *any* form of *supernaturalism*. The ultimacy of Bultmann's challenge rests exclusively on his emphasis on this latter sense of the term. To this extent, it may well be accepted that there is nothing really surprising in the fact that paradoxical results flow from Bultmann's 'revolution'. They flow *analytically* from the assumption on which the whole position is based.

To make this point, however, is to highlight the fact that, despite the apparent novelty of Bultmann's specifically *theological* conclusions, the basis of his position is an essentially *philosophical* stance – one which is, not only perennial in its challenge, but which also is as old as philosophy itself. It is, in fact, precisely the outlook, the new way of thinking, from which *philosophy*, as also *science*, originally arose in its opposition to, hitherto, all-pervasive *religious/mythopoeic thinking*.[2] It is, again, that which, in the fulness of time, gained classical expression in the thoroughgoing *materialism* of Democritus and which, later, finds full-blooded expression in such diverse thinkers as Hobbes and Marx; as well as coming to dominate the intellectual climate of the present day in, what may be loosely labelled as, *scientific materialism*. At the same time, the point must be emphasized that, no matter how clamorously asserted, it remains a *stance*. Further, that, notwithstanding its manifest importance, it is one which, through its very limitations,

14

has provoked profound reactions at seminal times in the history of philosophy. To mention the *two-world* views of Plato and Kant in this connexion is merely to underscore the point. Gathering up these threads, therefore, it may be seen that the implications of Bultmann's 'revolution' extend well beyond the realms of *theology* and *religion* to embrace the nature and autonomy of *philosophy* itself. For, if Bultmann is right in his assumption that *no* validity can be ascribed to *any* sense of *supernaturalism*, then this time-honoured discipline must be viewed as being entirely ancillary to the *scientific* enterprise. In short the position must be, as Kant clearly foresaw in the Preface to the (first edition) of his *Critique of Pure Reason* – that, unless *some* form of transcendentalism be accepted, then (in somewhat Freudian terms), *philosophy*, once, in pretension, at least, 'Queen of all the sciences', is reduced to a 'matron outcast and forsaken', a mere slave to the mastery of her sibling, all-powerful (*materialistic*) *science*.

These considerations serve, at the very least, to emphasize that the stakes involved in Bultmann's 'revolution' are extremely high. More particularly, they bring to the fore the importance of the idea which constitutes the main topic of the present discussion – that of the *miraculous*. For, it is *this* – the idea of the *supernatural* in its (putatively) *empirical*, that is personal and historical, exemplifications – whose rejection by Bultmann constitutes the real basis of his position:

> Modern man acknowledges as reality only such phenomena or events as are comprehensible within the framework of the rational order of the universe. He does not acknowledge miracles because they do not fit into this lawful order. When a strange or marvellous accident occurs, he does not rest until he has found a rational cause.[3]

Beyond this, however, is the fact that the *traditional/theological* idea of the *miraculous*, which is here rejected by Bultmann, is precisely that which constitutes the crux of Hume's own famous rejection of such events. That is, in the terms of his own classical definition: '*a transgression of a law of nature by a particular volition of the Deity*'.[4] To make this point is not to ignore, what has already been noted, that Hume's definition includes, also, the rider '*or by the interposition of some invisible agent*' (*HU*, p. 115n). Though largely ignored by Hume, as well as by most of his commentators, this is, as will be argued, a point of most particular importance. At the same time, it will be convenient, for immediate purposes, to restrict attention to the narrower definition given above which embraces, not only the traditional conception of the matter as formulated, for instance, by Aquinas, but, further, the main target of Hume's attack. On this basis attention may be turned to a consideration of what he has to say in this regard.

To begin, it is one of Hume's main contentions – as is also clearly implicit in the outlook of Bultmann – that the idea of the miraculous is immediately subject to the pressure of a powerful empirical consideration – one which, in its implications, demands a drastic revision of the former's presumed nature. There is, as he notes, the plain fact that a strong *socio-historical* correlation exists between the rise and dissemination of the scientific outlook and a decline in the belief in miracles – and, following from this, that the idea of the miraculous is to be seen as having its origin, not in any real basis in fact, but, purely and simply in the terms of a historically more rudimentary type of human understanding:

> It forms a strong presumption against all supernatural and miraculous relations, that they are observed chiefly to abound among ignorant and barbarous nations; or if a civilised people has ever given admission to any of them, that people will be found to have received them from ignorant and barbarous ancestors, who transmitted them with that inviolable sanction and authority, which always attend received opinions. (*HU*, p. 119)

and in continuing:

> When we peruse the first histories of all nations, we are apt to imagine ourselves transported into some new world; where the whole frame of nature is disjointed, and every element performs its operations in a different manner, from what it does at present. Battles, revolutions, pestilence, famine and death, are never the effect of those natural causes, which we experience. Prodigies, omens, oracles, judgements, quite obscure the few natural events, that are intermingled with them. But as the former grow thinner every page, in proportion as we advance nearer the enlightened ages, we soon learn, that there is nothing mysterious or supernatural in the case, but that all proceeds from the

usual propensity of mankind towards the marvellous, and that, though this inclination may at intervals receive a check from sense and learning, it can never be thoroughly extirpated from human nature. (*HU*, p. 119)

More particularly, then, as Hume holds, the idea of the miraculous is to be seen as having its roots in the purely *psychological* origin of human *credulity*.

Support for this claim, as he goes on, is abundantly demonstrated even in everyday affairs 'with regard to the most common and most credible events' (*HU*, p. 118), but no more so than in 'the many instances of forged miracles, and prophecies, and supernatural events, which, in all ages, have either been detected by contrary evidence, or which detect themselves by their absurdity' (*HU*, p. 118). The correlation in question is, thus, for Hume, one that is explained by the fact that a *scientific/rationalistic* outlook, and the intellectual climate which it engenders, presents a bulwark to the indiscriminate expression of this natural disposition. In the absence of such a counterweight, the position is simply, as he puts it, that 'the gazing populace receive greedily, without examination, whatever soothes superstition, and promotes wonder' (*HU*, p. 126). And, to the extent that 'the spirit of religion join itself to this [uninhibited] love of wonder', then, as he concludes, 'there is an end of common sense' (*HU*, p. 117). With this, too, there is, for Hume, a full and complete *naturalistic* explanation of the origin of the idea of the miraculous.

In commenting on this position, as it also relates to the claims of Bultmann, it may be accepted that human credulity is certainly one of the factors which must be taken into account in any estimation of the issue in hand. What may still be questioned, however, is whether such gullibility, or what Hume, more broadly, characterizes as 'the knavery and folly of men' (*HU*, p. 128), is of quite the wholesale kind that he really needs for his position. To this extent, the words of W. E. H. Lecky – written during the high rationalism of the latter half of the last century – are not without their force:

It is often and truly said that past ages were pre-eminently credulous, as compared with our own; yet the difference is not so much in the *amount* of the credulity, as in the *direction* it takes. Men are always prepared to accept, on very slight evidence, what they believe to be exceedingly probable.[5]

But even granting this objection, it might still be held that the substance of Hume's position remains unimpaired. For, whilst conceding that his account, as given above, is over-simplistic, it might still be contended that it is open to supplementation by other considerations of a like, *naturalistic*, nature.

Thus, following this line, and with a simple shift in emphasis, it might be held that man is not merely credulous by nature, but is also possessed of a neuro-physiological predisposition to a belief in the supernatural. Support for such a view might be taken as coming from the recent and highly publicized theory of Julian Janes regarding the historical origin of human consciousness. That is, more particularly, his contention that consciousness and the idea of the supernatural are ontologically related and are to be concomitantly explained in terms of the physio-biological development of the right hemisphere of the brain:

> Ancient peoples from Mesopotamia to Peru could not 'think' as we do today . . . Unable to introspect, they experienced auditory hallucinations . . . voices of gods, actually heard as in the Old Testament or the Iliad – which coming from the brain's right hemisphere, told a person what to do in circumstances of novelty or stress.[6]

Further, it might be held, following Freud in his famous *The Future of an Illusion* (1927), that man's belief in the supernatural (as also the miraculous) must have reference to the psychological disposition of *need* – the need and longing of humans for protection and comfort in a world where biological survival is constantly at risk. The sort of need, indeed, which is poignantly conveyed in the words of Aleksander Solzhenitsyn:

> Laugh as we may at miracles as long as we are strong, healthy and flourishing, let life become hopelessly wedged and crushed so that only a miracle can save us – and we shall believe in that one and only and altogether extraordinary miracle.[7]

To this, again, may be added the need of a developing social group for unity and cohesion and the clear role that myth (as this relates to stories of god(s) and miracles) has historically played in this. To this extent, it may well be that the very complication of some of the more dramatic of the recorded miracles is to be explained simply, as one recent writer puts it, as 'the progressive result of centuries of anxious parents trying to convince doubting children of false stories'.[8] It was, of course, Plato, in the *Republic*, who first delineated the importance of *myth* in the above sense, as well as the problem of human *incredulity* in its propagation. To return to the main discussion, however, the plain fact remains that, no matter to what degree such naturalistic considerations are extended, this can never make the world free from miracles in the sense needed for the matter in hand. For, though it be fully granted that all stories of the miraculous are open to explanation in such terms as the above, this does not establish the impossibility of miracles *per se*.

In point of fact, it is the mark of Hume's greatness that he clearly saw this; and that the main thrust of his essay is, not at all that given above, but, one, rather, which involves a philosophical or conceptual attack on the *idea* of the miraculous. His aim in this latter, and more fundamental, aspect of his argument is summarized – implacable opponent of the miraculous that he is – in the following way:

> Nothing is so convenient as a decisive argument of [the] kind, which must at least *silence* the most arrogant bigotry and superstition, and free us from their impertinent solicitations. I flatter myself, that I have discovered an argument of . . . [such a] . . . nature, which, if just, will, with the wise and learned, be an everlasting check to all kinds of superstitious delusion, and consequently, will be useful as long as the world endures. For so long, I presume, will the accounts of miracles and prodigies be found in all history, sacred and profane. (*HU*, p. 110)

It is Hume's originality as expressed here which, most particularly, makes his 'Of Miracles' the methodological starting point of any modern discussion of this question. The consideration is one which overrides any reservation there might be about the more general philosophical quality of the work – such as, for instance, is voiced by C. D. Broad in his remark that 'it has always seemed to me to be an over-rated work, and to fall below the extremely high standard of Hume's other philosophical writings'.[9] What Broad says here is undoubtedly bound up with the consideration that the essay contains, not one, but, what may be taken as, *two* conceptual or critical arguments relating to the miraculous. Further, that this fact raises difficulties with regard to Hume's wider philosophical position. Whether it *was* Hume's actual intention to offer more than one argument is open to question and will be the subject of later comment. What *is* clear is that the acceptance of the two adds to the richness, if not the consistency, of the work. They are interrelated in the context of Hume's exposition and both turn on the idea of 'a transgression of a law of nature'; but whereas one is concerned with *evidence*, the other is concerned with *possible events*. They are neatly summarized by a recent writer, Douglas Odegard, in the following way:

(1) There must be conclusive evidence against any violation of a law.
    A miracle violates a law.
    Therefore, there must be conclusive evidence against any miracle.
(2) Any violation of a law is, in some nonlogical sense, impossible.
    A miracle violates a law.
    Therefore, a miracle is impossible.[10]

It is the former which unquestionably dominates Hume's main intention, and it is, most certainly, to this that he refers in the claim noted above. At the same time it is the latter, sketchy though it is, which is more interesting and important for present purposes. They may be considered in turn.

The former (dominant) argument shows Hume with a firm grasp of the vital point that critical assessment of miracles – in the (limited) *traditional/theological* sense under present discussion – relates more especially to the field of *historical* methodology rather than to that of theology. In particular, it shows Hume as meeting head-on the central assumption of the standard apologetic of the time that the biblical miracles, and, in particular, the Resurrection, provide conclusive evidence for the authenticity of the Christian faith.[11] It is Hume's contention, in reply, that 'a miracle can *never* be *proved*, so as to be the foundation of [*any*] system of religion' (*HU*, p. 127, my italics).

Thus, as he argues, the testimony of others, is a crucial feature in the development and accumulation of human knowledge. This applies most obviously to historical enquiries. At the same time such (historical) testimony cannot be accepted uncritically. The maxim must always be that 'a wise man proportions his belief to the evidence' (*HU*, p. 110). And nowhere is this more relevant than with regard to the biblical miracles where the testimony never even relates to first-hand witnesses, but merely to books and traditions. As against (inferior) testimony of this kind must be set that relating to a man's own personal experience as this is encapsulated, most particularly, in the, so-called, *laws of nature*. That is to say, for Hume, those regularities in nature which have been established on the basis of induction from past experience and which, to the extent that they are 'proved' in this way, may be presumed as holding for future experience also – such laws, for instance, as 'heavy objects fall to the ground', 'water freezes when it gets very cold', 'men do not rise from the dead'. Now a miracle is, by definition, an event which contradicts or violates a law of nature in the above sense – for example, a man rising from the dead. To this extent, there is a conflict between two *kinds* of experience. On the one hand, the ground we have for a belief in a miracle is simply the experience we have as to *trustworthiness* of *testimony*. As against this must be set belief in the most basic experience of all – that is, the *regularities of laws of nature*. 'It is', as Hume writes, 'experience only, which gives authority to human testimony; and it is the same experience, which assures us of the laws of nature' (*HU*, p. 127). In such a circumstance, where 'these two kinds of experience are contrary', then, for Hume, 'we have nothing to do but subtract the one from the other' (*HU*, p. 127). That is, more positively, there is nothing to be done but consider the *weight* of the evidence; in which case the claims for the miraculous must be rejected. In summary, therefore, it is Hume's claim, in his 'everlasting check' on the miraculous, that 'no testimony is sufficient to establish a miracle, unless the testimony be of such a kind, that its falsehood would be more miraculous than the fact, which it endeavours to establish' (*HU*, p. 115–16). And since, by the very nature of the case, no testimony to a miracle can be of this kind then all such accounts must be rejected.

To obtain a full appreciation of the importance of what Hume says here it is only necessary to point to the fact that it effectively constitutes the starting point of the whole *liberal* movement in theology with its critical probing of the historical veracity of the biblical narratives. At the same time, it will be clear that the argument has only a very limited relevance to the culminating stance of this movement as it is instantiated in Bultmann's 'revolu-tion'. To establish that (historical) statements about miracles are the most intrinsically improbable of all historical statements is, certainly, to raise profound theological issues. But it does nothing to establish the intrinsic impossibility of the miraculous. It remains open that miracles, though real and falling under the definition given above, yet involve considerations far removed from the inherent implausibility of some of the more spectacular religious narratives. This is entertained by no less an authority than Hume himself:

> A miracle may either be discoverable by men or not. This alters not its nature and essence. The raising of a house or ship into the air is a visible miracle. The raising of a feather, when the wind wants ever so little of a force requisite for that purpose, is as real a miracle, though not so sensible with regard to us. (*HU*, p. 115n)

This leads to a further point – that Hume completely neglects the possibility that the evidence available might consist, not so much of the testimony of others, but, of a person's own direct observations. For, it might be that miracles, even though, perhaps, of a miniscule kind, occur at the present time; and that there are first-hand, though unpublicized, witnesses to such events. To make these points is, again, to do little more than emphasize the complexity of the topic under discussion and the need to come to closer grips with the issues involved. For the present, however, there must be reticence in any real endeavour in this direction. For, to the extent that the second of the arguments noted above is successful, all such effort would be entirely misplaced.

Hume's main argument to this point, as has been seen, is one which leaves open the possibility of miracles while, at the same time, insisting on the high *improbability* of such events; and, in particular, on the weakness of all historical testimony to their ever having occurred. The second argument may also be construed as relating to this main topic of testimony – but, in this case, as making the stronger claim that *no* possible testimony to a miracle could *ever* be conclusive. Most particularly, however, the interest of the argument lies in the claim that this impossibility with regard to testimony arises from the fact that miracles *per se* are impossible; and this for the reason that the laws of nature admit of no violations or exceptions. It is contained essentially in two short passages:

> A miracle is a violation of the laws of nature; and as a firm and
> unalterable experience has established these laws, the proof
> against a miracle, from the very nature of the fact, is as entire as
> any argument from experience can possibly be imagined. (*HU*,
> p. 114)

and:

> There must, therefore, be a uniform experience against every
> miraculous event, otherwise the event would not merit that
> appellation. And as a uniform experience amounts to a proof,
> there is here a direct and full *proof*, from the nature of the fact,
> against the existence of any miracle. (*HU*, p. 115)

What will be clear, at once, is that the sense of the term 'law of
nature' in this argument is quite different from the sense employed
earlier; as well as that which constitutes what is most distinctive
about Hume's general philosophical position. That is, the sense in
which such laws are conceived as inductive generalizations from
past experience; and which, as such, are always open to the *logical*
possibility of change in the future. To this extent C. S. Lewis is
entirely right in his remark that what Hume has to say in the
present connexion 'is quite inconsistent with the more radical, and
honourable, scepticism of his main work'.[12] So, too, Broad in his
conclusion that 'Hume, with his views of induction, has less right
to [maintain the position under discussion] than do most people'.[13]
This leads directly to the further point that the most obvious way
of discounting such inconsistency is by appeal to the consideration
that the extent of Hume's personal antipathy to the miraculous led
him to an unwitting overstatement of his case – as, for instance, is
suggested by another recent writer, Terence Penelhum:

> Hume's intemperance [of language] has weakened the appear-
> ance of his argument. In particular his insistence that the
> existence of natural laws makes it unreasonable to countenance
> miracle stories leads him to talk of 'a direct and full *proof*, from
> the nature of the fact, against the existence of any miracle'.[14]

At the same time, to raise these questions of general consistency is
to say nothing about the validity of the argument itself. This,

however, may be left for the following chapter. What may be emphasized is the argument's *historical* importance. For whether intended or not, it embraces a clear and decisive shift of emphasis with regard to the miraculous – from the sphere of *religion/theology/history* to that of *physical science*. It is this fact, in particular, which makes Hume's 'Of Miracles' the starting point of an important contemporary debate regarding the miraculous. It is to the intricacies of this debate – with all that it holds for Bultmann's 'revolution', as well as for philosophy of science – that attention may now be turned.

3

Miracles and Natural Necessity

It was T. H. Huxley, the arch-apostle of science, who wrote towards the end of the last century that 'no one is entitled to say *a priori* that any given so-called miraculous event is impossible'.[1] The interest of this statement for present purposes lies in the fact that contemporary philosophical discussion of the miraculous centres on attempts to offer just such *a priori* disproof. Whether such attempts are successful constitutes the main question to be faced in this chapter.

The discussion may be opened by returning to the argument of Hume noted at the conclusion of the previous chapter. Here, the point may be made at once that this argument, unlike those advanced in recent years, is clearly *not* intended as being of the *a priori* kind. It is not, and cannot be, Hume's position that miracles are inconceivable or that the very idea of such is logically self-contradictory. His examples, given earlier, of 'the raising of a house or ship into the air' and 'the raising of a feather, when the wind wants ever so little of a force requisite for that purpose' (*HU*, p. 115n), of themselves, rule out any such interpretation as this. The argument, rather, is, as he says, 'from ... the nature of the fact' (*HU*, p. 114). In short, in so far as it *is* Hume's intention to offer this argument – that natural law being, *in fact*, what it is, miracles, as *violations* of such law, are *physically* impossible.

To assert the putatively *empirical* character of this view of natural law, however, is not to establish its truth. Indeed, it is merely to make acute the vital question of what precisely is involved in such a claim. Even at the most rudimentary level the question arises as to how such a view could *ever* be empirically verified. More specifically, it brings to the fore the opposition between two quite different conceptions of the nature of such laws, the debate over which still constitutes the core issue of modern philosophy of science. Thus, on the one hand, there is the view that physical reality, although random and lawless in its ultimate nature, yet, out

25

of the very vastness of this randomness, yields *patterns of uniformity* or *laws*. This, as already indicated, is essentially the position of Hume – that the laws of nature are expressions of uniformities derived on the basis of induction and which, as such, are always open to the theoretical possibility of change in the future. It is the view which, again, has its roots in the philosophy of Democritus and which, in the present century, has had a great resurgence through its applicability to *quantum* mechanics. As against this, must be set the view that the paradigm instances of natural law are to be found, not, as above, in such probability statements as 'all bodies fall to the ground', but, in the explanatory hypotheses of natural science as exemplified, most spectacularly, in Newton's *laws of motion*. The view, that is, that the laws of nature are to be conceived as having the character of *mental constructions* – 'constructs' which, though formulated on the basis of past experience, yet, in some way, allow an unerring (or, at least, potentially unerring) prediction of future events. This is the conception which, as emanating primarily from Kant, was originally set forth in conscious opposition to the Humean standpoint and which, prior to the rise of the *quantum* mechanics in the present century, came close to exerting virtual dominion over scientific thinking. Without, for the moment, going any further into the vast issues raised by these two opposed positions, enough has been said to establish that the argument under present discussion (with its appeal to the *universality* and *necessity* of natural law) is, at the very least, in need of extensive amplification. As it stands it amounts to little more than what is summarized by Lewis in the following passage:

> The question, 'Do miracles occur?' and the question, 'Is the course of Nature absolutely uniform?' are the same question asked in two different ways. Hume, by sleight of hand, treats them as two different questions. He first answers, 'Yes', to the question whether Nature is absolutely uniform: and then uses this 'Yes' as a ground for answering, 'No', to the question, 'Do miracles occur?' ... He gets the answer to one form of the question by assuming the answer to another form of the same question.[2]

Whilst accepting the legitimacy of what Lewis says here the discussion may be continued by attending to whether any significant amplification of Hume's (putatively *empirical*) argument is forthcoming from more recent discussion of the miraculous.

The starting point of this contemporary debate may be seen in the claim that conflict over the miraculous is, in the last resort, merely *definitional*. More particularly, that the idea of a miracle as a violation of a law of nature is to be rejected on the ground that it involves a plain contradiction of terms, that is a *logical* contradiction. It is expressed by Antony Flew, one of Hume's most ardent supporters, in the following way:

> We are now ready to follow the scent of logical scandal left by the suggestion that there might be violations of laws of nature. There is indeed a stone of stumbling. For in what is in our time surely the dominant usage of the expression *law of nature* the suggestion of any genuine violation or overriding (as opposed to some built-in limitation of scope) is strictly self-contradictory.[3]

Despite Flew's reference to the 'dominant usage' of the term *law of nature*, the validity of the argument turns on the acceptance of the proposition that it is *analytically* or *self-evidently* true that such laws (whatever precisely these may be) are *necessarily/logically* inviolable. This, however, is plainly false. It is fully met by the words of Huxley, even though written nearly a century ago:

> Nobody can presume to say what the order of nature must be; all that the widest experience (even if it extended over all past time and through all space) that events had happened in a certain way could justify, would be a proportionally strong expectation that events will go on so happening, and the demand for a proportional strength of evidence in favour of any assertion that they had happened otherwise.[4]

The fact that what Huxley says here would be widely endorsed at the present time is of no immediate consequence. It is not the *truth* of this opposed conception of natural law which is required for present purposes. The rejection of Flew's argument follows simply from the mere *conceivability* of this alternative view.

Flew's argument, as may well be accepted, is oversimplistic. A more sophisticated attempt at an *a priori* rejection of the miraculous is forthcoming from Alastair McKinnon in his article '"Miracle" and "Paradox"'.[5] This, like Flew's, centres on the claim that 'the idea of a suspension of natural law is self-contradictory' (p. 309), but, at the same time, employs a different sense of *natural law* from that of the former. Thus, as McKinnon argues, 'natural law is not, as has been widely supposed, a kind of code for nature having legislative, and, perhaps particularly, prohibitive force' (p. 309). This is 'an outdated, untenable, and completely unscientific view' (p. 309). Rather, natural laws are to be conceived, most basically and simply, as 'highly generalized shorthand *descriptions* of *how things do in fact happen*' (p. 309, my italics). To say this is to highlight the tentative, provisional, corrigible character of such 'descriptions'. Laws in this sense are always open to being contradicted by new facts, including those of such an extraordinary kind as might lead to them being (erroneously) ascribed to the category of the miraculous. This, however, is not to allow the possibility of a 'violation' or 'suspension' of natural law. It is merely to acknowledge that the 'law' as originally formulated was not a *true* 'description' and that it must be replaced by one which more adequately represents what is, *in fact* (and no matter how extraordinary), the case. To this extent, there can be no suspensions of natural law – and, following from this, that the idea of a miracle (as involving just such a suspension) must be seen as entailing a contradiction in terms:

> The idea of a suspension of natural law is self-contradictory. . . . This contradiction may stand out more clearly if for *natural law* we substitute the expression *the actual course of events*. *Miracle* would then be defined as 'an event involving the suspension of the actual course of events.' And someone who insisted on describing an event as a miracle would be in the rather odd position of claiming that its occurrence was contrary to the actual course of events. (p. 309)

In short, as McKinnon concludes, the (true) laws of nature state what actually happens. As such, everything that happens, even the seemingly miraculous, must necessarily accord with them.

What may be accepted, is that, in this argument, McKinnon rightly draws attention to a feature of the idea of natural law which has received great emphasis in recent years, most particularly, through the writings of Karl Popper. That is to say, the point that such laws are more easily falsified than verified. Indeed, that, by their very nature, they can never be conclusively verified; and that what is most distinctive about them is their falsifiability. What may be accepted, too, is the further consideration that the triumphal march of science is intimately related to this characteristic of falsifiability. For it is the falsification of existing laws through the discovery of new facts which leads to ever-more comprehensive explanations; and, with this, to the scientific ideal that all facts will, in the fulness of time, be brought within the domain of scientific methodology and assimilated to natural law. Much more worrying in the argument is McKinnon's equation of natural law with *'descriptions* of how things do *in fact* happen' (my italics). This raises immediate difficulties with regard to the *predictive* character of scientific theories. For while the term *description* has a perfectly clear meaning with regard to the past and the present it hardly makes sense to apply it to what has not yet taken place. To this extent, talk of *description* with regard to the matter in hand most properly gives way, at this point, to that of *stipulation*.[6] However this may be, and whilst accepting the importance of each of the above points for philosophy of science, they may be put aside as being largely irrelevant to the immediate discussion and as merely serving to obscure the real basis of McKinnon's position. This, in short, is that 'the actual course of events' or 'how things do in fact happen' – and, no matter how extraordinary – is *always* open to explanation through the methodology of *science*. This, however, is precisely the point in need of proof. As such, the argument – and despite its sophistication – completely fails in its main intention as an *a priori* disproof of the miraculous. In essence it amounts, as with Bultmann's position, to no more than an assertion of complete and unbounded faith in the scientific outlook.

A variant of McKinnon's argument, as this rests on the assumption noted above, is to be found in the claim of another writer, Guy Robinson, that the whole scientific enterprise is, in some way, compromised by even allowing the possibility of the miraculous:

> Scientific development would either be stopped or else made completely capricious, because it would necessarily be a matter of whim whether one invoked the concept of a miracle ... to explain the awkward result, or, on the other hand, accepted the result as evidence of the need to modify the theory one was investigating.[7]

This argument, it will be clear, is exclusively heuristic and, to this extent, peripheral to the main discussion. At the same time, it may be met in ways that are highly relevant to this latter.

In the first place, it is *not* self-evident, as Robinson takes for granted, that the demands of science have a clear and undisputed priority over all other types of thinking. Man does not live by science alone and it might well be that, in the wider context of man's fuller being, the heuristic claim to the acceptance of (some sense of) the miraculous outweighs that of the scientist to its rejection. Secondly, it is simply not true that the acceptance of the above two classes of events necessarily leads to the disastrous consequences predicted by Robinson. Merely to mention the great Newton and the fact that his world-view embraced both natural and supernatural causation is sufficient to offer a complete counter to this claim. To add that Newton himself was steeped in, if not obsessed by, occultism is simply to press the point.[8] Whilst these general considerations are sufficient, of themselves, to counter the claim of Robinson they may be supplemented by a number of further points which relate, more specifically, to modern philosophy of science.

Thus, in this connexion, mention may be made of the view that an acceptance of the possibility of the miraculous might, under certain circumstances, be to the actual benefit of science. This is a position suggested by R. F. Holland who presents the fantastic, but imaginable, setting of a horse that continues to prosper without ever eating or drinking.[9] In such a case, as Holland maintains, it would be altogether more reasonable, and entirely in conformity with the scientific canon of simplicity, to *accept* a miracle rather than undertake a wholesale revision of the existing and well established (in this instance, physiological/biological) laws of nature. Most particularly, however, is the point made by Ninian Smart that it is plainly false to portray the scientist as being absorbed with each and every particular exception to existing scientific laws.[10] The fact is, as Smart argues, 'that science is not just observational: it is *experimental* (p. 40, my italic). As such, it is concerned with '*types* of situations' (p. 41) as these are established under *controlled* and, thereby, *repeatable* conditions (p. 40). To this extent, as he continues, it is not the single, isolated event which, for the scientist, 'produces the negative instance of deadly power' (p. 40), that is the instance that leads to the falsification of an existing law. It is 'the repeated, the sifted, the scrutinized experiment' (p. 40) which does this through the establishment of what are, in effect, '*small-scale* laws' (p. 41, my italics). The miraculous, in this respect, as Smart concludes, falls quite outside the realm of scientific methodology:

> The relevance of all this to miracles is readily apparent. Miracles are not experimental, repeatable. They are particular, peculiar events occurring in idiosyncratic human situations. They are not small-scale laws. Consequently they do not destroy large-scale laws. Formally, they may seem to destroy the 'Always' statements of the scientific laws; but they have not the genuine deadly power of the negative instance. (p. 41)

This argument constitutes not only an effective response to Robinson, but also provides an important amplification of what was said above in reply to McKinnon's rejection of the miraculous. Thus, as emphasized by Richard Swinburne:

> The upshot of all this is that – against McKinnon – laws of nature do not just describe what happens [i.e. 'the actual course of events']. They describe what happens in a regular and predictable way. When what happens is entirely irregular and unpredictable, its occurrence is not something describable by natural laws.[11]

To summarize, therefore, the positions of both Robinson and McKinnon are to be rejected for no less simple a reason (in addition to those already given) than that they involve an inadequate conception of what, in the context of scientific methodology, is meant by a *violation* or *suspension* of natural law.

With this, attention may be turned, finally, to the claim that the miraculous is open to *a priori* refutation on the simple ground that the very idea of the *super*-natural is logically self-negating. The position is argued, most notably, by Patrick Nowell-Smith[12] who, whilst rejecting the view (for example, of McKinnon) that miracle claims can be refuted on the basis of their being *exceptions* to *natural law*, notwithstanding, questions the validity of the distinction between the *natural* and the *supernatural* on which such claims are grounded:

> Let us grant ... that no scientist can at present explain certain phenomena. It does not follow that the phenomena are inexplicable by scientific methods, still less that they must be attributed

to supernatural agents . . . The problem is not whether science can explain everything in current terms, but whether the explanation of miracles requires a method quite different from that of science. Unless this latter thesis is proved, it is hard to see why miracles should be called 'supernatural'. (pp. 247, 248)

Thus, as Nowell-Smith contends, the problem of miracles is one that centres on the question of precisely 'what is involved in the notion of *explanation*' (p. 249, my italic). More particularly, as he continues, the term is meaningful only to the extent that it is limited exclusively to its *scientific* usage:

Let [an opponent] consider the meaning of the word 'explanation' and let him ask himself whether this notion does not involve that of a law or hypothesis capable of predictive expansion. And then let him ask himself whether such an explanation would not be natural in whatever terms it is couched, and how the notion of 'the supernatural' could play any part in it. (p. 253)

In short, as Nowell-Smith concludes, the idea of the miraculous (as this involves that of a 'supernaturally caused' event) is to be rejected for the simple reason that 'the phrase "supernatural explanation" is a contradiction in terms' (p. 252).

What may be seen, is that this conclusion, resting as it does on the central contention that *all* explanation must be of the *scientific* kind, approaches dangerously close to a simple begging of the question. Putting this aside, however, the argument is open to decisive rejection on two other grounds, both of which relate, more positively, to the possibility of *empirically* establishing the miraculous as a class of events radically different from the natural.

Thus, in the first place, there is the point that, even accepting Nowell-Smith's main premise that there is only one type of explanation, that is the scientific, it does not follow from this that all events must be *scientifically* explicable. There is nothing in what Nowell-Smith says to negate the possibility of some events being, by nature, (scientificially) *inexplicable*; and with this, as constituting a class separate from that of the natural. This, in point of fact, is amply, if obliquely, recognized by Nowell-Smith in a passage which, at one and the same time, highlights the essential circularity of his argument as well as a confusion in his use of the term *explanation*:

What I reject is the theory of science which makes it possible to claim that any phenomenon is essentially inexplicable, the leap to 'supernatural agencies', and the view that such agencies in fact explain the phenomena. If miracles are 'lawful' it should be possible to state the laws; if not the alleged explanation [i.e. the appeal to 'supernatural agencies'] amounts to a confession that they are inexplicable. (p. 251)

To this extent, therefore – and even within the terms of its own major premise – the argument may be seen as completely failing in its intention as an *a priori* refutation of the miraculous.

To the above may be added the second consideration – that the major premise itself is plainly false. Merely to mention Aristotle's time-honoured doctrine of the *four causes* is immediately to suggest a way in which this may be demonstrated. For the plain fact is, as Aristotle clearly saw, and has been continually emphasized since then, that, in addition to the sense of *explanation* stressed by Nowell-Smith, that is the *scientific*, there is also another straightforward and important sense of this term. That is, the sense which relates to an event having its origin in the *volitional* act of an agent. This is a point that is specifically urged against Nowell-Smith by Swinburne:

It is important [against this view] to make a distinction made by many modern philosophers between a scientific explanation of the occurrence of an event and an explanation of the occurrence of an event effected by the act of an agent, that is ordinarily a man, in terms of his purpose or intention in producing it, which I will term personal explanation.[13]

To make this distinction is not, of course, to deny the possibility of relations existing between the two types of explanation. It is not to deny, for instance, as Swinburne notes, 'that many events whose production can be explained by the intention or purpose of an agent can, also, be explained in scientific terms' (p. 55). Nor, again, 'that purposes and intentions are often predictable' (p. 55). Notwithstanding, as Swinburne rightly concludes, and as has been well argued in recent years, the point remains that crucial differences exist between the two. This leads to a further consideration. More specifically – that while discussion of volitional action is normally, and naturally, restricted to *human* purposes and intentions, this same sense of 'explanation' constitutes an essential (though often neglected) part of the definition of the miraculous which has guided the discussion so far. That is to say – the aspect embraced in Hume's reference to such an event being brought about by '*a particular volition of the Deity, or by the interposition of some invisible agent*' (*HU*, p. 105n). This immediately raises the possibility, as against Nowell-Smith, of distinguishing the *natural* from the *supernatural* on the basis that the latter, as opposed to the former, is to be conceived as having, in some extraordinary sense, the character of some kind of extraordinary *willing*. On this ground, again, therefore – and, no less than for the reasons already given – Nowell-Smith's argument is to be decisively rejected.

To summarize, therefore, it has been seen that the various arguments against the miraculous considered above, far from constituting *a priori* refutations of this idea, reduce, in the last resort, to what amount to, no more than, expressions of unfettered faith in the all-comprehensive legitimacy of the scientific enterprise. To this extent, they go no further than, and offer no support to, Bultmann's own basic stance. At the same time, while failing in their main intention, these arguments still serve to highlight the importance of another, more diffuse, question. That is – the *reasonableness* of accepting the idea of the miraculous; and with this, *two* kinds of exceptions to natural law. This is clearly a question which, returning to the quotation from Huxley given earlier, can only be settled on the basis of appeal to *empirical* considerations. As a condition of approaching this vital issue, however, a closer *conceptual* specification of what is involved in the idea of the miraculous is necessary. It is to this that attention may now be turned.

4

Miracles and Mind

While still, for immediate purposes, restricting the term *miraculous* to its traditional (biblical) connotation, attention may be drawn to a statement by Odegard which admirably summarizes the main thrust of the argument so far:

> The claim 'Anything decreed by a law is necessary unless a god does the contrary' becomes in effect the claim that, if a kind of thing is decreed by a law, there is absolutely no good reason to think that a contrary event ever occurs unless there is good reason to think that a god produces such an event. Thus, to say that a rod's turning into a serpent is impossible unless a god performs the transformation is in effect to say that, unless there is good reason to think that a god does such a thing, there is absolutely no good reason to think that such a thing ever occurs. And it implies that, if there is good reason to think that a god has done such a thing, there is absolutely no good reason to think that such a thing ever occurs otherwise. This is the epistemic point of saying that, although it is possible for a god to turn a rod into a serpent, such a thing is otherwise impossible.[1]

What Odegard says here clearly brings into focus the tension that exists in the idea of the *miraculous* between that of *natural law*, on the one hand, and that of the *super-natural*, on the other. It also highlights the conclusion of Chapter 3 regarding the failure of attempts to refute the idea of the miraculous by appeals to sophisticated conceptions of natural law. At the same time the passage is suggestive of two further points which are important for the development of the present discussion. They may be considered in turn.

Thus, in the first place, the passage brings into clear relief the question of the precise significance of the idea of natural law for the matter in hand. Enough has already been said to establish that a too-ready acceptance of its importance may easily lead to an over-hasty rejection of any form of supernaturalism. At the same time, there is the no less clear consideration that, without the idea of natural law, there can certainly be no conception of the miraculous. The fact is, as Lewis aptly remarks, that 'if you begin by ruling out the supernatural you will perceive no miracles ... [but] ... you will equally perceive no miracles until you believe that nature works according to regular laws'.[2] What may be added however, and what, Lewis would be the last to deny, is the point made by Broad. Namely, that 'the notion of a miracle belongs mainly to popular thought';[3] and, following from this – that it demands a much more basic and immediate sense of natural law than that discussed in the, for present purposes, esoteric terms of philosophy of science. Thus, to return to what Odegard says in the above passage – and accepting that the turning of a rod into a serpent would count as a miracle – a vital element of the miraculous, as portrayed here, as, also, in so many narratives of such events, is a sense of natural law which is open to full and immediate appreciation by even the most *ordinary* intelligence.

Pursuing the consideration further, the bizarre and extraordinary nature of such (putative) events follows precisely from this fact – as opposed, for instance, to what happens in the hidden vestibules of the scientist's laboratory. That there is such a sense of natural law is fully emphasized, if it needs to be, by Smart:

> It is not true that people are unacquainted with laws of nature. You don't need to have any scientific expertise to know that people do not rise from the dead, that water freezes when it gets very cold, that heavy objects tend to fall towards the earth, and so on.[4]

It is stressed, again, in more aggressive terms, by Lewis in talking, more specifically, about the narrative of the Virgin Birth:

> You and I may not agree ... as to whether miracles happen or not. But at least let us not talk nonsense. Let us not allow vague rhetoric about the march of science to fool us into supposing that the most complicated account of birth, in terms of genes and spermatozoa leaves us any more convinced than we were before that *nature* does not send babies to young women who 'know not a man'.[5]

And, further, in relation to the consideration raised earlier regarding the *credulity* of people in bygone times:

> The idea that the progress of science has somehow altered the
> question [of what is possible] is closely bound up with the idea
> that people 'in olden times' believed in [miracles] 'because they
> didn't know the laws of Nature'. Thus you will hear people say
> 'The early Christians believed that Christ was the son of a virgin,
> but we know that this is a scientific impossibility'. Such people
> seem to have an idea that belief in miracles arose at a period
> when men were so ignorant of the course of nature that they did
> not perceive a miracle to be contrary to it. A moment's thought
> shows this to be nonsense: and the story of the Virgin Birth is a
> particularly striking example ... Why? Because Joseph knew just
> as well as any modern gynaecologist that in the ordinary course
> of nature women do not have babies unless they have lain with
> men.[6]

With this, therefore, there is, in effect, a return to the earlier
discussion of Hume; and to the fact that it is *his* straightforward
and unsophisticated (though, within its limits, thoroughly legitimate) conception of natural law which is most fundamental in any
attempt to delineate the idea of the miraculous. That is to say – the
idea of regularity and order in nature as this impresses itself, most
basically, at the *common-sense* level of observation.

The second main point that may be extracted from the above
passage from Odegard is that a further vital aspect of the miraculous is to be found in the fact that such (putative) events suggest, in
some way, the interposition of some (invisible) *super-human* agency, that is, for immediate purposes, *God*. To this extent, it is not
sufficient that such events be simply bizarre or extraordinary – that
is, merely 'exceptions to' or 'violations of' natural law in the above,
rudimentary, sense of the term. The fact is, as Lewis notes again,
that 'the progress of science has ... (and greatly to our benefit)
made all sorts of things incredible which our ancestors believed;
man-eating ants and gryphons in Scythia, men with one single
gigantic foot, magnetic islands that draw all ships towards them,
mermaids and fire-breathing dragons' (p. 58). But, as he goes on,
'those things were never put forward as supernatural interruptions
of the course of nature' (p. 58). They were put forward, rather, 'as
items within her ordinary course – in fact as "science"' (p. 58). To
this may be added, reciprocally, the consideration that certain

phenomena, now scientifically established as natural, for example floods, pestilences, earthquakes, were, at one time – and so, still, in many parts of the world – regarded as evidence of supernatural activity. The juxtaposition of this point with that of Lewis serves to bring out what is of most importance for immediate purposes and what is clearly implicit in the above passage from Odegard. In short, that what is most fundamental to the idea of the miraculous is, not (a) any overriding entailment about the primacy of *natural law*, but, rather, (b) the conception of some kind of super-human *volitional* control over the natural order.

This, significantly enough, is vividly delineated by Hume himself in a passage which immediately precedes his definition of a miracle:

> Sometimes an event may not, *in itself, seem* to be contrary to the laws of nature, and yet, if it were real, it might, by reason of some circumstance, be denominated a miracle; because, in *fact*, it is contrary to these laws. Thus if a person, claiming a divine authority, should command a sick person to be well, a healthful man to fall down dead, the clouds to pour rain, the winds to blow, in short, should order many natural events, which immediately follow upon his command; these might justly be esteemed miracles, because they are really, in this case, contrary to the laws of nature. For if any suspicion remain, that the event and command concurred by accident, there is no miracle and no transgression of the laws of nature. If this suspicion be removed, there is evidently a miracle, and a transgression of these laws; *because nothing can be more contrary to nature than that the voice or command of a man should have such an influence.* (*HU*, p. 115, my final italics)

The conclusion from the above, therefore – as this is also implicit in the epistemic condition summarized by Odegard – is that, though the idea of the miraculous involves a (rudimentary) sense of natural law as a *necessary* aspect of its connotation, its *sufficiency* springs from something over and above this. That is to say – from the idea of some kind of super-human intelligence which is capable of manifesting an arresting control over the natural order of things.

The consideration is, of course, open to full illustration by appeal to the biblical narratives. To mention the stories of Moses' wonder-workings at the court of Pharaoh and the performance of Elijah in the elaborate setting at Carmel is but to give two examples out of many from the Old Testament. The healing miracles of the New Testament abundantly demonstrate the same point. So, also, the so-called 'nature' miracles – the calming of the storm, the turning of water into wine, the blighting of the fig tree, and so on. It may be acknowledged that the narratives of the Virgin Birth and the Resurrection have the added interest of illustrating the direct, as opposed to the mediate, intervention of God. At the same time, there is still the fact that any appreciation of the significance of these (theologically) higher miracles is plainly to be seen as being derivative from a logically prior understanding of the preceding, more basic, sense of the term. However this may be, the point to be emphasized is that already drawn. That is, as summarized by Broad – 'To say that a law of nature is true, but that there are miraculous exceptions to it, comes, therefore, to this: the law is true independently of all conditions in the material world, but it may be suspended by something acting upon matter or other minds in the same direct way as our minds seem to act on our bodies and on themselves.'[7]

In point of fact, this conclusion has come to occupy a position of central importance in recent discussion of the idea of the miraculous. It is summarized, for instance, by (Paul) Dietl:

> We are dealing [here] with requests and answers, that is thoughts, and thoughts not as psychological occurrences but as understood ... [That is, with] ... an understanding that can grasp the request and then bring it about that a natural law be broken.[8]

And, further, in responding to the claims of Nowell-Smith noted earlier:

> But surely it has become obvious that there is nothing which could be pinned down as the independent variable in a scientific explanation ... [of the miraculous]; for no conceivable candidate is necessary. The prophet asks God to do miracle No. 4 at midnight and then goes to sleep. Or he asks God to do whatever miracle turns up at whatever hour turns up and then dies ... No natural law will do because only vehicles of thought could function as the natural *explanans* and no such vehicle is necessary ... That is why if a new department is set up [to investigate

such events] it will not be with the science faculties at all. It will be a department of religion.[9]

Again, there is the same point as given by (Margaret) Boden in framing the example of a man who is capable of instantly curing cases of leprosy by uttering certain incantations:

> [Granted that such is empirically validated] . . . would we not be absolutely justified in saying that such a thing is *scientifically impossible*? Could we reasonably suggest, with all our knowledge – imperfect though it may be – of the nature of tissue-growth and cell-differentiation, and of the ravages of the leprosy bacillus within the human body, that such an 'anomalous' event might one day be scientifically explained? I think not: such a suggestion would be at least as blatant an act of faith as the wildest claim ever made in the name of religion.[10]

As may be seen, therefore, both the above writers use the point under discussion as a criterion for distinguishing what has traditionally been labelled the *miraculous* from the class of the *natural*, as this has been steadily assimilated to the sphere of the scientist.

At the same time, what is entirely lacking in the foregoing is any explanation as to precisely *why* the miraculous, in the above sense, should be regarded as permanently and necessarily falling outside the domain of the scientist. That is, as being by its very nature, '*scientifically* impossible'. Despite the fact that this question is left open by Dietl and Boden an answer is forthcoming.

It is, indeed already implicit in the important, though rarely quoted, passage, *HU*, p. 115n, from Hume quoted above. For besides offering a *criterion* of the miraculous as this is contained in the idea of an event's being brought about by (what appears to be) some kind of super-natural *willing*, the passage also highlights another vital consideration. That is – that what is involved in such (super-normal) *willing* is such as to be more appropriately characterized in contemporary terms as (a) *transcending the parameters of (materialistic) science*, than (b) *violating the laws of nature*. The point is plainly to be seen in the two senses of the term *laws of nature* which are instantiated in the reference to the event in question being 'in fact' (as opposed to, merely, 'not seeming') contrary to such laws. It is to be seen, again, in the final remark that '*nothing* can be *more contrary to nature* than that the voice of a man should have such influence' (my italics). Most particularly for immediate purposes, however, attention may be drawn to the way in which it is expressed by Broad in an essay on precisely this very topic.[11]

Thus, as Broad argues, there are 'certain limiting principles', or, as they may be called, *Basic Limiting Principles* which 'we [in the West] unhesitatingly take for granted as the framework within which all our practical activities and our scientific theories are confined' (p. 7). Some of these 'seem to be self-evident' (p. 7). Others 'are so overwhelmingly supported by all the empirical facts which fall within the range of ordinary experience and the scientific elaborations of it (including under this heading orthodox psychology) that it hardly enters our heads to question them' (p. 7). Taken together, these principles do, as Broad summarizes the point, 'cover very satisfactorily an enormous range of well-established facts of the most varied kind' (pp. 8–9). Further, as he goes on, the situation has developed where

> we are quite naturally inclined to think that they must be all-embracing ... [and where] we are correspondingly loth to accept any alleged fact which seems to conflict with them; and, [where, again] if we are forced to accept it, we strive desperately to house it within the accepted framework. (p. 9)

They are, in short, principles which, as developed most principally over the course of the past four hundred years, have come to be unquestioningly accepted, not merely as the *parameters* of the Western way of thinking, but, also (in the West), as *constitutive* of the nature of reality itself.

With regard to the principles themselves, and without claiming his list to be exhaustive, Broad identifies nine such which he classifies under four main heads. Of the nine it is sufficient for present purposes simply to mention that three are given under, what he calls, *General Principles of Causation* (pp. 9–10) and four under *Limitations on Ways of acquiring Knowledge* (pp. 10–12). The remaining two may be stated more fully. First – *Dependence of Mind on Brain*:

> A necessary, even if not a sufficient, immediate condition of any mental event is an event in the brain of a living body. (p. 10)

Secondly – *Limitations on the Action of Mind on Matter*:

> It is impossible for an event in a person's mind to produce *directly* any change in the material world except certain changes in his own brain. (p. 9)

And further, in amplifying its connexion with the other main divisions:

> It is true that it seems to ... [the agent] ... that many of his volitions produce directly certain movements of his fingers, feet, throat, tongue, etc. These are what he wills, and he knows nothing about the changes in his brain. Nevertheless it is these brain-changes which are the immediate consequences of his volitions; and the willed movements of his fingers, etc., follow, if they do so, only as rather remote causal descendants. (p. 10)

It is, as may be seen, this latter principle which is of most direct relevance in the present connexion. For to accept it, as one must, as a *Basic Limiting Principle* in Broad's sense of the term, is, at the same time, to provide an answer to the main question under discussion. That is – as to *why* the miraculous (in the sense of an event brought about by some kind of super-human *willing*) is to be conceived as constituting a *logically* separate class from that of the *natural*. The point is simply that it is excluded from the latter on *definitional* grounds. In short – *by the self-imposed limitations of science itself.*

This conclusion, it will be clear, is not negated by the possibility raised earlier that miracles (in some significant sense of this term) might be open to *empirical* investigation. Neither, and more particularly – by the view of Nowell-Smith that, in the very act of being accepted as a possible object of empirical enquiry, the (putatively) miraculous is automatically assimilated to the sphere of the *natural*. Any difficulty that might arise in this connexion is fully met by making a distinction between (a) the *validation*, and (b) the *explanation* of any such phenomenon. It is the former, that is the *establishment* of a miracle as an actual happening, which is most fundamental with regard to the matter in hand. It is this, alone, which is sufficient to mark off such an event from the 'natural' in the sense of this term used so far. The question of *explicability* is merely incidental to the phenomenology of the happening itself. This is a point that is clearly anticipated by Broad in accepting the possibility of the miraculous being subject to (*mind/matter*) *laws* which, though not yet known, are, in principle, knowable:

It is not necessary to assume that ... [the miraculous] ... obeys
no laws; we should still call events due to the volitions of God, or
an angel or devil or magician, miracles, even if we knew that
these volitions obeyed among themselves psychological laws.[12]

To allow this is merely to highlight the possibility that the domain
of *science* – with all its assumptions, parameters and methodology
(as, also, all its triumphant successes achieved on this basis) –
might merely be part of a wider realm of the (potentially) *knowable*.
To this extent, the main point remains. That is, that the (putatively)
miraculous – whether explicable or not – is *definitionally* excluded
from the *natural* as this is conceived under the *heuristic* demands of
the (currently existing) *scientific* endeavour.

It remains to offer an anecdotal amplification of this conclusion,
the significance of which will be taken up more fully later. It
concerns the influence exerted, particularly with regard to physiology and psychology, by the so-called 'Helmholtz' School of Medicine whose most famous members were Emil Du Bois-Reymond
(1818–96), Ernst Brücke (1819–92), Carl Ludwig (1816–95) and
Hermann Helmholtz (1821–94). The 'amazing story' of the far-
reaching influence exerted by these men is recounted by Sir Ernest
Jones in his account of Freud's student days under Brücke.[13] Thus,
as Jones recalls, the above four men formed a small private club,
imbued with 'a veritable crusading spirit' which had, as its main
objective, the complete eradication of any trace of *mentalism/
vitalism* from human thought. In 1845 this was enlarged to form the
Berliner Physikalische Geselltschaft which had, as a condition of
membership, subscription to the following oath:

No other forces than the common physical and chemical ones
are active within the organism. In those cases which cannot at
the time be explained by these forces one has either to find the
specific way or form of their action by means of the physical-
mathematical method or to assume new forces equal in dignity
to the chemical-physical forces inherent in matter, reducible to
the force of attraction and repulsion.

The enormous influence of this movement is attested by Jones in
his remark that 'Du Bois-Reymond, Brücke, Helmholtz and Ludwig remained life-long friends' and that 'within twenty-five or
thirty years they achieved complete domination over the thinking

of the German physiologists and medical teachers' as well as giving 'intensive stimulus to science everywhere'. From the vantage point of the contemporary scene, there can be no question that the dogmatic *materialism* expressed here has led to a vast extension of knowledge over the past hundred years. Whether this is balanced in terms that relate to the wider aspects of human life is more doubtful. Most important for present purposes, however, is the point that, whatever its *heuristic* importance, it is a stance which is theoretically open to challenge, in the most direct way, by the possibility of the *miraculous* as delineated above and as may be developed more fully in the course of what follows.

5

Miracles as a Mode of the Super-normal

In the course of the discussion to this point, attention has been confined to the sense of the term *miracle* which is most commonly taken for granted and whose derivation springs, most obviously, from the biblical narratives of such (putative) happenings. In continuing the argument, it will be the object of the present chapter to explore the possibility of extending the idea, as developed so far, beyond the *historical/theological* constraints of its traditional connotation.

The scope of the issue may be brought into focus by returning to Bultmann and to a summary statement, in his own words, of the underlying basis of his theological 'revolution':

> [The mythological conception of the world] is different from the conception of the world which has been formed and developed by science since its inception in ancient Greece and which has been accepted by all modern men. In this modern conception of the world the cause-and-effect nexus is fundamental . . . Modern science does not believe that the course of nature can be interrupted or so to speak, perforated, by supernatural powers.[1]

Enough has been said to establish that this assertion is to be viewed as being more in the nature of an expression of faith than of established fact. It assumes the very point in need of proof and is, to this extent, entirely inadequate to support the structure it has to bear. At the same time – and as has been fully acknowledged – it still poses the residual and fundamental challenge of the *reasonableness* of appeal to any kind of *supernatural* agency; and, with this, *two* categories of exceptions to *natural law*.

Here it may be said, at once, that, in so far as the idea of the miraculous is restricted, as is generally taken for granted, to the traditional (biblical) sense of this term, the balance must be accepted as being heavily weighted on the side of Bultmann. The plain fact is that the modern world would appear to be singularly bereft of events of the bizarre and spectacular nature recorded in the biblical narratives. The trouble about miracles in this sense of the term, as Broad pertinently notes, 'is not that no evidence *could* prove one, but that no evidence *has* proved one'.[2] In this connexion, too, the supporter of the view that there can only be one kind of exception to natural law, that is the *natural*, can point to another important consideration in his favour. That is, the fact that much of what, in bygone times, was attributed to supernatural agency has, through the march of science, been brought under natural/physical law. Granted this – or, so it may be argued – it is entirely reasonable to assume that, given only time, all phenomena, even the most bizarre and extraordinary, will eventually yield to the methodology of the scientist. To this extent, Bultmann's conclusion, together with Hume's, that the biblical narratives of the miraculous are to be explained in terms of a more rudimentary type of understanding, might well appear as being entirely justified and thoroughly in accord with the scientific criterion of simplicity.

Concomitantly, however – and, again, as has already been made plain – this specifically *theological* aspect of Bultmann's 'revolution' is inextricably interrelated in the context of his exposition with, what is, in effect, a *metaphysical* stance. That is, the contention that *no* possible sense of *supernaturalism* can have any basis in reality. This is a claim which, as already noted, extends well beyond the spheres of theology and historical scholarship to strike at the very heart, not only of *religion* but, also, of *philosophy* itself. Bultmann himself undoubtedly confuses these two, quite separate, aspects of his position. Indeed, it is from this very fact that the provocativeness of his writings essentially springs. They are, however, clearly, if only implicitly, distinguished by an early respondent to his original manifesto, Julius Schniewind:

> Modern man is by no means the first to feel the difficulty of accepting the faith of the Christians [as this involves the *miraculous*]. The great majority of mankind have always been ready and willing enough to accept a vague and general belief in God [and with this, for present purposes, the *supernatural*] which makes no specific demands upon them, but the more definite Christian belief in Christ [and the biblical sense of the *miraculous*] they prefer to reject as a myth. The cultured scorn of a Celsus and the coarse ribaldry of the nineteenth and twentieth centuries are at one in this.[3]

It is, of course, Bultmann's underlying *metaphysical* assumption – as opposed to his (perhaps, justified) claim, as a liberal theologian, regarding the mythological character of the biblical miracles – which constitutes the crux of the whole of the present discussion. More particularly for the moment, however, is the fact that it brings into sharp relief what is, in effect, the main concern of the immediate chapter. That is, the question of whether – in opposition to the position assumed by Bultmann – a sense of the *miraculous* may be specified which, even though, perhaps, removed from its traditional, biblical, connotation, is open to the possibility of some kind of (empirical) *validation*.

There may be pause to reiterate the far-reaching significance of the issue. Thus, with regard to the realm of science there is, at once, the point that the idea of establishing a class of supernatural exceptions to natural law reciprocally opens up no less a possibility than that of attaining a decisive refutation of, what – as instantiated, for instance, in the terms of the Helmoltzian oath – may be labelled as *scientific/materialistic* orthodoxy. Further, in this connexion – of invoking, also, a drastic revision of the ethical/psychological/social/political doctrines associated with this dominant metaphysical stance. Whilst noting the vastness of these implications, the point must not go unnoticed that they are essentially *philosophical* in nature and present no threat whatsoever to the practical autonomy of the scientist. As against this, the impact of the same idea on the spheres of religion and theology is much more direct. In one respect, of course, it is clearly to be welcomed. In another, however, it raises the spectre of a challenge which is, potentially, quite as disturbing to the traditional Christian consciousness as the reductionist aspect of Bultmann's position. For, if Bultmann is *theologically* right in his questioning of the biblical narratives and, at the same time, *factually* wrong in his outright rejection of *any* form of *supernaturalism*, then his conclusion regarding a move to existentialist ethics may well be very wide of the mark. What might be called for, rather, is a complete *theological* rethinking of some of the most fundamental tenets of the Christian faith. Such, indeed, is the substance of the conclusion of another early respondent to Bultmann's manifesto, Helmut Thielicke:

> Bultmann has thrown down a serious challenge to the very foundations of the Church [and] we therefore owe [him] a debt of gratitude . . . If we understand him aright, the most remark-

able fact about his thesis is that it cannot remain stationary. Either it must advance in the direction of Kamlah and cease in the end to be Christian, or there must be radical examination of the whole problem of myth from within the Church. By such an examination the Church may finally win a new freedom in the truth.[4]

What may be reiterated, therefore, is the extent of the challenge arising from the central concern of the present chapter. That is – from whether the idea of the miraculous is open to development beyond the, for present purposes, *sterile*, (historical/theological) connotations assumed so far.

In turning, more specifically, to this latter, a start may be made by highlighting the point already noted in discussing the views of Hume – that miracles need not necessarily be conceived as relating exclusively to such grand-scale affairs as are recorded in the biblical narratives and in the annals of Church history. Coupled with this is the further consideration that neither need such (putative) events be conceived as being necessarily rare in the manner of their occurrence. This is a point which is strongly, and rightly, emphasized by a recent writer, George Landrum:

> One tends to think of miracles as being rare – perhaps very rare indeed . . . Now it may well be that miracles are and always have been rare; but I can not see that it is part of the concept of a miracle that they are rare . . . One cannot, therefore, *define* 'miracle' so as to make it *a priori* impossible that common events should be miraculous.[5]

Taken together the two considerations raise the (conceptual) possibility that miracles might, indeed, be relatively common and happening at the present time – though because of their miniscularity (or, in Hume's phrase, because they are 'not so sensible with regard to us' (*HU*, p. 115n)) pass largely unnoticed, particularly in an intellectual climate antipathetic to their reality. It might even be, as many practising Christians believe, that intercessionary prayer is, itself, capable of producing miracles in this more limited sense. To the above extent, therefore, there is the main point that scale and bizarreness – though, perhaps, (and, certainly, traditionally), of religious importance – are, philosophically, merely of incidental significance to the idea of the miraculous *per se*.

This conclusion leads directly to a further, and more basic, restriction imposed on the idea in question by a too-close attention to the biblical model of such events. This concerns the assumption that miracles are to be conceived as being, in some way, necessarily related to the All-Powerful (theistic) *God* of the Judæo-Christian faith. It is to be seen, for instance, in the definition of the miraculous given in the *Oxford Dictionary of the Christian Church*: 'A miracle according to the traditional view is a sensible fact produced by the special intervention of God for a religious end, transcending the normal order of things usually termed the Law of Nature.'[6] Historically it is epitomized, in its most extreme form, in the claim of Aquinas that no created thing is capable of generating a miracle; and that God, as alone uncreated, has this sole power.[7] It is expressed again, more loosely, in the contention that the power to perform miracles, though stemming ultimately and exclusively from (the One and Only) *God*, is, yet, capable of being mediately exercised through lesser supernatural beings such as 'gods'/angels, and even, exceptionally, through human agents acting under special dispensation from such latter beings. Such, indeed, is the teaching which, as set forth by Pope Benedict XIV in his *De Miraculus* (1738), constitutes standard Roman Catholic doctrine on this issue. To this extent, there may be full acceptance of the point made by Lecky regarding the *historical* correlation between (Judæo-Christian) *theism*, on the one hand, and the (traditional) idea of the *miraculous*, on the other:

> The predisposition in favour of miracles grows out of, and can only be adequately explained by, certain conceptions of the nature of the Supreme Being, and of the habitual governance of the universe, which invariably accompany the earlier, or, as it may be termed, anthropomorphic, stage of development.[8]

What may be questioned, however, is the *philosophical* validity of this correlation. Here, there is the point, at once, that, within the precise terms of the foregoing context, there is, also, necessary appeal to agents of a more perverse kind than 'gods'/angels – that is, to 'gods'/devils, and, with this, their influence on men. As such, therefore, there is the clear conclusion that any purely *theistic* circumscription of the *miraculous* is to be seen as having no more than merely *definitional* force.

Pursuing the point further – and, again, as has been fully argued

– what is most fundamental to the idea of the miraculous is the *phenomenological* manifestation of some kind of super-naturalistic *volitional* agency. The moral nature of this power, as this may be contingently assessable from the particular circumstances surrounding any (putative) miracle, is merely incidental to the *sufficiency* of this, more basic, characteristic. Indeed, any (speculative) assessment as to the nature of such agency must, in the most literal way, be immediately subject to the spectral possibility raised by Descartes in his idea of a 'malignant deceiver'. The substance of the above is, in fact, fully anticipated by Hume in the postulation of the latter disjunct of his own classical definition of the miraculous. That is, in his perception that overriding the (theistically *loaded*) idea of (a) *a particular volition of the Deity* in this definition, is the wider (and theistically *neutral*) conception of (b) *the interposition of some invisible agent*. To this extent, again, therefore, the idea of the miraculous may be freed from its traditional (biblical) connotations. There is, in short, the conclusion that the idea of the miraculous, though having strong *contingent* links with *theism*, is not *necessarily* related to this deeply entrenched, specifically *religious*, outlook.

There is, however, another main point implicit in the above. It may be brought out by drawing attention to two senses of the term *supernatural/super-natural* which are to be found juxtaposed in the preceding discussion. Thus, in the first place, and obviously enough, there is (a) the sense which may be characterized for present purposes as necessarily involving reference to *an invisible realm of 'God(s)'*. Secondly, there is (b) the sense which centres on the basic *phenomenological* characteristic of the miraculous as this is to be found in the idea of a direct *mental* (and with this, *super/para-normal*) control over physical nature. That there is a strong contingent relation between (a) and (b) is obvious enough. It is plainly to be seen in the widely accepted religious assumption that evidence with regard to (b) constitutes a basis for belief in (a). At the same time, it is no less clearly the case that there is no *necessary* connexion between the two. Sense (a), for instance, might well be accepted without any rider regarding (b) – as, for example, in the view that, though there are 'gods', they may have neither the interest nor power to intervene in the affairs of men. Again, there is no need to assume from the acceptance of (b) that there is necessarily a realm of the *supernatural* in sense (a). Conversely, to postulate (b) is not necessarily to negate (a). These considerations serve to highlight, once more, the confusion in Bultmann's own use of this key term. More immediately, however, there is the vital point that the *sufficiency* of the idea of the miraculous is to be seen as turning, in the last resort, on (b) above rather than on (a). It turns, in short, on the (phenomenological) *super-normality* of the happening itself, as opposed to any presumed *supernaturalistic* ascription as to cause.

On the basis of the above, therefore, there is the clear conclusion that the *miraculous* need not necessarily be conceived in the exclusive terms of the biblical model of such events. What is *philosophically* most basic to the idea is, not any contingent feature relating to scale or bizarreness, nor any, necessarily speculative, claim as to origin, but, rather, the factor of some kind of super/para-normal *willing*. That is, more specifically – the phenomenological manifestation of purely *mental*, that is unmediated, control over physical nature. With this, too, there is the point that, as conceived in this way, there is nothing to negate the possibility of such events being brought about – even though, perhaps, only exceptionally, and not necessarily exclusively – by the *direct* volitional activity of *embodied* rational, that is *human*, agents. Nor, again, in this connexion, is there any necessity to relegate such events exclusively to the past. It might (conceivably) be the case that they are happening at the present time. Even, indeed, (again, conceivably) that they are, to some degree, repeatable.

In themselves, of course, these considerations provide no direct answer to the question raised earlier regarding the *reasonableness* of entertaining the miraculous as a class of events logically separate from the natural. At the same time they do open up the possibility of a new approach to this question. For the fact is that, contemporaneously, there exist two widely acknowledged – if, notwithstanding, highly controversial – classes of (putative) events which, to all intents and purposes, clearly fall under the (theologically neutral) sense of the miraculous delineated above. For immediate purposes they may be merely indicated. Thus, in the first place, there is the vast and nebulous class of (putative) events which have traditionally been associated with such labels as magic, sorcery, charm cures, witchcraft and which, for present purposes, may be taken as falling under the latter heading of *witchcraft*. Secondly, there is the class which, as falling under what, over the course of the past century, has come to be known as 'psychical research', may be called the *psychical*. To this extent, therefore – and, as constituting a vital link in the chain of the main argument – the two may be added to the class of the (biblical) miraculous as *modes* of, what has been delineated in the course of the foregoing as, the *super-* or *para-normal*.

To conclude with a number of points in supplementation of the above, attention may be drawn, first, to the way in which the preceding conclusion is endorsed, if only obliquely, by Swinburne in his own, *religiously* oriented, assessment of the miraculous.

Extraordinary events lacking religious significance are more appropriately characterized as *magical* or *psychic* phenomena rather than *miracles*.[9]

The point, too, may be taken as reflecting the division between the two senses of the term 'supernatural' which constitutes the core of the discussion of the present chapter. More specifically – that the *philosophical* sufficiency of the idea of the *miraculous* (as this embraces, also, *witchcraft/magic* and the *psychical*) is to be found, not in any *supernaturalistic* ascription as to *cause*; but rather in the (phenomenological) *super-naturalism* of the event itself, as this involves the *physical* manifestation of some form of super/para-normal *volitional* activity.

Further, and with regard to the distinction drawn between *witchcraft and the psychical*, there is the consideration that it is the latter which is, by far, of most importance for the present purpose. This follows directly from the fact that a whole variety of claims falling under the general label of the *psychical* have been the subject of sustained and highly refereed investigation ever since 1882 when the Society for Psychical Research was specifically established for this very purpose. With mention that this is a point to which it will be necessary to return, note, at least, must be made of the consideration that, from a wider perspective than that of the moment, *witchcraft*, too – and despite the esotericism of the title – is not without its challenge. For besides being a phenomenon/ practice that antedates man's recorded history, it remains one that continues to have an immense following. One, indeed, that to some degree or other, constitutes an integral part of the daily life of, what is, probably, a majority of the world's population. It must be fully acknowledged, in deference to Hume, that this majority undoubtedly makes up the least educated portion of the human race. With this, further, must come the acceptance of a general, and, perhaps, wholly justified, *scientific* prejudice against any possibility of its factual reality. At the same time, the consideration stands that the practice itself – as this relates to a vast realm of healing, no less than to intents of a more sinister nature – contemporaneously presents a boundless, and, largely, virgin, field for empirical investigation, most obviously, at the hands of the social scientist. This said, the concern in what follows will be exclusively with the *psychical*.

Finally, for the moment, there is the pressure of another point. Namely – the need for a widening of the idea of the *super-normal/psychical* beyond that assumed for the purposes so far. To this stage – and following the dominant model presented by the biblical *miracles* (as, also, the popular conception of *witchcraft*) – it has been taken as being identified, pretty well exclusively, with the idea of some kind of super/para-normal *volition*. It must now be extended to cover, further, the complementary conception of (various forms of) super/para-normal *cognition*. There is nothing arbitrary about this move. It has already been touched upon in the earlier discussion of Broad's 'Basic Limiting Principles'. But beyond this is the plain historical fact that claims to extraordinary powers of *seeing* or *knowing* – as embraced under such labels as omens, divinations, portents, prophecies, visions, revelations – have constituted vital elements of *witchcraft/magic*, as well as the *miraculous*, right down the ages. In a similar way, parallel claims – as falling under the heads of *clairvoyance, telepathy, pre-cognition* (or, more generally, *extra-sensory perception*) – embrace, at the present, certain of the most widely investigated aspects of the *psychical*. To this extent, therefore, a dichotomy may be drawn between, what may be characterized as, the *physicalistic* and *mentalistic* modes of the (putatively) *super-normal/psychical*. Or, in the terms of Arthur Schopenhauer (1788–1860), whose views will assume increasing prominence in the course of what is to follow – (a) *actio in distans* and (b) *visio in distans*.[10]

With this, the discussion may be turned to more empirically-based considerations.

6

Super-normality as a Mode of the Real

It will be seen from the preceding discussion that, to the extent that Bultmann's 'revolution' is open to challenge on a wider basis than strictly *religious/theological* grounds, this is to be found, most particularly, in the idea of the *psychical*. Further – that it is the *super-normal*, in this sense, which, as constituting a logically separate class from the *natural/normal*, presents a direct (theoretical) threat to the *heuristic* parameters of (*materialistic*) *science* itself. The concern in this chapter and in Chapters 7 and 8 will be with the *empirical* significance of this challenge. In other words, with the *evidential* legitimacy of regarding the *super-normal/psychical*, as delineated in the course of what has been said, as a *mode* of the (*physically/common-sensically*) *real*.

The discussion may be opened by appeal to the views of Lecky and, in particular, the central thesis of his classical survey. More specifically – his proclamation of a correlation between (a) the decline of belief in the *miraculous* and (b) the accelerating ascendancy of the spirit of modern *rationalism*. Thus:

> There is certainly no change in the history of the last 300 years more striking, or suggestive of more curious enquiries, than that which has taken place in the estimate of the miraculous ... All history shows that, in exact proportion as nations advance in civilization, the accounts of miracles taking place among them become rarer and rarer, until at last they entirely cease ... The plain fact is, that the progress of civilization produces invariably a certain tone and habit of thought, which makes men recoil from miraculous narratives with an instinctive and immediate repugnance, as though they were essentially incredible, independently of any definite arguments, and in spite of dogmatic [religious] teaching.[1]

With no attribution to Lecky himself, two widely-accepted presumptions may be extrapolated from the correlation indicated here. First – that (a), in its relation to (b), is to be seen as marking a decisive victory for the shades of Democritan/Epicurean *materialism* in its two thousand year battle with the forces of religious/ theological *supernaturalism*. Secondly – that (b), in its relation to (a), is to be viewed as being allied to the powers of a progressive *humanism*, in its opposition to the retrogressive influences of religious/theological *obscurantism*. As to truth, however, it must be immediately tempered by the distinction drawn earlier between: (x) (*religious/theological*) *supernaturalism*, and (y) (*phenomenological*) *super/para-normality*. For, though, as all the evidence suggests, there is a clear historical link between the rise of *rationalism* and the decline of (x), there is no such obvious connexion in the case of (y). Indeed, with respect to the nineteenth century, as, also, the period of the high Enlightenment which preceded it, the truth of the matter is the very opposite. In short – that (y), in its divorce from (x), constitutes a factor of vital and progressive importance in the cultural milieu of the time.

It is a point which may be decisively illustrated by attending to the circumstances surrounding two movements, in particular – (a) the diffuse and pervasive influence which flourished well up to, and beyond, the middle of the last century under the banner of *mesmerism* or *animal magnetism*; and (b) the spectacular social phenomenon of the latter half of the century which attracted the attention of a vast audience on both sides of the Atlantic under the name of *spiritualism/spiritism*. Of interdisciplinary dimensions, the matter is one whose full importance is still only in the process of being realized; mainly, at this stage, by social historians and historians of psychology.[2] With this, too, must go the fact of its significance in embracing, not only the genesis of modern *psychiatry*, but, also, the practical discovery and popularization of one of the most momentous ideas of all time – that is the *unconscious*. Most directly for the main purpose, however, is a further consideration. Namely – that it was precisely the pressure of events arising from the above which led to the formation, in 1882, of the previously mentioned Society for Psychical Research with its avowed objective of investigating

that large body of debateable phenomena designated by such terms as *mesmeric*, *psychical* and *Spiritualistic* ... without pre- judice or prepossession of any kind, and in the same spirit of exact and unimpassioned inquiry which has enabled Science to solve so many problems, once not less obscure nor less hotly debated.[3]

With mention that this is a consideration to which it will be necessary to return, the objective for the present must be with a delineation of the extent of the challenge arising respectively from (a) and (b) above. On this basis, and for convenience of exposition, the discussion may be offered in three continuously related sections.

I

To begin with a historical sweep of *mesmerism*, the movement itself may be seen as having its origin in Munich in the year 1775 when its founder, Franz Anton Mesmer (1734–1815), a physician by training, was instrumental in inflicting a decisive personal defeat on a famed local priest, Johann Joseph Gassner (1727–79). The setting of the clash was a commission arranged by the Prince-Elector Max Joseph of Bavaria to enquire into Gassner's activities in procuring, what, within the present context, may be legitimately labelled as, happenings of a super/para-normal kind. In the instance, dramatic healings of the sort recorded in the New Testament narratives. To this commission, Mesmer had been invited as specialist adviser. What, however, gives an immediate twist to the account, is that the confrontation was in no way related to the question of whether seemingly miraculous cures had actually taken place. It was accepted on all sides that Gassner possessed healing gifts of the most remarkable kind. To this must be added the point that Mesmer's own standing at the commission derived, not from his specialist training as a physician, but, precisely from the fact that he, too, had triumphantly established himself as a man of just such powers as those of Gassner. What was at issue, rather, was ascription as to *cause* – how the cures were to be *explained*. Here, Gassner was clearly cast as the representative of an outmoded, and, through the 'witch-craze', discredited, form of *supernaturalism*.[4] His position, in the briefest terms, was one which rested on a belief in the 'exorcism' of 'devils'. Mesmer's claims, on the other hand, made a direct appeal to the new spirit of the times. The cures, he proclaimed, had a *scientific/rationalistic* basis. More specifically, as he declared, they were brought about by the special manipulation of a particular *physical* force (a kind of super-fine, invisible 'fluid') of which he was the discoverer and to which, following the analogy with (*physical*) magnetism, he gave the name *animal magnetism*.[5] Whether justice was done to Gassner need not be pursued. Suffice it to say, that the outlook for him was an order drastically curtailing his healing ministry and, whether from this or some other cause, an early demise. Beyond this, the point for the main purpose is simply the fact that *mesmerism/animal magnetism* is clearly to be seen as being born out of a curious mixture of (a) (anti-supernaturalistic) *rationalism*, on the one hand, and (b) what may well be accepted as (super/para-normalistic) *thaumaturgy*, on the other.[6]

In drawing this conclusion, there is the immediate point as made by a notable writer on the history of 'mental' healing – Frank Podmore, whose name will be the subject of later reference. 'Mesmer's first claim to our remembrance lies in this – that he wrested the privilege of healing from the Churches, and gave it to mankind as a universal possession.'[7] More for the main concern, however, is the fact that, failing to find recognition for his Munich achievement in his home city of Vienna, Mesmer moved, in 1778, to Paris where he quickly established both fame and fortune through his spectacular 'crisis' healings. So great, indeed, was his success that he was eventually led to institute a highly extravagant group-healing therapy involving, at times, hundreds of patients. With this, too, came the foundation of his Société de l'Harmonie – a semi-secret brotherhood devoted to the teaching and practice of the master's healing methods in exchange for the parting of substantial sums on the side of the initiates. It was a venture which, in the event, proved so successful that, within a year, branches had been established, not only in Paris, but in towns and cities throughout France. What must be added is that, as in the case of Gassner, Mesmer's very success led to his undoing. In 1784, following agitation over the activities of his movement, the king appointed no less than two commissions to enquire into the legitimacy of his claims regarding 'magnetism'. The one was made up of members of the Académie des Sciences and the Académie de Médecine; the other of members of the Société Royale. Together, they comprised some of the foremost scientists of the day including the astronomer Bailly, the chemist Lavoisier, the physician Guillotin and the American ambassador, Benjamin Franklin.

Again, as in the case of Gassner, the issue was *not* over whether seemingly super/para-normal cures had actually been effected. It was simply and straightforwardly over whether any new *physical* force had been discovered. The verdict was decisively against Mesmer – that no evidence whatsoever could be found for the existence of such a force. The episode effectively marks the end of Mesmer's involvement with the movement that was to bear his name into the next century. He left Paris at the beginning of 1785 to disappear into an oblivion about which very little is known. He died thirty years later, still wealthy, but, also, still resentful at being thwarted over what he believed to be rightfully his own.

Here, there may be pause to highlight the relevance of a consideration brought to the fore by a recent writer on Mesmer, the historian, Robert Darnton:

> Extravagant as it seems today, mesmerism has not warranted the neglect of historians, for it corresponded perfectly to the interests of literate Frenchmen in the 1780s. Science had captivated Mesmer's contemporaries by revealing to them that they were surrounded by wonderful, invisible forces; Newton's gravity, made intelligible by Voltaire; Franklin's electricity, popularized by a fad for lightning rods and by demonstrations in the fashionable lyceums and museums of Paris; and the miraculous gases of the Charlières and Montgolfières that astonished Europe by lifting man into the air for the first time in 1783.[8]

And, in continuing:

> Mesmer's invisible fluid seemed no more miraculous, and who could say that it was less real than the phlogiston that Lavoisier was attempting to banish from the universe, or the caloric that he was apparently substituting for it, or the ether, the 'animal heat', the 'inner mold', the 'organic molecules', the fire soul, and the other fictitious powers that one meets like ghosts inhabiting the dead treatises of such respectable eighteenth-century scientists as Bailly, Buffon, Euler, La Place, and Macquer. Frenchmen could read descriptions of fluids, very like Mesmer's under the articles 'fire' and 'electricity' in the *Encyclopédie*. If they desired inspiration from a still greater authority, they could read Newton's description of the 'most subtle spirit which pervades and lies hid in all gross bodies' in the fantastic last paragraph of his

Principia (1713 edition) or in the later queries of the *Opticks*.[9]

Returning, however, to the main discussion, there is the point that the year 1784 was as fateful for Mesmer as 1775 had been for Gassner – and this, as with the latter, over the issue of *how* the seemingly super-normal was to be *explained*. At the same time – and with another twist – it was also the year that was to give to the movement which Mesmer had founded a vital new impetus. One indeed, that was, not only to ensure its survival, but, further, open up a vast and exciting new realm, i.e. the *mental*, to practical experimentation.

The story, as it now unfolds, centres on one of Mesmer's most able and loyal followers, Armand-Marie-Jacques de Chastenet, Marquis de Puységur (1751–1825) and his discovery of 'magnetic' or 'artificial' *somnambulism*.[10] In experiments with a retainer from his estate, one Victor Race, Puységur came to notice 'magnetic' effects of a kind far removed from those of the model presented by Mesmer. For Mesmer, with his *physicalistic* outlook, it was the object of the 'magnetizer' to 'manipulate' the 'magnetic fluid' in such a way as to bring about a *physiological* 'crisis' in the patient. This crisis – involving, as it often did, violent physical effects of the kind which form a theme in the New Testament healing miracles – was regarded by Mesmer as an essential prelude to the 'fluid' attaining the more equable distribution necessary for recovery. As against this, the condition that Puységur noticed in the 'magnetized' Race was one which strongly resembled *sleep*, but with a crucial difference. It was one, too, in which the patient displayed a lucidity in answering questions that, in many respects, surpassed that of his waking state. Of particular interest was the fact that Race was able to diagnose the nature of his illness, give a prognosis of its likely development and prescribe treatment – though seemingly remaining completely amnesic to these, as well as other, details of his 'crisis' on return to (normal) consciousness.[11] Continued experiments with Race, as well as others, consolidated these findings. They, further, led to the establishment of the fact that the new kind of 'crisis' was much more easily and reliably induced than that which characterized Mesmer's own highly idiosyncratic procedures.

Against this background – and to complete these delineatory details – Puységur was led to two main conclusions. First, at the practical level – that what he had discovered was, not only a more perfect kind of 'crisis' than that which had constituted the corner-stone of Mesmer's teachings, but, also, a completely new kind of medical therapy where treatment was open to prescription by the 'magnetized' patient. Secondly, and more philosophically – that the new kind of 'crisis' was essentially *mental* in nature. It was one which – as he gropingly grasped – turned on the *will* of the 'magnetizer' in its relation to the *mind* of the patient; and had nothing whatsoever to do with the manipulation of any particular (*physical*) fluid as Mesmer so passionately believed. The latter, theoretical, aspect of Puységur's discovery was to remain a matter of desultory debate among 'magnetizers' throughout the remaining history of the movement. Regarding the former claim, however-er, there was little room for any such equivocation. With the promise of demonstrably easier procedures and fascinating poten-tialities, it was the object of immediate and enthusiastic endorse-ment. Henceforward, it was to be Puységur's 'magnetic *sleep*', and not Mesmer's *physiological* type of 'crisis' that was to be the hallmark and *raison d'être* of the mesmeric movement for the rest of its existence.

It is necessary to make clear at this point that what Puységur had discovered in 'magnetic sleep' was precisely that which – with all the potent nebulousness of its challenge – would eventually come to attain a degree of *scientific* respectability under the more restrained label of *hypnotism*. In particular, it was the phenomenon which, under this title, was to be the subject of intense *scientific/medical* interest in the 1880s through the competing personalities of Jean-Martin Charcot (1835–93) and Hippolyte Bernheim (1840–1919) at their respective schools of the Salpêtrière and Nancy. Moreover – the effect whose *mentalistic* nature was to be finally established through the strength of the latter's culminating triumph over the *materialistic/physiological* ascriptions of the former. These are considerations to which it will be necessary to return. More for the present are a number of points relating to the subsequent history of the movement.

To begin, there is the fact that, as events were to transpire, Puységur's discovery was to have barely five years to make its impact. To this extent, reference may be made to his work during this period in establishing the Société Harmonique des Amis Réunis at Strasbourg – an organization which, as an extension of Mesmer's institutes, had, as its objectives, the training of 'magne-tizers' in his own methods and the setting up of centres for treatment. The point has a relevance which may be marked in two respects. First – that, by 1789, the body had come to count no less than two hundred members, including the élite of the Alsation aristocracy who pledged to give their treatments gratuitously. Second – that, unlike other mesmeric centres, the Strasbourg Society published annual reports (still extant) listing the cures with short case histories covering the names of the practitioner and patient, and the nature of the illness.[12] The fact to be added is that the movement came to a complete end in 1789 when the fury of the French revolution swept away forever the Société de l'Harmonie with all its branches. Many of its members met their end on the guillotine. Puységur himself was to spend two years in prison. Thereafter, France was to be engulfed in war on a grand scale for nearly a quarter of a century. Notwithstanding, following all this turmoil, a second generation of 'magnetizers' eventually emerged who looked to Puységur as their natural and unquestioned leader. As to Puységur himself, his end came in 1825 following the rigours of attending the coronation of Charles X at Rheims. He died still loyal to Mesmer, thus contributing to the perpetuation of a confusion in the term *animal magnetism* which has persisted to this day.

Secondly, there is also the fact that the very scale of the upheaval in France led to Puységur's discovery taking its deepest immediate root in the more settled soil of neighbouring Germany. Just how rapid was its spread in this country is attested by (Henri F.) Ellenberger in his remark that '[even] as early as 1790, animal magnetism had become so widespread ... that it was almost common practice to consult somnambulists for problems of disease and health, for practical advice, and sometimes for spiritual guidance'.[13] Moreover, it was not only at the popular level that mesmerism took hold in Germany. At the academic level, too, it gained early acceptance. German universities were quick to show an interest and, following a favourable report on the subject published by the Prussian government in 1816, Chairs in 'magnetism' were established at both Berlin and Bonn. With this, also, is the fact that the subject of 'magnetism' was set as the topic for the 1819 Essay Competition of the Berlin Academy of Science. This, again, has particular relevance since it was the subsequent publication of two of the unsuccessful entries for this competition – those, respectively, of Alexandre Bertrand (1795–1831), with his dual training as a physician/engineer, and François (later, General

François) Noizet (*c.*?), both supporters of the *mental* nature of the phenomenon – which came to play a vital, if circuitous, role in Bernheim's later victory over Charcot on the nature of *hypnotism*.[14] This aside, the fact of the above developments taking place in the land of Mesmer's own first great triumph may be plausibly accepted as a further reason for the continued association of his name with the (new) 'magnetism' of Puységur.

Thirdly, attention may be drawn to certain main features relating to the respective developments of mesmerism in France and Germany, the countries of its firmest grounding. In France, the emphasis was to remain throughout, as it started, almost exclusively, on the *therapeutic* aspects of 'magnetism' – the same interest, indeed, which, following decades of medical opposition, was to be belatedly revived towards the end of the century by Charcot and Bernheim. In contrast, the course of its development in the more exuberant intellectual climate of Germany was to lead ever more in the direction of an unfettered exploration of the strange and exciting effects asssociated with the condition of 'magnetic lucidity'. As time went by, and as the movement became more diffuse, this interest became increasingly associated with claims tinged with the aura of *supernaturalism*. Three specific points are worthy of note. First, that two figures, in particular, came to evoke a great deal of attention in the 1820s for the visions which they proclaimed whilst in the condition of 'magnetic sleep' – Katharina Emmerich (1774–1824), a poor peasant woman, formerly a nun, who bore the stigmata of the Passion; and Friedericke Hauffe (1801–29), the 'Seeress of Prevorst', in whose presence were reported, moreover, the spontaneous displacement of physical objects.[15] Further, that the two women became the subjects of sustained, on-the-spot, studies by two notable figures of the time – respectively, the poet Clemens Brentano (1778–1842) and the poet-physician Justinius Kerner (1786–1862). Finally, and most especially, Kerner's study, besides establishing itself as a work of clinical interest, came to reach a wide popular audience in Germany, as well as, later, in translation, in the United States.[16] Beyond these details, however, is the fact that the movement also brought in its train an ever-growing band of entertainers whose stock-in-trade was the uninhibited exploitation of 'magnetic sleep' for the purpose of well-paying stage performances. These developments were more than sufficient to eventually call forth a clerical opposition to mesmerism that was to match and add to the longer sustained antagonism of the medical profession. By 1850, the hey-day of the movement was over in Germany, as it already was in France. Thereafter, it went into a rapid decline as a new mood of positivism came to dominate German thought.

Finally, for the moment, mention may be made of a number of points relating to the development of 'magnetism' in Britain and North America. With regard, first, to the latter, its original introduction came early with the establishment of a flourishing mesmeric society in the (then) French City of New Orleans.[17] More generally, however, the movement's diffusion was slow until the 1840s when, following the increasing popularity of mesmeric stage demonstrations and the fame achieved by a number of notable figures as healers and 'seers', there was a rapid acceleration of interest in the subject.[18] In Britain, too, the movement made but little headway until the 1840s, mainly due to the entrenched and virulent opposition of both religious and medical factions. Notwithstanding, it was in this country that an initial, even though very limited, medical interest was eventually sparked. Thus, it was the Manchester physician, James Braid (1795–1860), who, in 1843, coined the less provocative term *hypnotism* as a synonym for 'magnetic sleep' after having been convinced of the reality of the phenomenon by a visiting French 'magnetizer'. Further, and, again, during the 1840s, it was two British medical men – John Elliotson (1791–1868) and James Esdaile (1809–59), the latter working in India – who, prior to the discovery of chemical anaesthesia, reported on their successful use of 'magnetic sleep' as an anaesthetic for even major surgery.[19] These technicalities apart, the movement may be taken as reaching its peak in Britain in 1851 when, following widespread Scottish interest in the phenomenon, Hume's own city of Edinburgh, together with a number of other centres, became scenes of a veritable *psychic* 'epidemic'.[20] With this, in Britain, as in the United States, any future that mesmerism might have had was rapidly overtaken by events which will be taken up more fully below.

To summarize, therefore, the point that may be seen as emerging from the above is a distinction between (a) the dominant healing mission of the mesmeric movement as it originated and developed in France, and (b) claims to effects of a more esoteric nature as these emanated, most particularly, from Germany and the United States. In reiterating that it will be necessary to return to the culminating significance of (a), the discussion may be continued by pursuing the historical merging of (b) with the movement which constitutes the second main topic of the present concern – that is, *spiritualism*.

II

A start may be made by reference to the words of Schopenhauer. Thus, his scathing indictment of the retrogressive influence exerted by the English clerical establishment in its opposition to the facts of 'magnetism':

> By opposing with incredible insolence and impudence every form of scientific knowledge so that the matter has gradually become a scandal to our continent, obscurantist English parsondom is mainly guilty of injustice through its encouraging and cherishing all prejudices that favour the 'cold superstition that it calls its religion' and through its hostility to truths that are opposed thereto. Animal magnetism must have suffered such an injustice in England where, after it had been acknowledged in theory and practice in Germany and France for forty years, it was still untested and, with the confidence of ignorance, laughed at and condemned as a clumsy fraud. 'Whoever believes in animal magnetism cannot believe in God' was a remark made to me by a young English parson even in 1850; *hinc illae lacrimae!*[21]

There is no need to take issue with anything that Schopenhauer says in this passage. The point to be emphasized, rather, is one that relates to the subsequent change in the intellectual climate of the country which he here so berates for its theological obscurantism. More particularly, that, within the space of little more than two decades of the above being penned, this milieu had altered so dramatically as to make Britain the very centre of academic, as well as popular, turmoil over the reality of the *super-normal*.

In any estimation of what brought about this shift, it is, of course, impossible to under-rate the massiveness of the impact of the Darwinism revolution in undermining the religious/theological orthodoxy of the time. To this extent, it is not without interest to note Schopenhauer's own anticipatory delineation of this very catharsis in his diatribe against 'English parsondom':

That by the crudest bigotry those parsons degrade the most intelligent nation, which is in almost every respect the first in Europe, to the lowest level and thus make it an object of *contempt* is something that should no longer be tolerated ... Here their impudence goes to the length of attacking with wrath, sneers, and shallow ridicule in newspapers even the positive and universal results of *geology*. For they are anxious in all seriousness, to uphold the Mosaic myth of creation, oblivious of the fact that in such attacks they are merely hitting an iron pot with an earthenware ... [and] ... when, through recent historical and geological discoveries (for instance, the pyramid of Cheops being a thousand years older than the Great Flood), they are deprived of the factual and historical elements in the Old Testament, their whole religion also falls to the ground.[22]

At the same time – and more particularly for the main purpose – there is the fact to which reference has already been made. In short: that, over and above the climactic effects of this high peak of nineteenth century *rationalism*, the period under discussion was characterized, also, by a vast and ever-increasing interest in events which, as arising from the burgeoning of the *spiritualist* movement, cut across the entrenched opposition of both *religious* and *scientific* factions.

The bizarreness of the circumstances surrounding the movement makes it necessary to temper the reader's mind, at the outset, with a number of remarks which underscore the extent of its *cultural* significance. Thus, there is, first, the fact of its very *scale* – as, for instance, is attested by R. Lawrence Moore with regard to the land of its birth, the United States:

> Scarcely another cultural phenomenon affected as many people or stimulated as much interest as did spiritualism in the ten years before the Civil War and, for that matter, through the subsequent decades of the nineteenth century.[23]

Secondly, and in the light of the preceding reference to the Darwinian debate, mention may be made of a direct if little recognized, historical link between the latter and the rise of the movement in hand. More specifically, there is the fact that Alfred Russel Wallace (1823–1913), co-founder, with Darwin, of the theory of *natural selection*, became an early and prominent convert to the cause of spiritualism.[24] Further – that this constituted the major factor in his break with Darwin over the vital issue of man's own evolution; with Wallace, in opposition to Darwin, maintaining the, still, live line that a *spiritual* essence, over and against *mechanical* selection, must be postulated to account for the higher aspects of human development. Finally, for the moment, there is the point made by Alan Gauld regarding the actual *pressure* of testimony to the reality of spiritualistic effects as this gave rise to the formation of the Society for Psychical Research:

> There is no doubt that the S.P.R. answered a need of the times. This is evidenced not so much by the growth in its membership (membership rose from 150 at the beginning of 1883, to 707 in January 1890, and 946 in January 1900) as by the quality of those who joined. Among its early supporters were persons of outstanding eminence from nearly every field. In 1887 its Council Members and Honorary Members included a past Prime Minister (Gladstone . . .), and a future Prime Minister (Arthur Balfour); eight F.R.S.s – Wallace, Couch Adams, Lord Rayleigh, Oliver Lodge, A. Macalister, J. Venn, Balfour Stewart and J. J. Thomson; two bishops; and Tennyson and Ruskin, two of the outstanding literary figures of the day.[25]

With these initial comments, attention may be turned to a detailing of certain of the more esoteric aspects of the spiritualistic challenge.

With regard, first, to the origin of the movement, this may be dated from the winter of 1848 when a family in the hamlet of Hydesville, upper New York State – John D. Fox, a poor but respectable Methodist farmer, his wife Margaret, and their daughters Margaretta (aged fourteen) and Catherine (aged twelve) – became the victims of protracted periods of rappings emanating from the shared bedroom of the house which they had recently come to occupy. The climax of these events came on the evening of March 31 when, in response to questioning, the rappings yielded primitive codal replies to the effect that the 'communicator' was a 'person' who had met a violent death in the house. The subsequent details of the story, though interesting in their own right, need not be pursued in the current context beyond mention that, in later 'messages', the 'communicator' claimed that he had been an itinerant pedlar who had been murdered for his money and whose remains were buried in the cellar of the house.[26] On this basis, the main point is simply the straightforward historical fact that from the spark of the Hydesville happenings burst the flame of, what must remain as, one of the most startling claims of the modern world. In short – the central spiritualistic contention that communication with 'spirits' of the dead is not only possible, but also *empirically* demonstrable.

The local interest aroused by the above events was to achieve national significance two years later following the publicity arising from the association of the Fox sisters with the famous showman, P. T. Barnum, in New York. By this time Margaretta and Catherine had been joined by an older (and lately widowed) sister, Leah Fish, and, whether by design or not, the three very soon came to be established as the founding members of, what was to blossom into, a brand-new profession – that of the paid (spiritualistic) *medium*. Thereafter, the spiritualistic creed spread with enormous speed. Mediums proliferated and were sought out by vast numbers of people of all stations and walks. Thus, to quote Moore:

> Beginning in 1850, spiritualism became vastly popular in . . . [the United States] . . . Americans in astounding numbers studied the reputations of a growing roster of professional mediums and crowded into the séance rooms of those they judged the best . . . It was not just the half-baked, the uneducated and the credulous who appeared at séances or spirit circles. The number of prominent people who attended spiritualist meetings in the 1850s is [also] impressive.[27]

Techniques of 'communication' underwent rapid development, not only in terms of (physical) codal systems, but, also, through the means of automatic writing and the trance condition. There was, further, a relentless advance in the direction of dramatic *physical* effects – a development which, as the century wore on, was to become an increasingly accentuated aspect of the movement.

Very soon, too, a spiritualistic *philosophy* came to emerge, ostensibly on the basis of 'spirit' teachings, but, notwithstanding, also highly reflective of the social/democratic optimism of the period. Thus – that spirits had a benevolent concern (as, also, pity) for the human condition; that 'love' and 'development' were the keynotes of 'spiritual' existence; that, within this scheme of things, no 'soul' would ever be ultimately 'lost' or 'cast away'; that Jesus (among other great spiritual teachers) was a 'spirit' who had, out of love, become carnate in order to lead human-kind out of its 'darkness'; and that (spiritualistic) *physical* effects were to be taken as *empirical* assurances of the reality of this other 'realm'. Such, indeed, was the virility of the movement that, by 1856, the suggestive possibility was raised by Theodore Parker, one of the foremost religious thinkers of the time – and himself, not a spiritualist – of it actually becoming the new religion of the United States:

> In 1856, it seems more likely that spiritualism would become the religion of America than in 156 that Christianity would be the religion of the Roman Empire, or in 756 that Mohammedanism would be that of the Arabian population . . . It has more *evidence for its wonders* than any historic form of religion, hitherto.[28]

And, further:

> It has more *evidence for its wonders* than any historic form of religion, hitherto. It is thoroughly *democratic*, with no hierarchy, but inspiration is open to all. It is no *fixed fact*, has no *punctum stans*, but a *punctum fluens*; not a finality, but opens a great vista for the future. Its present condition is no finality. It admits all the truths of religion and morality in all the world-sects.[29]

The conclusion to be drawn, therefore, is that within less than a decade after its humble beginnings in the Hydesville 'rappings', spiritualism had come to be firmly established in the United States as a religious-social phenomenon of the very first order of cultural significance.

Returning to the Fox sisters, the discussion may be continued with a highlighting of the significance of *physical* effects as these came to follow them in the history of the movement. In the words, once again, of Moore:

> After the triumphs of the Fox sisters in New York City, the variety of spirit manifestations increased with amazing rapidity. For example, during the summer of 1850, some one hundred mediums blossomed in Auburn, New York, a town near Hydesville. Most of the spirits were rappers, but already some had learned to do other things. Aside from making rapped replies to

questions, spirits could rely on automatic writing, slate writing, and control of the medium's voice to get their message through – or they could skip the message altogether and depend entirely on physical effects. Table-raising remained an impressive display throughout the nineteenth century, as did the playing of untouched musical instruments. Sometimes spirits levitated the body of the medium or of one of the sitters. After the Civil War, spirit photography and materialization séances considerably expanded the medium's repertoire.[30]

The various claims delineated here, like those surrounding the Hydesville 'rappings' themselves, bring to the fore, in the sharpest possible way, the overriding concern of the present discussion as it relates to the ultimate (*philosophical*) *nature/status* of the *physical/ common-sensical* world. At the same time, there can be no denying the intellectual embarrassment arising from the mere mention of possibilities as outlandish as the foregoing. To this extent, it is necessary to emphasize that it certainly forms no part of the current endeavour to indulge in any special pleading beyond what can be sustained by the strength of strictly critical considerations. With this, too, must go the fact of the vastness of the testimony lying behind Moore's synopsis – testimony which, as embracing the so-called 'great age' of the *physical* mediums, covers figures and events on both sides of the Atlantic extending over more than three decades. And, again – that this very plenitude, coupled, as it invariably is, with charges of deceit and counter-charges of unfairness and bigotry, presents a particularly intractable barrier to any summary evaluation. In the light of the foregoing, the concern in what follows will be limited to a single, though entirely adequate, main objective. Namely, that of characterizing the strength of the challenge arising from, what Gauld, in his own scholarly appraisal, singles out as amongst the most provocative of all the evidence of the time for the reality of the *physically* psychical.[31]

The case in point is one that involves a shift of scene from the United States to Britain and relates, most particularly, to claims arising from a series of 'sittings' (eleven in all) with the renowned American medium Daniel Dunglas Home (1833–86) which took place between May 1871 and April 1874. There may be a marking of Home's significance. Thus, Gauld:

What is astonishing (one is almost tempted to say appalling) about D. D. Home is the sheer *number* of seemingly disinterested persons who were prepared to testify that he had in good or passable light produced startling phenomena before their very eyes.[32]

In this regard, too, there is the fact that the claims themselves, though extraordinary in the extreme, are, yet, to be seen as commonplace enough in the context of the time. Again, as summarized by Gauld:

Movements and levitations of the table and of other objects; the appearance of materialised hands and figures; the handling of red-hot coals; mysterious playing of an accordion; and the rapping out of messages ostensibly from dead persons.[33]

To highlight the full drama of the situation, however, is another consideration. That is – that the 'sitter' and protagonist to these happenings was no less a figure than William (later, Sir William) Crookes (1832–1919), one of the foremost chemists and physicists of the time.

The significance of the point may be amplified. Best known, perhaps, as the discoverer of the element thallium and the inventor of, what is still popularly known as, 'Crookes' tube', Crookes – though of little formal education – was elected Fellow of the Royal Society in 1863 at the early age of 31 and became President in 1913. He was knighted in 1897, just prior to his Presidency of the British Association, and was admitted to the exclusive Order of Merit in 1910, nine years before his death in 1919. Beyond these biographical details are two other considerations, both involving reference to the organ *Quarterly Journal of Science* of which he had editorial control during the period under discussion. There is, first, the bibliographical point that, though, as events transpired, Crookes' complete notes on his experiments with Home were not made public until their appearance in the *Proceedings of the Society for Psychical Research* in 1889, a full intimation of their substance had already been given by him in the pages of the *Quarterly Journal* for January 1874; as, also, to a lesser degree, in two earlier articles in 1871.[34] Secondly, there is the historical fact of the academic furore which followed the publication of these articles – a storm which, at its height, brought aspersions as to Crookes' fitness for membership of the scientific community and reverberations which continued right down to, and beyond, the end of his life. With this, again, comes the force of a further point. More specifically – that Crookes' claims were the subject of full endorsement by Wallace who was himself present at certain of the main happenings.[35] To the above extent, therefore, the conclusion to be extracted is the full force of a dramatic dilemma. In short – that either (a) *physicalistic* events (among them, some of the most embarrassingly bizarre nature) must be given credence, or (b) the character/ability of men of the scientific stature of Crookes and Wallace must be impugned.

The acuity of the dilemma may be heightened by a number of further considerations. In the first place, there is the power of Crookes' words, as taken from the *Quarterly Journal* for October 1871, in defending his claims against the initial rumblings of his critics:

> In his opening address before the British Association at Edinburgh this year, Sir William Thomson said, 'Science is bound by the everlasting law of honour to face fearlessly every problem which can fairly be presented to it.' My object in thus placing on record the results of a very remarkable series of experiments is to present such a problem, which, according to Sir William Thomson, 'Science is bound by the everlasting law of honour to face fearlessly.' It will not do merely to deny its existence, or try to sneer it down. Remember, I hazard no hypothesis or theory whatsoever; I merely vouch for certain facts, my only object being – the *truth*. Doubt, but do not deny; point out, by the severest criticism, what are considered fallacies in my experimental tests, and suggest more conclusive trials; but do not let us hastily call our senses lying witnesses merely because they testify against preconceptions. I say to my critics, try the experiments; investigate with care and patience as I have done. If having examined, you discover imposture or delusion, proclaim it, and say how it was done. But, if you find it to be a fact, avow it fearlessly, as 'by the everlasting law of honour' you are bound to do.[36]

And, again, a few months later, in echoing, what might well be seen as, the earlier claims of Mesmer:

> That a hitherto unrecognized form of Force – whether it can be called a psychic force or *x* force is of very little consequence – is

involved . . . is not with me a matter of opinion, but of absolute knowledge; but the nature of that force, or the cause which immediately excites its activity, forms a subject on which I do not feel competent to offer an opinion.[37]

Secondly, there is the fact of his later stand regarding the truth of his testimony. Thus, his proclamation, more than a quarter of a century on, in concluding his Presidential Address to the British Association in 1898:

These, then, are some of the subjects, weighty and far-reaching, on which my own attention has been chiefly concentrated. Upon one other interest I have not yet touched – to me the weightiest and the farthest reaching of all. No incident in my scientific career is more widely known than the part I took many years ago in certain psychic researches. Thirty years have passed since I published an account of experiments tending to show that outside our scientific knowledge there exists a force exercised by intelligence differing from the ordinary intelligence common to mortals. This fact in my life is of course well understood by those who honoured me with the invitation to become your President. Perhaps among my audience some may feel curious as to whether I shall speak out or be silent. I elect to speak, although briefly. . . . To ignore the subject would be an act of cowardice – an act of cowardice I feel no temptation to commit. . . . I have nothing to retract. I adhere to my already published statements. Indeed, I might add much thereto. I regret only a certain crudity in those early expositions which, no doubt justly, militated against their acceptance by the scientific world.[38]

Finally, for the moment, there is a point which may be developed more fully below.

It is one which relates to the fact that, despite the extraordinary nature of Crookes' claims, there were, indeed, other prominent scientific figures of the time, in addition to Wallace, who came to support the truth of what he had to say. Among these, especial mention may be made of J. C. Friedrich Zöllner (1834–82), Professor of Physical Astronomy at Leipzig, who, following Crookes' lead, had come to conduct experiments of his own with another celebrated American medium, Henry Slade (d. 1905). Of particular relevance are two passages from his findings regarding such effects of Slade's as slate-writing (by an 'invisible hand') and the 'invisible tying' of knots in an endless cord. First: the challenge of his words as backed by the famed names of Gustav Theodor Fechner (1801–87) and Wilhelm Weber (1804–91). Thus, in the *Quarterly Journal* for April 1878:[39]

> I reserve to later publication, in my own treatises, the description of further experiments obtained by me in twelve *séances* with Mr. Slade, and, as I am expressly authorized to mention, in the presence of my friends and colleagues, Professor Fechner, Professor Wilhelm Weber, the celebrated electrician from Göttingen, and Herr Scheibner, Professor of Mathematics in the University of Leipzig, who are *perfectly* convinced of the reality of the observed facts, altogether excluding imposture or prestidigitation.[40]

Secondly, his words in the Dedication of his promised treatise to 'William Crookes, F.R.S.':

> By a strange conjunction our scientific endeavours have met upon the same field of light, and of a new class of physical phenomena which proclaim to astonished mankind, with assurance no longer doubtful, the existence of another material and intelligent world. As two solitary wanderers on high mountains joyfully greet one another at their encounter, when passing storm and clouds veil the summit to which they aspire, so I rejoice to have met you, undismayed champion, upon this new province of science;[41]

and, in concluding:

> To you, also, ingratitude and scorn have been abundantly dealt out by the blind representatives of modern science, and by the multitude befooled through their erroneous teaching ... With these consolatory words ... accept, my honoured friend, the present work as a token of the sincere esteem of the Author.[42]

What may be extracted, therefore, is not only the fact of the foregoing involving reference to events as extraordinary and bizarre as anything recorded in the biblical miracles, but, also, of the testimony to their reality being asserted by figures who were to the forefront of the scientific establishment of the time.

The conclusion may be taken as a crystallization of the main objective of the argument so far, and as the starting point of Chapters 7 and 8 where the discussion will be continued respectively under two main heads: (a) the critical significance of the Society for Psychical Research in responding to the force of the above, and (b) the relevance of contemporary testimony to the reality of *physicalistic* effects. It remains to complete the present concern by returning to the climactic significance of the Charcot-Bernheim confrontation in the *therapeutic* tradition of the mesmeric movement.

III

By way of continuity, there may be a highlighting of the entrenched medical opposition to 'magnetism' which is to be seen as being pervasive throughout the whole history of the tradition. It was within this context that Braid's affirmation of the reality of the phenomenon, and his ascription to it of the label *hypnotism*, met but short-lived and mainly local interest. So, too, the exciting prospects raised by Elliotson and Esdaile for the relief of pain; and, this, notwithstanding the fact that the latter's work had already led to the establishment of a government sponsored Mesmeric Hospital in India.[43] With this, again, there may be mention that Elliotson – a dominant figure of the time, and one who was progressive enough to introduce both the stethoscope and the clinical lecture into Britain – was forced into resigning his Chair at University College, London, through his espousal of mesmerism.[44] This latter consideration, in particular, may be taken as symptomatic of the aggressively punitive attitude to the phenomenon which, going beyond any merely lethargic opposition, increasingly came to take hold of medical thought during the second half of the nineteenth century. So, also – as presaging the enormous influence which came to be exerted by the 'Helmholtz' School of Medicine with its virulent (and *a priori*) rejection of *any* form of *mentalism*. The point that may be brought to the fore, therefore, is that, by the time of the third quarter of the century, the spirit of (*materialistic*) *rationalism* had come to establish itself to such a degree in both Germany and France as to make any interest in 'magnetism'/*hypnotism*, not merely unfashionable, but, also, in many quarters, a matter of professional ostracism.

It is against this general background that, in 1881, Charcot – with all the prestige attaching to his world-famous achievements in the spheres of *physiology/neurology* and *hysteria*, as well as the full panoply of his power as head of the Salpêtrière – delivered his paper 'On the Various Nervous States Determined by Hypnotization in Hysterics' to the Académie des Sciences in Paris.[45] The paper, coming, as it did, from one of France's very greatest men of science, raises, at once, the question of what had led him to an interest in the eschewed phenomenon. Here, as all the evidence suggests, his experimentation in the field arose through the fertile influence of Charles Richet (1850–1935) who, following his own discovery of the effect through the medium of a popular hypnotic entertainer (in the instance, the highly newsworthy *Donato*), had already alerted medical attention to the provocativeness of the happening.[46] Beyond this, however, is the consideration that the significance of Charcot's paper is hardly to be seen as turning on its implicative *validation* of the latter. More to the tune of the time is the fact of his claim that, despite the phenomenon's aura of the *thaumaturgical*, it was, yet, open to full *explanation* in the *naturalistic* terms of his own *neuro-physiological* researches.

The point is one which may be illustrated by the virtually contemporaneous, but earlier, words of a prominent German physiologist in responding to local excitement over another mesmeric performer of the day, *Hansen*. Thus, the claim of Rudolf Heidenhain (1834–97) of Breslau:

I hope I have succeeded in convincing you that, in Mr. Hansen's performances, we have not to deal with any unknown specific force, but with the establishment of physiologically definable conditions of the cerebral organs, which are dependent on stimulation of sensory apparatus; and which can be judged of in the light of the knowledge we at present possess of the functions of the nervous system, without our being obliged to take refuge in any kind of mysticism ... Any one who, a hundred and fifty years ago, had publicly exhibited such experiments as Mr. Hansen does daily ... would have infallibly been proceeded against for witchcraft. Fifty years ago, such ... demonstration[s] would certainly have led to a new kind of superstition, as indeed took place when the excitement about animal magnetism was at its highest. We owe it to the rapid advance of experimental physiology that we, today, can guard ourselves against such deception.[47]

At the same time – and returning to Charcot – there is, also, the pressure of a further point. More specifically – that what he purported to offer was not just an *explanation* of the troublesome happening, but, one, moreover, that involved its *degradation*. There is, in short, the conclusion that central to the applause which greeted Charcot's paper was his contention that the 'magnetic'/ *hypnotic* state, with all the challenge it presented to established medicine, was reducible, in the last resort, to, no more than, a mere condition of *morbidity* indicative of incipient *hysteria*.

With respect to the basis of the claim, it is necessary to remark that, due, mainly, to Charcot's own work among hysterical patients at the Salpêtrière, the disorder of *hysteria* had come to be accepted as having, at the very least, strong associative links with the *muscular* (neuro-physiological) disease of *catalepsy*. Beyond this, his linking of *hypnotism* to *hysteria* is to be seen as stemming exclusively from the fact that the *cataleptic* state, with its strange *muscular* effects, could be *artificially* induced in the *hypnotic* condition.[48] The gross *non-sequitur* of the conclusion which Charcot drew from these connexions was to be fully exposed over the course of the next ten years.[49] It was to be a process ending in deep disillusionment and sudden death in 1893. At the same time, it was also one in which the greatness of the man would be displayed in discoveries that were to forever change the face of medical science. In particular, is the fact of his revolutionary work in the years 1884–5 in demonstrating the *psycho*-genesis of certain paralyses. Further – in shifting the very meaning of the word *neurosis* in a direction away from its original *physiological* etymology.[50] With this, again, is the profound influence which he came to exert on the young Freud who visited him on study leave in late 1885. In thus indicating the extent of Charcot's subsequent move away from the unsoundness of his original *pathological* understanding of the phenomenon, there may be a return to the main concern with another point: that is, the nature of the opposition which came to be exerted by his antagonist, Bernheim – Professor of Internal Medicine at Nancy, with his established reputation in the fields of typhoid fever and heart and pulmonary diseases – in bringing about this change.

The challenge itself is to be seen as receiving its formulation in a paper which Bernheim read to the Medical Society of Nancy in 1883 and which later reached a wider audience through a short book published in 1884.[51] Here, in stark opposition to the central contention of Charcot's celebrated paper, he maintained that the hypnotic state was, not a condition of morbidity found only in hysterics, but, one to which *all* humans were susceptible to some degree. It was, he claimed, a condition of *sleep* brought about by *suggestion*. Moreover – one with *therapeutic* implications, even for certain illnesses of a plainly organic nature. These ideas were developed more fully by Bernheim, under the general label of *psycho-therapeutics*, in a textbook on hypnotism which appeared in 1886.[52] It was a work whose very success made it the instrument by which Nancy came to be established as a distinct, if diffuse, school set in opposition to the entrenched stance of the monolithic Salpêtrière. One, too, whose wider cultural/academic importance is marked by the consideration that a German translation by Freud himself appeared in 1888, a few months before he travelled to meet Bernheim and his colleagues at Nancy, and, thereafter going on to attend the first International Congress on Hypnotism in Paris.[53] With these details, the point to be brought to the fore is the fact of the book's command in its attack on Charcot. The consideration is one which may be illustrated by reference to three bare passages.

First – the barb of Bernheim's comment that Charcot's world-renowned experiments with hypnotized hysterics were no more than mere artifacts:

> Once only did I see a subject who exhibited perfectly ... [Charcot's] three periods of lethargy, catalepsy and somnambulism. It was a young girl who had been at the Salpêtrière for three years.[54]

Further – in explaining the case:

> Subjected to a special training by manipulations, imitating the phenomena which she saw produced in other somnambulists of the same school, taught by imitation to exhibit reflex phenomena in a certain typical order, the case was no longer one of natural

hypnotism, but a product of false training, a true *suggestive hypnotic neurosis.*[55]

And, again, in affirming the validity of his own position:

No one regards the work of the Salpêtrière School more justly than I do. I am too much a pupil of M. Charcot, I owe him too great a part of my medical education, not to render the homage which is due to the eminent master, whose name will always be an honour to the French School of Medicine. But I do not accept blindly – does the master himself do so?[56]

With this, therefore, there may be a reiteration of the point already indicated. In short – that by the time of Charcot's death in 1893, the position of the Salpêtrière had come to be so completely eroded as to leave the field of hypnotism entirely to Bernheim and his School of Nancy.

The above, as may be accepted, is wholly sufficient to highlight the importance of Bernheim as titular head of the Nancy School with its commitment to the *psycho-therapeutic*, as opposed to *neuro-physico/morbidic*, view of hypnotism. It is indicative, too, of Bernheim's profound influence on Freud in the latter's own journey from his original base in the field of *neuro-physiology* to the realm of *mind*. At the same time, it does nothing to answer the main question for the matter in hand – that of the basis and justification of this outlook. For this attention must be turned to another vital figure in the history of hypnotism – Ambroise Liébeault (1823–1904).

Of poor origins – the twelfth child of a Lorrainean peasant family – Liébeault was a man who, by dint of hard work, came to establish himself as a country doctor in a village just outside Nancy.[57] In this, he proved so remarkably successful that, within the span of ten years, he had earned, what, for him, amounted to, a modest fortune. At this stage whilst in his thirties, and brooking the full flood of the intellectual tide of the time, he turned his attention to 'magnetic'/*hypnotic* healing. The critical issue of what led him to this, though to some degree conjectural, will be taken up below. More immediately, there is the point that his patients were largely poor and that, as an inducement for them to submit to hypnotism, he offered his treatment gratuitously. There can be little question that, as with the earlier 'magnetizers', this was of the very crudest form. Invariably, it amounted to little more than the public and indiscriminate assurance to the hypnotized patient of the relief of his/her symptoms. Notwithstanding, his success was such that, within a few years, he was in the position of having a vast practice with little in the way of remuneration for his services. His response was to give up work in order to write a book on his procedures and successes. This appeared in 1866 and, in the event, was a disastrous failure.[58] Thereafter, Liébeault returned to his practice, again concentrating on 'magnetic'/*hypnotic* therapy, but, this time, accepting such fees as were offered to him by his patients. Though largely ostracized by his medical colleagues, his reputation as a remarkable healer steadily grew over the years. So much so, indeed, that, in 1882 – following the interest in hypnotism that arose from Charcot's paper – he was visited by Bernheim who became fully converted to his ideas. From this arose his belated fame. He was fêted and fulsomely acknowledged by Bernheim as his original inspiration, practical adviser, close collaborator and trusted friend. His methods were introduced into the University Hospital at Nancy. His book was rescued from oblivion and became widely read with a revised edition under a new title appearing in 1889.[59] To summarize – with Bernheim as his fully recognized *academic/rationalistic/scientific* spokesman, he emerged, from all his obscurity, to occupy the undisputed role of spiritual father of the Nancy School.

Returning to the critical issue of the circumstances surrounding the source of Liébeault's interest in mesmeric healing, a point that must not go unmentioned is the general legacy of Puységur's earlier work in the region of Alsace-Lorraine. More particularly, however, is the fact of Liébeault's own testimony that he was first drawn to the subject in his student days through reading an old book on 'magnetism'. This latter, as all the evidence suggests, was the treatise which had constituted Bertrand's submission for the Essay Competition of the Berlin Academy – a work which, as previously noted, received its publication in 1823. At the same time, in accepting this, the question remains as to why Liébeault was stimulated to a renewed interest in the subject in the mid-1850s. Whilst there can be no certainty, a suggestion with more than a hint of plausibility is that arising from another point already made. That is, the belated (and privately sponsored) publication by (General) Noizet, in 1854, of what – as in the case of his old friend Bertrand – had originally been conceived as an entry for the 1819

Berlin Academy competition. Be this as it may, what is beyond dispute is that – with regard to both practical technique and commitment to the *mental* nature of the phenomenon – the ideas of Noizet are plainly to be seen as being reflected in the work of Liébeault, as, also, later, in that of Bernheim.[60] There is, in short, the conclusion that a clear line of connexion may be drawn from Bernheim, through Liébeault, to, what amounts to, some of the very best theoretical work of the old mesmeric tradition.[61]

It was, of course, this link with the past that gave Bernheim his victory over Charcot who, from the sheer brilliance of his own clinical mind, sought to explain the phenomenon completely *de novo*. Just *how* much Bernheim owed to this 'thaumalurgical' line is made plain in the fact that the whole substance of what he has to say is, in no way *explanatory*, but, purely and simply, *descriptive/ validational*. The point is one that is open to immediate illustration by appeal to his use of the key term *suggestion* – where, as he says, 'the phenomena of so-called animal-magnetism are simply the phenomena of suggestion'.[62] So, also, in the presumed novelty of his claim to the *mental* character of the effect: 'It is the doctrine of Braid or Braidism, the doctrine of suggestion which is deduced from observation, contrary to the doctrine of Mesmer or Mesmerism; the doctrine of a mesmeric or magnetic fluid.'[63] Most particularly, in this regard, however, are his *clinical/observational* endorsements of the *efficacy* of his *suggestive* theory. Not gainsaying their truth, they amount to, what might well be taken as issuing more from the mouth of a 'thaumaturgical' shaman, than from the work of a leading figure of Europe's medical establishment.

Thus, with regard to the Nancy method of treatment:

> The patient is *put to sleep by means of suggestion*, that is by making the idea of sleep penetrate the mind. He is *treated by means of suggestion*, that is by making the idea of cure penetrate the mind. The subject being hypnotized, M. Liébeault's method consists *in affirming in a loud voice the disappearance of his symptoms*.[64]

Further – with respect to results:

> Since 1882 I have experimented with the suggestive method which I had seen used by M. Liébeault, though timidly at first and without any confidence. Today it is daily used in my clinic; I practice it before my students; perhaps no day passes in which I

do not show them some functional trouble, pain, paresis, uneasiness, insomnia, either moderated or instantly suppressed by suggestion ... Muscular pains, the painful points in phthisis, certain dynamic contractures, even though bound up with organic affections of the nervous centres, certain movements which remain after chorea, incontinence of urine, which children suffer from at night, etc., – *often disappear as if by enchantment after a single suggestion, or after several.*[65]

And, again, more generally, in terms reminiscent of the earlier claims of Crookes:

I can honestly say, that I have made my observations coolly, without any predisposition to either side, and without enthusiasm. But when after many hundred observations in all classes of society, in the hospital and in the city, I have seen constant, uniform phenomena induced, and when, on the other hand, I know that everyone who has studied the question in an unbiased manner, has observed facts identical or analogous to those I have observed, am I to admit that all our subjects have leagued together to mystify us? Certain minds have a horror of the marvellous. They are right: but they are wrong when they consider as marvellous and systematically deny, facts which they have not verified, just because these facts do not agree with the *a priori* conceptions in their minds. The facts are undeniable: the interpretation of them follows; if that is faulty, do not blame the facts, but the insufficiency of our knowledge of psychology and nervous physiology.[66]

What may be brought to the fore, therefore, is the clear conclusion that no *strong/explanatory* sense of the term 'scientific' is to be seen as emerging from the famed medical victory of the School of Nancy over the Salpêtrière. More specifically, there is the point that, as with his claim to the *mental* nature of hypnotism, so, also, regarding its *therapeutic* implications, the substance of what Bernheim has to say is entirely *phenomenological* or *validational* in character. There is, in short, the fact that the whole basis of Bernheim's triumph over Charcot is to be found in, no more and no less than, the unequivocal *affirmation* by one of the foremost medical personages of his day, of the *reality* of that which, for more than the span of a century, had been the prerogative of 'thaumalurgical' *mesmerists*.

It remains to bring the chapter to a close with a few extra points that supplement what has already been put forward.

Thus, there is, first, the fact that the therapeutic successes of the Nancy School, as detailed and authenticated by Bernheim in the foregoing passages, are to be seen as being not a jot more 'scientific' than the healing *miracles* recorded in the biblical narratives – or, for that matter, those falling under the general heading of *witchcraft*. To this extent, the very strength of his testimony, as this rests on the broader backing of the whole mesmeric tradition, may be taken, at the very least, as supportive of the possible reality of these (or, certain of these) latter. With this, too, arises – as in the claims of Crookes and Zöllner – what may be legitimately viewed as, a necessary corrective to the famous claim of Hume regarding the innate and fatal weakness of *any* historical testimony to the reality of the *miraculous/super-normal*. To make these points is neither to endorse *supernaturalism* nor the view that such happenings must forever defy *explanation*.[67] Rather, it is simply to affirm the entirely reasonable point which – as expressed by Crookes and Zöllner, as well as Bernheim – constitutes the central theme of the present concern. In short – that whether there are happenings which are *thaumaturgical/super-normal* (or, even, to use the, now, common, term – '*psycho*-somatic') in the sense that they transcend the parameters of established (*materialistic*) *science*, is determined *not* by these *parameters*, but by the *facts*.

Secondly, and with regard to the *nature* of the phenomenon, mention may be made of the enormous *academic/scientific* interest in the effect which, following its long era of neglect arose, as a concomitant to the Charcot–Bernheim controversy. This is nowhere more clearly attested than by a bibliography on the subject which appeared in 1888 and which, whilst originally containing no less than 800 recent titles, was supplemented, only two years later, by a further list of nearly 400 new writings.[68] So firmly, indeed, did the potentialities of the newly established happening implant themselves on the consciousness of the time that there was hasty resort to laws – hardly since relaxed – for its social control. The full irony of the situation is noted by a prominent contemporary of the scene. Thus, William James (1842–1910):

> [The facts of] 'animal magnetism' . . . were stoutly dismissed as a pack of lies by academic medical science the world over, until the non-mystical theory of 'hypnotic suggestion' was found for them, – when they were admitted to be so excessively and

dangerously common that special penal laws, forsooth, must be passed to keep all persons unequipped with medical diplomas from taking part in their production.[69]

What may be added, however, is that sustained interest in the subject did not long outlast the Charcot-Bernheim confrontation; with the phenomenon, thereafter, being relegated once more to the realm of the academically 'unrespectable'. As to the reasons for this abrupt switch, the salutary case of Charcot's own fateful involvement with the challenge is one that cannot go without notice. So, also, the critical importance of Freud's own abandonment of his early clinical interest in the effect in favour of the more scientifically orthodox method of *free association*. Yet another reason is undoubtedly to be found in the quick realization of the point already made regarding Bernheim's use of the term *suggestion* – that, though putatively *explanatory*, it is, in truth, merely *descriptive*. However this may be, there is, notwithstanding, the conclusion that current assessment of the nature of the effect goes little beyond the substance of what has been said. The position, in brief, is no more than that summarized in the contemporary words of F. L. Marcuse – 'That hypnosis exists has become accepted: what it is . . . is generally disputed.'[70]

Finally, and following from the above, there is the culminating significance of the point that the phenomenon, though the continuing object of gross *academic/scientific* neglect, pre-eminently remains as a persisting challenge to the heuristic parameters of the whole frame of *scientific/materialistic* orthodoxy. In particular, it is such as to bring into sharp focus the words of Schopenhauer written nearly a century and a half ago in the final years of the mesmeric era:

> Considered, of course, not from the economical and technological, but the philosophical point of view, animal magnetism is the most significant and pregnant of all the discoveries that have ever been made, although for the time being it propounds rather than solves riddles.[71]

The wider relevance of the consideration will be the subject of later remark. More immediately, the discussion may be continued by turning to the challenge of the foregoing as it led to the circumstances of its systematic investigation.

7

The Systematic Investigation of the Super-normal

The discussion may be opened with passing mention of the fact that the reverberations of Crookes' involvement in the realm of the so-called *spiritualistic* have continued right down to the present with the claim of one contemporary writer that Crookes was, in some way, coerced into betraying his scientific probity through his (putatively) illicit liaison with a young medium, one, Florence Cooke, of Hackney.[1] The plausibility of this contention – and whatever the details of Crookes' love life – must be left for the judgement of the reader. More for the immediate purpose is the scope of the *ad hominem* attack which took place within the context of Crookes' own time.

In the event, it was initiated, most notably, by an article which appeared anonymously towards the end of 1871, but which was quickly identified as issuing from the pen of the distinguished naturalist and evolutionist, W. B. Carpenter (1813–85), author, among other works, of the leading (English) physiological textbook of the day, and, at the time, Registrar of London University.[2] It was met, as may be added, by a massive reply by Crookes who, in a special pamphlet, not only offered an exhaustive, point-by-point, refutation of all the charges laid against him, but, also, in the process, subjected his assailant to a devastating personal castigation.[3] It is not without relevance to note the measure of Crookes' command in this exchange – as, for instance, is captured in the cutting acerbity of his attack on the (essentially mechanistic) theory of mind of his 'anonymous' critic:

It is curious to note how Dr. Carpenter is made to pervade the *Quarterly Review* article. The reviewer throughout the article unconsciously manifests his implicit conviction that Dr. Carpenter is to be regarded as the paramount authority in reference to the subtle psychological questions involved in the so-called spiritualistic phenomena. The theories of the profound psychologists of Germany, to say nothing of those of our own countrymen, are made quite subsidiary to the hypotheses of Dr. William Carpenter. An unquestioning and infatuated belief in what Dr. Carpenter says concerning our mental operations has led the reviewer wholly to ignore the fact that these speculations are not accepted by the best minds devoted to psychological inquiries. I mean no disrespect to Dr. Carpenter, who, in certain departments, has done some excellent scientific work, not always perhaps in a simple and undogmatic spirit, when I 'speak advisedly' that his mind lacks that acute, generalising, philosophic quality which would fit him to unravel the intricate problems which lie hid in the structure of the human brain.[4]

At the same time – and notwithstanding the publicity attaching to this debate, or the scale of Crookes' victory over Carpenter – the episode is, yet, to be seen as no more than symptomatic of a deeper and more dominant response which is nowhere better summarized than in the *ex cathedra* pronouncement of W. K. Clifford (1845–79), another leading evolutionist of the time:

> There is no evidence which amounts to a *prima facie* case against the dynamical uniformity of Nature; and I make no exception in favour of that *slykick* force which fills existing lunatic asylums and makes private homes into new ones.[5]

What may be reiterated, therefore, is the nature of this prevailing response; as, also, its *ad hominem* recursivity. In short, that – then as now – it is one which involves an outright and *a priori* rejection of all such claims as those of Crookes on the simple and unquestioned ground of so-called '*scientific* impossibility'.

It would, of course, be easy to find pragmatic reasons for the support of this outlook, particularly in view of the very extravagance of Crookes' claims. This is a point that has already been fully acknowledged. At the same time, and whatever sympathy there might be for such a position, it is, yet, to be viewed as thoroughly inadequate, as well as completedly *unscientific*, as a response to the demands of the situation. For the plain fact is – as, again, has been sufficiently addressed – that whether or not there are events of the kind attested by Crookes (as, also, Wallace, Zöllner, Fechner and

Weber) is not such as could ever be open to purely *a priori* resolution. Rather, like Galileo's own historic claim regarding the existence of 'spots' on the sun, it is one which, by its very nature, is only answerable by appeal to the relevant facts. That is, and no matter how long or involved the process – by the method of *empirical/scientific* investigation. It is precisely this point which constitutes the substance of Crookes' plea in the passage from the *Quarterly Journal* quoted earlier, as, again, that of Bernheim regarding *hypnotic* therapy. It is also the point which is expressed in the clearest possible way by the young William James in responding to the turmoil over spiritualistic claims in his native United States. Thus, in one of his earliest writings, while still a senior at the Harvard Medical School:

> The present attitude of society on the whole question [of spiritualistic claims] is as extraordinary and anomalous as it is discreditable to the pretensions of an age which prides itself on enlightenment and the diffusion of knowledge. We see tens of thousands of respectable people on the one hand admitting as facts of everyday certainty what tens of thousands of others equally respectable claim to be an abject and contemptible delusion; while other tens of thousands are content to stand passively in the dark between these two hosts and in doubt, the matter meanwhile being – rightfully considered – one of really transcendent interest.[6]

Most particularly for present purposes, however, is the fact of the above as this led, in 1882, to the formation of the previously mentioned Society for Psychical Research.

In bringing to the fore the question of the degree of credibility which is to be seen as attaching to the pretensions of this new and scientifically motivated enterprise, the issue is one which may be approached through the figure of Henry Sidgwick (1838–1900) – Fellow of Trinity College, Cambridge; holder, from 1883, of the Knightsbridge Chair of Moral Philosophy at the University; and the man who, as well as being the Society's first President, was also to remain its dominating influence for the first two decades of its existence.[7] The wider ramifications of these biographical details may be pursued by mention of the significance of Crookes' experiments of the early 1870s – and, in particular, the publication of his *Researches in the Phenomena of Spiritualism* – in awakening

Sidgwick to the full extent of the challenge of the psychical. There occurred a further impact of these experiments, either directly or indirectly, on a number of other Fellows of Trinity – most notably, Lord Rayleigh (1842–1919), Arthur J. Balfour (1848–1930), his brother Gerald W. Balfour (1853–1945), Frederic W. H. Myers (1843–1901), Edmund Gurney (1847–88) and Walter Leaf (1852–1927).[8] The point has a significance which is reflected in two additional considerations.

Thus, there is, first, the fact that, even as early as 1874, an informal association of the above had already been established – on the initiative of Myers and under the leadership of Sidgwick – for the systematic investigation of spiritualistic claims. Secondly, that it was this same élite and closely-knit cadre, with especial emphasis on Sidgwick, Myers and Gurney, together with certain other notable additions, which was to continue as the main driving force of the later Society.[9] With this, too, it is necessary to remark on two highly-gifted women, sisters of the Balfours, who were also closely associated with, what came to be known as, the 'Sidgwick group' – Evelyn (Lady) Rayleigh, wife of Lord Rayleigh, and Eleanor, who married Sidgwick in 1876.[10] Of the two, it is the latter, Mrs Sidgwick (1845–1936), who is, by far, of most importance for present purposes – partly, for the prominence which she came to attain as Principal of Newnham College, Cambridge (1892–1910), but, mainly, for the magnitude of her contribution to the work of the Society, not least, as this continued over a period of more than three decades after her husband's death. What may be extracted from these details is, therefore, not only (a) the fact of the intellectual calibre of the Sidgwick group being of the very highest order, but also (b) the point, as summarized by Gauld, regarding the Sidgwicks themselves – 'To say that the Sidgwicks had friends in high places would be an enormous understatement. They were also, I should guess, among the most intellectual couples of the century.'[11]

It is worth emphasizing the significance of the latter, not least for the reason, to quote Gauld again, that 'Sidgwick's reputation throughout the country was such that no one would think that a Society of which he was head could be composed mainly of cranks or knaves.'[12] The same, moreover, might be said of a whole litany of notable figures who, in addition to Myers, the two Balfours and Mrs Sidgwick, came to succeed Sidgwick in the Presidency of the Society – Balfour Stewart, William James, Sir William Crookes, OM,

Sir Oliver Lodge, Charles Richet, (Bishop) W. Boyd Carpenter, Henri Bergson, F. C. S. Schiller, Lord Rayleigh, OM, Sir Arthur Conan Doyle, William McDougall, Camille Flammarion, Gilbert Murray, OM, C. D. Broad, H. H. Price, Sir Alister Hardy, to name only the most famous.[13] At the same time, it is also necessary to remark that the original inspiration for the formation of the Society did not come from the Sidgwick group itself. Rather, the prime movers in this respect were William F. (later, Sir William) Barrett (1844–1925), Professor of Physics at the Royal College of Science, Dublin; and certain prominent spiritualists of the time, of whom especial mention may be made of Rev. William Stainton Moses (1839–92), author, through automatic writing, of the classic of its genre, *Spirit Teachings*.[14] Two further points may be made in this regard. First, that of these originators, the latter faction was to resign from the Society within a few years over, what they came to regard as, the excessive intellectualism of the Sidgwick group; while Barrett, though remaining a member, never came to be part of its ruling clique. Second, that Barrett is to be seen, further, as being instrumental in the establishment of a similar Society in the United States – a body which, though short-lived (it was formed in January 1885 and amalgamated with the British Society in December 1889) has a crucial importance since it was graced by the figure of James as its leading light. With mention that this is a point to which it will be necessary to return, there is, more immediately, the conclusion that the stamp of the future development of the Society is already to be seen in the uncompromising insistence of its dominant founding element, that is the Trinity/Cambridge group, on the appointment of Sidgwick to its leadership – a role he continued to exercise, inside and outside the Presidency, right up to the time of his death.

In supplementation of the above, it is necessary to mention that Barrett, like Sidgwick himself, was originally awakened to a decisive interest in the psychical through the publicity attaching to Crookes' experiments with spiritualistic mediums. Further – that, following this lead, he came to conduct pioneering experiments of his own in the field of 'thought transference'; and that, in 1876, a paper by him on this subject was actually accepted (though never subsequently published) by the British Association for the Advancement of Science.[15] This, again, is a point having particular relevance since it is precisely this idea under the label of *telepathy*, given to it by Myers in 1882, which came to dominate the interest and work of the early Society as well as constitute the core of the group's most lasting achievements.

With this, too, there may be note of the especial significance of Moses – an ordinand of the Church of England, a master at University College School, London, and a man of altogether outstanding moral probity – in the history of spiritualistic claims. First: for the reason of his early impact on the Trinity/Cambridge investigators. Thus, to quote Gauld:

> On 9th May 1874 Moses talked with, and showed his notebooks to, two enquirers of high academic standing, Edmund Gurney and F. W. H. Myers . . . [who] . . . both . . . felt that if Spiritualistic phenomena could be attested by a person of such pre-eminent respectability and such monumental seriousness of mind, there must indeed be something in them worthy of investigation.[16]

Secondly, and, again, as given by Gauld – for his role in the development of so-called *veridical* or *evidential* data:

> Moses' automatic writings are important . . . for reasons [other than] the relative literary merit of *Spirit Teachings* . . . In amongst them are various cases of 'evidential' communications – communications, that is, containing correct information about deceased persons which, on the face of it, could not have been known to the medium . . . [Such] cases . . . were then rare, and Moses' standing and high character made them impressive, even to persons who might otherwise have been sceptical.[17]

In accepting the critical significance of this latter for (x) the idea of ('naturalistic') *telepathic* interchange between specifically *carnate* minds, no less than for (y) *supernaturalistic* claims as to the reality of *spirit* communication, attention may be turned to a third main point which is taken up below.

The consideration is one which, in its most general form, may be seen as reflecting the overriding theme of the main discussion as this turns on the challenge of Bultmann. More specifically, it involves the delineation of a number of points which bear on the motivation of the Sidgwick group. In the first place, there is the plain historical fact of the crisis in *religious/theological* thinking which followed in the wake of the Darwinian revolution. To this may be added the fact that, of the foregoing Trinity figures, the two most vitally affected by the depth of this hiatus were Sidgwick himself and, even more decisively, for present purposes, Myers.

Pursuing the point further, and with regard, first, to Sidgwick, the extent of his own religious heartsearchings during this period is drawn by Broad, a later Fellow of Trinity, as well as holder of the former's old Chair:

> During the sixties Sidgwick was engaged in a desperate internal struggle with the intellectual difficulties which the Christian religion, as then understood in England, presented to honest and instructed minds. In the course of these inquiries he gained a thorough mastery of Hebrew and Arabic, made an elaborate study of theology, and immersed himself in philosophy;[18]

and, further, in recounting certain more practical consequences of this personal turmoil:

> At that time it was a condition of holding a fellowship that the holder should declare himself to be a '*bona fide* member of the Church of England'. This obligation was not usually taken very seriously, but Sidgwick was an exceptionally conscientious man. By June 1869 he had come to the conclusion that he did not fill the condition literally enough to justify him in holding a paid office on these terms. He therefore resigned his fellowship and assistant tutorship at Trinity. The college accepted his resignation with deep regret and did what it could to compensate him by creating a lectureship in Moral Science, without theological conditions, and appointing him to it. Nevertheless, Sidgwick suffered a considerable loss of income and amenities for a number of years.[19]

What may be seen, too, is the fact of Sidgwick's early interest in spiritualistic claims being a clear function of this crisis of faith. Thus, to quote, again, Broad:

> The first period of Sidgwick's investigations into Spiritualism extends roughly from 1865 to 1875. In 1863 he writes to his friend Dakyns: 'I have not yet investigated Spiritualism, but I am still bent on doing so as soon as I get an opportunity.' ... He writes [again] to Dakyns [in 1864] saying: 'As to Spiritualism I have not progressed, but am in painful doubt. Still, I have some personal

experiences and much testimony, and I find it hard to believe that I shall not discover some unknown laws, psychological or other.[20]

And, continuing with details which have a particular relevance for the wider theme of the present discussion:

> Writing to Roden Noel in December 1866, he makes some interesting comments on the effects which his recent reading of Lecky's *History of Rationalism* has had on him. The book had set him to consider the *evidence* for medieval miracles, a topic which Lecky explicitly ignored. Sidgwick was considerably impressed by this evidence, and he writes to Noel as follows: 'I dimly foresee that I shall have to entirely alter my whole view of the universe and admit the 'miraculous' ... as a *permanent* element in human history and experience...' He suggests that these reflexions link up with his interest in Spiritualism, and that together they may throw a light on the origin of all religions.[21]

On this basis, therefore, a point which may be brought to the fore is the strength of the specifically *religious* dimension attaching to Sidgwick's pioneering interest in the psychical.[22]

Turning to the second of the above figures, an immediate assessment of his importance for the matter in hand is given by Gauld in his comment that '[it is very much to be doubted] whether Sidgwick's investigations would have been so extensive or so prolonged as they in fact were had it not been for the influence upon him of ... Frederic Myers ... a person whose temperament was far more eager than his own'.[23] Part of what Gauld says here is certainly to be taken as marking the dedicatory zeal of the latter in following Sidgwick's own, more measured, involvement with spiritualistic claims. But beyond this, is a further consideration which is also embraced in Gauld's remark. That is, more specifically – the vital fact of Myers' visionary conception, soon endorsed by the rest of his circle, of the *spiritualistic/psychical* as constituting the firm *empirical/scientific/intellectual* basis of a new *religious* synthesis centring on the *demonstrable* reality of *post-mortem* survival.

In marking the intensity of Myers' concern with this question, passing mention may be made of the fact that this interest was certainly heightened, following 1876, by the tragic circumstances surrounding the death of a young woman with whom, as all the evidence suggests, Myers was deeply in love. At the same time, this is to be seen as but expressive of a deeper dispositional concern. Thus, in this connexion, it is not without interest to note an early intimation of the passion of this later preoccupation: namely, as given in his recollection of the drama of a night-time swim across the Niagara River, just below the Falls, when on a tour of Canada and the United States in 1865:

> As I stood on a rock, choosing my place to plunge into the boiling whiteness, I asked myself with urgency, 'What if I die?' For once the answer was blank of emotion. I have often looked back on this apathy in the brief interspace of religions as my only subjective key to the indifference which I observe in so many of mankind ... I emerged on the American side, and looked back on the tossing gulf. May death, I dimly thought, be such a transit, terrifying but easy, and leading to nothing new? *Coelum non animum mutant* may be true of that change as well.[24]

Most particularly, however, are the words in which Myers recalls the conscious dawn of his inspiration, and, thereafter, life-long work. He dates the event as taking place in December 1869:

> In a star-light walk which I shall not forget ... I asked him [Sidgwick], almost with trembling, whether he thought that when Tradition, Intuition, Metaphysic, had failed to solve the riddle of the Universe, there was still a chance that from any actual observable phenomena – ghosts, spirits – whatsoever there might be drawn as to a World Unseen. Already, it seemed, he had thought that this was sensible; steadily, though in no sanguine fashion, he indicated some last grounds of hope; and from the night onwards I resolved to pursue this quest, if it might be, at his side.[25]

What may be seen, therefore – and to complete these amplificatory details – is, not only a definite *religious/ethical* dimension to the motivating vision of the Sidgwick group, but, also, the strength of the challenge (emanating, most principally, from Myers) of seeking, through the (putatively) *super-normal*, a specifically *scientific* resolution of what, until only a few decades earlier, had been unquestioningly assumed as falling within the realm of (either *religious* or *metaphysical*) *faith*. In other words, the idea, no less, of conducting an *empirical* investigation into the most momentous of all questions – that of 'immortality' or *post-mortem* survival.[26]

On the foregoing basis, enough has been said for the clear establishment of (a) the strength of the academic/intellectual credentials of the founding leaders of the, now, long established Society for Psychical Research; as also (b) the urgency of the latter's mission in the context of the time which saw its inception. What has emerged, further, are two, quite separate, though closely interrelated, aspects of the Society's aims. They may be delineated more fully.

In the first place, and most obviously, there is the central concern of the latter with the need for a thoroughgoing *empirical/scientific* investigation into the reality of the super-normal *per se*. Thus, as proclaimed by Sidgwick in the terms of his Presidential Address to the new organization:

> We are all agreed that the present state of things is a scandal to the enlightened age in which we live. That the dispute as to the reality of these marvellous phenomena – of which it is quite impossible to exaggerate the scientific importance, if only a tenth part of what has been alleged by generally credible witnesses could be shown to be true – I say it is a scandal that the dispute as to the reality of these phenomena should still be going on, that so many competent witnesses should have declared their belief in them, that so many others should be profoundly interested in having the question determined, and yet that the educated world, as a body, should still be simply in the attitude of incredulity ... The primary aim of our Society, the thing with which we all unite to promote, whether as believers or non-believers, is to make a sustained and systematic attempt to remove this scandal in one way or another.[27]

And, again, in laying down the methodological strategy of the Society:

> Scientific incredulity has been so long in growing, and has so many and so strong roots, that we shall only kill it, if we are able to kill it at all ... by burying it alive under a heap of facts ... We must keep 'pegging away', as Lincoln said; we must accumulate fact upon fact, and add experiment upon experiment [and] trust

to the mass of evidence for conviction ... We have done all that we can when the critic has nothing left to allege except that the investigator is in the trick ... We shall, I hope, make a point of bringing no evidence before the public until we have got it to this point of cogency ... We must drive the objector into the position of being forced either to admit the phenomena as inexplicable, at least by him, or to accuse the investigators either of lying or cheating or of a blindness or forgetfulness incompatible with any intellectual condition except absolute idiocy.[28]

To this extent, there is (x) the overriding concern of the Society as this relates to the far-reaching, and essentially *philosophical*, concern of seeking, through the establishment of the *super-normal*, a decisive refutation of the prevailing and entrenched *materialism* of the age. Beyond this, however, there is (y) the narrower, and more specifically, *religious*, aspect of the Society's aims. That is to say, the aspect which, over and above the foregoing concern with the *super-normal* as such, involves, also, the objective of validating the reality of *life-after-death*. It is, of course (x) rather than (y) which is of most direct importance for present purposes, as also for its relation to the proclamation of Schopenhauer noted earlier regarding the significance of *mesmeric/hypnotic* effects. At the same time, it is so intimately intertwined with (y) in the history of the Society's researches that no adequate treatment of either is possible without, at least, cursory, reference to both.

In the light of the above – and turning, next, to methodological considerations – there may be an immediate highlighting of the general antipathy of the Sidgwick circle to claims falling under the head of the *physically* psychical. To make this point is not to suggest a complete and utter abrogation by the body of any interest whatsoever in the extravagance of such (putative) effects. Against this must be set, at once – and notwithstanding the uniformly negative results – the extended list of researches in this area which were pursued, most principally, by the aggressively critical minds of Mrs Sidgwick and Hodgson, and which included the 'exposure' by the latter of theosophical claims surrounding the flamboyant figure of Madame Blavatsky in India.[29] In this connexion, too, especial mention may be made of the investigations which absorbed the attention of the whole Sidgwick group, as well as other leading associates, for more than a year over the period 1894–5; and which, as involving the celebrated Neapolitan medium

Eusapia Palladino (1854–1918), came to attain a lasting if ambivalent fame in the Society's annals as the *affaire Palladino*. More for the present, however, is the group's prevailing suspicion and caution regarding such claims – an attitude which, certainly, at times, approached very close to a stance of *a priori* rejection.

In vivid amplification of the point made here, it is only necessary to quote the words of Podmore:

> Very few critical accounts of the earlier seances have been preserved: but they are not needed. The accounts given by the Spiritualists themselves, when they condescend upon detail, are sufficient to show that we need look for no other cause for the results described than trickery of the most trivial and vulgar kind – trickery for the most part too obvious to need a commentary.[30]

It was, indeed, the pressure of this attitude which led, in the winter of 1886–7, to the mass exodus from the organization of its founding spiritualist faction whose own main and vested interest lay in the reality of just such happenings. In itself, this might appear as raising something of an anomaly. For, as already indicated, it was precisely claims of this kind which – as voiced, for instance, by figures of the stature of Crookes and Wallace – had been so largely instrumental in leading to the original establishment of the Society. Part of the reason for this is undoubtedly to be found in the natural distaste of individuals whose own interests were overwhelmingly intellectual for involvement in concerns geared, first and foremost, to the exposure of crude (or, not so crude) chicanery. At the same time, there is also the fact that the investigations in this area which had been carried out, mainly by Gurney, Myers and Sidgwick, in the 1870s, had already led, and despite spiritualistic presuppositions to the contrary, to the quite definite conclusion that this was not a fruitful avenue of approach with regard to (y) above. More specifically, as came to be seen – that, whatever the degree of (presumed) *super-normality* in such cases, this, in itself, carried no entailment as to *supernaturalistic* cause.

But beyond this were two other conclusions which – as relating to (x) as well as (y) – had also come to be accepted as consequences of these early enquiries. First – that, as falling within the virtually exclusive preserve of the (paid) professional medium, they carried with them, right from the start, the presumptive aura of trickery and fraud.[31] To this extent, and as came to be fully accepted, they belonged to a realm where the established scientific canons of *reproducibility* and *control* were necessarily at a discount; and, where, accordingly, as in the case of Crookes, any claims arising therefrom were such as to be inherently and chronically vulnerable to peremptory *ad hominem* dismissal. The attitude, in brief, was one which saw involvement in the sphere of the *physicalistic* as, not only predominantly unfruitful with regard to (y), but, also, in large measure, as positively inimical to the more general objective of the Society as embraced under (x).

There may be mention at this point that the seeming anomaly of, what was characterized above as, the *affaire Palladino* is not to be taken as compromising the attachment of Sidgwick and his circle to the intrinsic importance of these considerations. The position, rather, is simply that the *affaire*, with all its culminating confusion and intellectual embarrassment, came to be seen as but confirmatory, in the most decisive manner, of the validity of the group's longer-term vision. At the same time – and from a perspective wider than that of the purely methodological – it must not pass unnoticed that the detailed evidence relating to the investigations continues, to this day, to present difficulties every bit as perplexing as those surrounding the earlier claims of Crookes. Further, that these are to be seen as arising, not least, from the intransigence of certain of the group – and of Hodgson and Johnson in particular – to the bare idea of the *physically* psychical. The point is one that need not be laboured beyond mention of a number of factual details.

First, and with regard to the 'sittings' themselves – that these took place at the summer home of Richet (at the time, Professor of Physiology at Paris), on his private island of Roubaud, off the south coast of France, and at the Myers' residence in Cambridge, where, in each case, Palladino had been invited as a house guest. Secondly, that of the 'sitters'/researchers at these sessions, mention may be made of (Lord) Rayleigh, J. J. (later, Sir J. J.) Thomson and Francis Darwin, as well as the main figures of Richet, Myers, the Sidgwicks, Hodgson, Johnson, and the prominent physicist Oliver (later, Sir Oliver) Lodge (1851–1940). Finally, and with regard to Palladino herself – that, as the last of the so-called 'great *physical* mediums', she was brought to the sudden attention of the academic world in 1890, following a personal testament similar to that of Crookes nearly two decades earlier. In the instance, the declaration of Cesare Lombroso (1836–1909), the noted recidivist/criminologist and Professor of Psychiatry at Turin (as, moreover, a determined and highly publicized sceptic) that he had become a convert to the reality of dramatic *physical* effects after 'sittings' with her. With this, too, must go the point that Richet (as, also, Lodge) came to follow Lombroso in declaring his conviction in the genuineness of, certain, at least, of, the Palladino effects – a position he strenuously maintained for the rest of his long life.[32] This said, there may be a return to the main discussion with a reiteration of the point that the achievements of the Society, in the great era of its first two decades under the leadership of the Sidgwick group, are to be seen as belonging overwhelmingly, if not exclusively, to the realm of the *mentalistic*. In short – to what James, in his Presidential Address to the Society in 1896, approvingly refers to as (a) the 'calm air of delightful studies' as opposed to what, with the Palladino debacle in mind, he colourfully (if, not altogether fairly) labels (b) 'phenomena of the dark-sitting and rat-hole type'.[33]

The conclusion may be taken as marking a transition from the elaboration of essentially preliminary details to the overriding objective of the discussion as this relates to the actual accomplishments of the Sidgwick group in its predominant concern with the sphere of (a) above.

In this regard, there is, at once, the very extent/intensity of this effort – a consideration which is further heightened when set within the context of the early death of Gurney in 1888, and those, all premature, of Sidgwick, Myers and Hodgson, respectively, in 1900, 1901 and 1905. It is conveyed by Gauld in a passage which is useful, also, for the reason of its reference to two major works – one (mainly) by Gurney, the other by Myers – which arose from the pressure of this vast co-operative enterprise:

What impresses one perhaps most of all about the Sidgwick group is their sheer industry, and the scope and scale of their work. Between the S.P.R.'s foundation in 1882 and the end of 1900, the S.P.R. published some 11,000 pages of *Proceedings* and *Journal* to which must in effect be added the 1,416 pages of [Gurney's] *Phantasms of the Living* and the 1,360 pages of Myers' *Human Personality and its Survival of Bodily Death*. Of these 14,000 pages at least fifty per cent were contributed by the small group of close friends – the Sidgwicks, Hodgson, Gurney and Myers – who were also the S.P.R.'s principal organisers. When one reflects that most of their papers were based on arduous experiments or case investigations which they had themselves conducted, and that only two of the five – Gurney and Hodgson – were in a position to give the whole, or anything like the whole, of their time and energy to the work, one's amazement passes into something like despair.[34]

In this connexion, too, there may be a highlighting of the wider cultural, as well as scientific, importance of this religiously/*ethically* motivated enterprise as it contributed, in a most vital way, to the development of the modern idea of the *unconscious*. Though little recognized nowadays, it is a consideration whose anticipatory significance is drawn by James with especial regard to the work of Myers:

> It is at any rate a possibility, and I am disposed to think it a probability, that Frederic Myers will always be remembered in psychology as the pioneer who staked out a vast tract of mental wilderness and planted the flag of genuine science upon it.[35]

It is a consideration, further, which has been echoed more recently by Aldous Huxley in setting the breadth of Myers' conception of the *unconscious* against the more pathologically based outlooks of the now 'household' names of Freud and Jung:

> Myers' account of the unconscious [in his *Human Personality*] is superior to Freud's in at least one respect; it is more comprehensive and truer to the data of experience. It is also, it seems to me, superior to Jung's account in being more richly documented with concrete facts and less encumbered with those psycho-anthropologico–pseudo-genetic speculations which becloud the writings of the sage of Zurich ... How strange and how unfortunate it is that this amazingly rich, profound and stimulating book should have been neglected in favour of descriptions of human nature less complete and of explanations less adequate to the given facts.[36]

In deliberately setting aside any further pursuit of the above, there is, more particularly, a consideration which has already been the subject of mention. That is, the dominating and vital importance of the super-normalistic idea of *telepathy* in the work of the Sidgwick group.[37]

The degree to which this idea has entered into the popular consciousness since the time of Barrett's first experimentation in the field and the coining of the actual term by Myers will be obvious enough. So, too, is the widespread acceptance of the idea's phenomenal reality – at least, as set within the limits of fleeting moments of individual/personal experience. To make these points is not, of course, to suggest anything like a *fait accompli* with regard to validation. What may be asserted, however, is the contemporary prevalence of a conception which, as stemming, most principally, from the early endeavours of the Society for Psychical Research, is the continuing object of sustained and virulent opposition by the entrenched forces of *scientific/materialistic* orthodoxy. Nor, indeed, is the strength of this antagonism merely nominal. For, in so far as 'thought' may be considered as a 'signal' (as, *philosophically*, it has every right to be), then the very possibility of (instantaneous) 'thought transference'/*telepathy* is such as to present a direct (theoretical) threat to one of the main pillars of the whole edifice of modern (physical) science – that is the presupposition that there can be no 'signal' faster than the speed of *light*. In thus indicating the challenge of the idea – a matter whose significance will attain prominence in a later chapter – the discussion may be continued by attending to the mode of its development at the hands of the Sidgwick group.

Here, an immediate division may be drawn between two, quite distinct, strands of this enterprise. On the one hand, there is the *practical/experimental* aspect of the endeavour – the side which, following the lead of Barrett, had, as its main objective the (empirical/scientific) *validation* of the phenomenon. On this, little further need be said beyond passing mention of two points. First, the *extent* of these early experiments – as indicated, for instance, in the list, together with associated references, collated by Gauld.[38] Secondly, and by way of 'flavour' – the summary given by James of one of the most provocative of these experiments. Thus, one conducted by Gurney on a hypnotized subject:

> The subject's hands are thrust through a blanket, which screens the operator from his eyes, and his mind is absorbed in conversation with a third person. The operator meanwhile points with his finger to one of the fingers of the subject, which finger alone responds to this silent selection by becoming stiff or anaesthetic, as the case may be. The interpretation is difficult,

but the phenomenon, which I have myself witnessed, seems authentic.[39]

Returning, however, to the main concern, this must be seen as lying with the *theoretical* development of the idea as this emerged from the group's main preoccupation with the question of *post-mortem* survival.

The matter is one which may be approached through reference to the fact that among the first acts of the Society following its formation was the setting up of six separate investigative committees for the pursuit of various aspects of the (putatively) supernormal. Further, that, of these, it was the so-called Literary Committee – charged with the collection and collation of evidence relating to, what, in Myers' terms, may be characterized as, 'ghosts, spirits, [etc.]' – which accomplished incomparably the most work during the early years of the organization's existence. A measure of the extent of this effort – borne mainly by Gurney and Myers, and especially the former – is conveyed in the remark of Gauld that 'in the year 1883 alone the six members of the Committee wrote more than 10 000 letters, and correspondence was only part of their activities. They had also often to travel in order to interview crucial witnesses, and to visit libraries and Record Offices.'[40] At the same time, and following from the above, there is also the significance of a vital twist. The fact, namely, that out of the massive effort of the Literary Committee's first endeavours, arose, not the sought-after, and avidly hoped-for, evidence for *post-mortem* survival, but something decidedly and unexpectedly different.

The intellectual impact of the discovery indicated here is recounted by Gurney and Myers as joint authors of the (first) 'Report of the Literary Committee' which was presented in December 1882:

Those who are used, as most of us have been all our lives, to hearing now and again a stray story at third or fourth hand, with the usual commentary of vague wonderment or shallow explanation, but without any suggestion of analysing or probing it, can scarcely imagine the effect on the mind of a sudden, large accumulation of direct, well-attested, and harmonious testimony. The similarities of unlooked-for detail which bind the phenomena together into distinct groups, the very similarities which make the accounts of them monotonous reading, give the strength of a faggot to the dispersed units which looked as if the mere dead weight of uninquiring incredulity might easily break them.[41]

Pursuing the point further, the vital fact which came to be realized was that by far the largest single class of cases collected by the Committee related to, what came to be labelled as, *crisis apparitions* – cases which are summarized by Gauld in the following way:

> At a given time a certain person, the *percipient*, sees the figure, or hears the voice, of another person (in the majority of cases someone well known to him), whom we will call the *agent*. It transpires that at or about the time when the percipient thought he saw the agent or thought he heard his voice, the agent was in a totally different place, and was undergoing some singular crisis in his affairs – generally death.[42]

What may be added is that by August 1883 the evidence under discussion had become so extensive that a decision was taken to prepare a book on the subject with Gurney, Myers and Podmore as the projected joint authors. In the event, this plan was later changed – mainly through Sidgwick's insistence on the necessity for individuating responsibility – and the authorship entrusted entirely to Gurney, with Podmore being assigned the role of investigative assistant and Myers the task of writing an extended introduction.[43] So was born the work which appeared in October 1886 under the title *Phantasms of the Living*. More specifically, the work which – as constituting the culmination of the Society's first major project – had, as its overriding thesis, the original and highly provocative claim that (seemingly *super-naturalistic*) *crisis apparitions* are to be explained *naturalistically*, even if, at the same time, *super/para-normalistically*. In short – as hallucinations generated in the percipient by the receipt of a *telepathic* 'message' from the crisis-ridden (and, usually, dying) agent.

There can be no doubt of the intensity of Gurney's effort in the writing of this work; nor of its subsequent status as a classic in the field of psychical research and of *telepathy* in particular. In this connexion, too, there is, no less, the fact of its pioneering significance in the development of *statistical* methodology in general. Of especial interest in this regard is the attack on the basis of Gurney's findings which issued from one of the foremost logicians of the day, C. S. Peirce (1839–1914). More specifically, his claim, in a critique of the former's work which appeared in the *Proceedings of the American Society for Psychical Research* for December 1887, that each of the cases cited by Gurney violated one or more of what he held to be eighteen criteria of evidential acceptability. Further – the care with which, in the last months of his life, Gurney responded to, and met, most of these criticisms. Setting aside these details, however, there is the point of main concern. Namely, that, following Gurney's death, the outstanding terms of Peirce's challenge – as these turned, in each case, on the need for a wider sampling base – were taken up by the other members of his circle in a second vast project which came to be known as the 'Census of Hallucinations'.

The undertaking – which Gurney himself had already entertained and which was planned in connexion with the projected International Congresses of Psychology (Paris, 1889; London, 1892; Munich, 1896; Paris, 1900) – was begun in the spring of 1889 under the primary direction of Mrs Sidgwick and Alice Johnson with the initial and ambitious object of obtaining 50 000 answers to the 'Census Question', namely:

Have you ever, when believing yourself to be completely awake, had a vivid impression of seeing or being touched by a living being or inanimate object, or of hearing a voice; which impression, so far as you could discover, was not due to any external physical cause?

In the event, the target sample proved to be beyond practical attainment and the final findings of the Census Committee, as these appeared in 1894 under the title 'Report on the Census of Hallucinations', were based on a figure of 17 000 respondents of whom 2272 answered in the affirmative.[44] For various reasons this number was reduced to 1684 persons who, between them, laid claim to 1942 hallucinations. Of the latter, rather more than 300 were identified as relating to visual hallucinations of persons known to the percipient, with, most particularly, 80 coinciding within twelve hours each way of the deaths of the supposed agents, and with 32 of these proving to be much better evidenced than the rest. On this basis – that is using a sampling base of 17 000 and taking the minimal figure of 32 as the working number for *crisis apparitions* in the preceding sense – there is the main conclusion of the (nearly 400-page) Report. In short – and as founded on the best statistical tools of the day – that this represented a probability ratio of more than 400:1 over chance coincidence, and hence evidence of a powerful nature for an associative link with the theory of 'thought exchange'/*telepathy*.

There is neither need nor intention to pursue this conclusion beyond the highlighting of three brief points. First, and in reiteration of what has already been said, there is the clear fact of the intellectual thoroughness of the effort which went into its establishment. Secondly, there is the altogether balanced assessment of Gauld regarding its lasting significance:

> The methods by which the Census was conducted were of course antiquated and would certainly not be regarded as satisfactory today. None the less it was a work on a considerable scale, and one cannot easily point to any conclusions drawn by the Census Committee which the data do not justify. The *Report on the Census of Hallucinations* without doubt threw the onus on the critic. It was no longer up to psychical researchers to give reasons for supposing that there is a correlation between deaths and crisis apparitions. It was up to whoever disputed this to find stratagems ingenious enough to explain away the evidence.[45]

Finally, and most importantly for the course of what is to follow, there is the fact that, whatever the ultimacy of its final strength, it is, yet, to be seen as but part of a wider spectrum of evidence asserted by the Sidgwick group regarding the matter in hand.

Thus, in this regard, there is, at once, the support which is to be seen as arising from the minutiae of common personal experience – support which, though hardly scientific, was, yet, such as to make the idea the topic of widespread popular understanding and interest within the context of the time. Further, there were the results of practical experimentation in the field, such as had been undertaken, most notably by Barrett and Gurney, but also by others. Beyond this, again, was the group's clear insight that the theory of *telepathic* communication (between specifically *carnate* minds) constituted a more *economical/scientific* explanation of a whole range of seemingly preternatural *mentalistic* effects than the extravagance of appeal to 'spirit' agency. With this, too, came the reflexivity of another crucial consideration which will be pursued more fully below. The fact, in brief, that, within the final scheme of the group's overriding preoccupation with the question of *post-mortem* survival, the postulation of *telepathy*, in the foregoing ('naturalistic') sense, became a matter, not simply of necessary *presupposition*, but also of technical *discount*. Whilst, thus, emphasizing the breadth of the evidential base offered by the Sidgwick group for the phenomenon in hand, the main discussion may be closed with an amplification of the last of the preceding points.

The matter is one which relates to the culminating phase of the group's endeavours as this came to settle, following 1890, on the full extent of the challenge arising from the phenomenon of so-called *evidential* or *veridical* (mediumistic) data – that is, as already noted, mediumistic 'communications' of a veridical (if inconsequential) nature whose purported source was a deceased relative or friend of the 'sitter'. It will be obvious enough that the provocativeness of such 'messages' had already been the subject of deep interest by the group from the earliest days of its inception. At the same time, there is, no less clearly, the fact that, as seen from the standpoint of this early period, there were seemingly intractable barriers to any theoretical progress in this direction. Thus, there was the immediate limitation imposed by the stark paucity of material of this kind during the period in hand. Coupled with this was the difficulty arising from the general cloud of suspicion which hung over the virtually exclusive source of such data – that is the paid, professional, medium. Beyond this, again, lay the intransigence of the possibility that the phenomenon, if not the product of deliberate fraud, was, yet, to be explained in the (*naturalistic*) terms of some kind of prodigious *memorizing* ability – or, in Gauld's words, that 'mediums *might* be, not people with the faculty of communicating with deceased persons, or even with clairvoyant gifts, but simply people with unusually sticky subconscious memories.'[46] With these considerations in mind, the main point for the moment concerns the new vistas for research which were opened up, following 1884, by James' discovery of the Boston medium, Mrs Leonora E. Piper (1859–1950).

There can be no question of Mrs Piper being set apart from the stereotypical medium of the day. Of striking good looks she was – if of no great education – a woman of refinement and pre-eminent married respectability with two young children and a husband in the employ of a large Boston store.[47] In this connexion, too, there is the clear dating of the origination of her mediumistic ability – as this arose, quite spontaneously, in 1884, when visiting a blind healing medium on a matter of personal health. Most particularly, however, is a point centring on the phenomenology of her mediumship, namely the seeming prodigality of her ability whilst in a condition of (self-induced) trance to produce 'messages' of just the kind under discussion.[48] To this may be added a number of further considerations. First – that the local fame which soon arose from the practice of this gift (mainly with friends and relatives) brought her to the attention of James who, in the interests of research, obtained an anonymous 'sitting' with her towards the end of 1884. Secondly – that this meeting so intrigued James that he continued with further sessions in 1885, as well as supplementing the information gained in this way with that derived from some twenty-five other persons for whom he arranged 'sittings' under pseudonyms. Finally, for the moment, there is the fact that the culmination of these studies came in 1886 with a short paper by James in the *Proceedings of the American Society for Psychical Research* in which he expressed his complete conviction in the genuineness of Mrs. Piper's trances, as well as the super-normality of (some, at least, of) her 'messages'.[49] Thus, in this regard, his unequivocal conclusion was as follows:

> I repeat again what I have said before that taking everything that I know of Mrs. Piper into account, the result is to make me feel as absolutely certain as I am of any personal fact in the world that she knows things in her trances which she cannot possibly have heard in her waking state, and that the definite philosophy of her trances is yet to be found.[50]

With this, too, arose the challenge of Mrs Piper's mediumship – as set forth by one of the founding fathers of modern psychology – being officially conveyed to the Sidgwick group in England.

To the above extent, the claim of James was – certainly at the practical level – that, in the figure of Mrs Piper, he had discovered a medium with the capacity to produce *evidential* data, if not quite to order, at least, on a scale hitherto considered only as an ideal. Further – of her ability to do this even under conditions of strict control. The response to this claim was not long in coming. In May 1887, Hodgson – by common consent, the Sidgwick group's most able detector of fraud – arrived in Boston to take up the secretaryship of the fledgling American Society. At this stage, as all the evidence suggests, he had little thought of the matter of Mrs Piper ending in any way other than as just one more instance of plain duplicity. In the event – and despite resort to such lengths as having Mrs Piper and her family 'shadowed' by a detective for several weeks – no hint of a resolution of this kind was forthcoming. Rather, the startling *evidentiality* of some of the 'messages' received in anonymous 'sittings' during the remainder of 1887, as well as a later series of sessions over the period 1888–9, resulted in a full endorsement of the conclusions of James.[51] This, in turn, led to an additional round of investigations and, following a suggestion by Hodgson/James, Mrs Piper being invited by the Sidgwick group to submit herself to further tests in the completely new environment of England. This she accepted, with the visit taking place in the winter of 1889–90 under the arrangement and control of a special research committee consisting of Myers, Leaf and Lodge. Beyond these details, however, is the investigative outcome of this visit. In short – that it was entirely confirmatory of the earlier findings of James and Hodgson.[52]

What may be seen, therefore, is that, by the turn of the 1890s, the Sidgwick group was in possession – if, of nothing else – of two firm conclusions arising out of the extended studies of Mrs Piper's mediumship. First – the fulsome validation of the phenomenon of so-called *evidential* data. Secondly – and following from the circumstances of this validation, the elimination of the sufficiency of the hypothesis of some kind of extended *memory* as to necessary cause. In thus accepting the *super-normality* of some, at least, of the mediumistic 'messages', the group was led to conduct, what was to be, its final assault on the question of *post-mortem* survival.

In the event, the vanguard of this endeavour was, again, to be Mrs Piper and Hodgson. Following her return to the United States, the former entered into an agreement with the American Branch of the Society giving Hodgson a large measure of control over her professional activities in return for a modest retaining fee. Thereafter, Hodgson was to devote most of the remaining years of his life to the challenge of her ability – at times under conditions of the most extreme financial duress. It was to be a process marked by striking developments. In 1892, Hodgson began receiving, through Mrs Piper, *veridical* data of an order which altogether surpassed anything previously obtained. This was accompanied by a change in the physical aspects of Mrs Piper's mediumship, as this moved from oral 'communication' to (mainly) that of automatic writing. The period, too, was characterized by the participation of other 'sitters' – always introduced under conditions of anonymity and with the fullest precautions being taken to preserve this. Complete notes of the proceedings were kept, generally by Hodgson or his secretary, with the transcripts being annotated by the 'sitters' with regard to accuracy. To bring the above together, the result was the accumulation of a detailed (and, at the time, unique) set of seance records which came to constitute the basis of a second (book-length) paper by Hodgson, which appeared in 1898 with parts of it being read by him to the General Meeting of the Society in March of that year.[53]

The paper may be viewed as marking a watershed in the history of the Sidgwick group. What may be taken for granted, of course, is the general acceptance by the latter of the importance of Hodgson's painstaking study of Mrs Piper as this had extended, at the time of the paper, over the span of more than a decade. By common consent, this had led to the firm establishment of the indubitable *super-normality* of Mrs Piper's 'messages'. More for the present, however, is the change which the years had brought in Hodgson's attitude to the *explanation* of the phenomenon. At the time of his first paper in 1892, he had been more than content to ascribe the matter to some complicated process of *unconscious* mind. More specifically, it was his view – shared by the other members of his circle – that the 'naturalistic' idea of *telepathy* (though, perhaps, in some extended form involving a 'pool' of *unconscious*, if still, *carnate*, thought) offered the most productive possibility of approach to the problem. As against this, he was far from accepting the spiritualistic hypothesis as to cause. The 'personalities' of the 'communicators', as he made plain, were much too 'fragmented' to allow resort to any explanation of this kind. To this extent, his position, at this stage, certainly went no further than that summarized by James, writing in 1893, in bringing the phenomenon of Mrs Piper's mediumship to popular attention:

> In the case of Mrs. Piper, not a physical but a trance medium, we seem to have no choice offered at all. Mr. Hodgson and others have made prolonged study of this lady's trances, and are all convinced that super-normal powers of cognition are displayed therein. These are *prima facie* due to 'spirit-control'. But the conditions are so complex that a dogmatic decision either for or against the spirit hypothesis must as yet be postponed.[54]

With this, therefore, there may be a return to the far-reaching import of Hodgson's second paper with the point that, not only was this overwhelmingly confirmatory, once more, of the *super-normality* of Mrs Piper's ability, it was also proclamatory of a decisive shift in his view as to *cause*. That is, no less, of his conversion to the hypothesis that the 'communicators' were, indeed, as 'they' claimed, the surviving 'spirits' of deceased persons.

In setting aside the details of Hodgson's argument, it suffices merely to say that, despite the full endorsement by the other members of the group of the undoubted strength of his case, there was, yet, a general reluctance to accept it as exhaustive in its own right. In particular – and returning to the reflexivity of the point made earlier – it was met by the position urged by Sidgwick. More specifically – that, whatever the degree of Hodgson's *personal* conviction in the matter, following his extended, first-hand, experience of Mrs Piper's mediumship, no fully adequate *theoretical* resolution of the problem was possible without a decisive *elimination* of the alternative hypothesis of ('naturalistic') *telepathic* interchange. The difficulty was one which was to absorb the virtually exclusive attention of the group for the remaining years of its existence.

In the event, it was a process which – though largely incidental to the primary concern – may be marked with the mention of three bare points. First, the fact that (putatively) definitive progress towards this goal was only forthcoming following the deaths, in quick succession, of the main figures of Sidgwick, Myers and Hodgson. Secondly, that this advance was intimately bound up with the phenomenon of what came to be known as *Cross-Correspondences* – that is the phenomenon (with 'Gurney', once more, as a leading 'participator') which is summarized by Gauld in the following way:

> Parallel or interlinked communications obtained through different mediums and automatists, and allegedly devised by the spirits of deceased members of the Sidgwick group for the benefit of their colleagues still in the flesh.[55]

Thirdly, and as a foil to the esotericism of the two preceding points, there is the fact of Broad's own measured, if oblique, reference to the seeming outcome of these efforts. Thus, his words in assessing the significance of a contemporary product of automatic writing:

> These automatic scripts are a very important addition to the vast mass of such material which *prima facie* suggests rather strongly that certain human beings have survived the death of their physical bodies and have been able to communicate with certain others who are still in the flesh.[56]

To summarize, however – and whatever the final standing of the above – the point to be emphasized in bringing the discussion to a close is that made earlier regarding the *reflexive* importance of the idea of *telepathy* in the work of the Sidgwick group. More specifically – that, not only did this latter derive support of a potentially decisive nature from the exhaustiveness of Hodgson's demonstration of the *super-normality* of Mrs Piper's 'messages'; it, also, through the very *strength* of this evidence, came to stand as a positive *barrier* to the acceptance of what was really of most consequence for the group – that is the force of Hodgson's case for the reality of *post-mortem* survival.[57]

To complete the present survey, there may be mentioned the strength of Broad's anticipatory response to any merely peremptory rejection of the above:

> I suppose that it is inevitable that some clever fool should triumphantly remark that the fact that Sidgwick [and his group] approached the subject of psychical research from [the angle of *post-mortem* survival] discounts the value of [their] work. It should be a sufficient answer to point out that in fact Sidgwick reached a purely negative conclusion about the evidence produced by psychical research for human survival. And, if I may pass from the particular to the general, I would conclude with the following observation. A conscientious and critical person who realizes the immense importance of human survival is much more likely to weight the scales against *prima facie* evidence for it than to accept such evidence lightly. His desire that it may be true, and that it may be proved to be so, will indeed make him persevere and constantly return to the attack after each set-back and disappointment. This effect it did have on Sidgwick. But he will be so anxious lest his desires should trick him into accepting fairy gold that he will be in some danger of

rejecting real gold if it should be ever offered to him.[58]

With this, too, there may be the addition of a number of concluding points relating, more specifically, to the contemporary standing of the group's pioneering, if incidental, establishment of the phenomenon of *telepathy*.

Thus, to continue, there is the fact that, despite the inhospitability of the intellectual climate which took increasing hold following the turn of the century, academic interest in its challenge did not recede quite so completely as happened in the corresponding case of *hypnotism*. In particular, there is the way in which, over the span of the past half-century, the phenomenon has been kept in the public mind through the sustained and highly publicized researches associated with the name of the psychologist J. B. Rhine.[59] With this, too, there may be a highlighting of the fulsome, if still, virtually singular, recognition given to the phenomenon by a prominent figure of the scientific establishment – namely, Sir Alister Hardy. Thus, there are his words from his Gifford Lectures for 1963–5, in arguing for the potentiality of the phenomenon as a link between the, otherwise opposed, Darwinian and Lamarckian theories of evolution:

> If telepathy is proved to exist in man, and I believe that the evidence is overwhelming, and if we believe that man is one with the stream of life then it seems most unlikely that so remarkable a phenomenon should be confined to just a few individuals of just one species of animal.[60]

To make these points is not to draw from them more than they can bear. Neither is it to ignore the virulence of the charge of so-called 'scientific impossibility' – as, for instance, is captured in the anecdotal remark of Nowell-Smith of '[knowing] a very distinguished physicist to explain that Dr Rhine's experimental results in "parapsychology" must be false because such things just cannot happen.'[61] At the same time – and whatever the extent of this deeply entrenched stance – enough has been said for the firm establishment of (two clear aspects of) a single main point. In short, and due, not least, to the efforts of the Sidgwick group – that the sheer weight of the evidence for the phenomenon is such as not only to (a) completely pre-empt the foregoing use of *impossible*, but also (b) call into sharp question the associated sense of *scientific* from which it derives its entire vestige of plausibility.

In noting that both (a) and (b) above will be topics of later concern, there is, more immediately, the second of the considerations raised earlier; that is – and deliberately setting aside the breadth of the subsequent work of the Society – the continuing pressure of contemporary testimony to the reality of effects falling under the more dramatically provocative label of the *physically* psychical. It is to this latter consideration – with its shades of such famous names as Crookes, Wallace, Zöllner, Fechner, Weber, Richet, Lombroso, as well as others – that attention may now be turned.

8

Super-normality as a Mode of the Present

The topic for this chapter is one which the reader will have little difficulty in associating with the name of the Israeli entertainer Uri Geller and the highly publicized controversy of the past decade over his claim to the reality of so-called 'metal-bending'. That is, more specifically, his claim to the demonstrability of his capacity to bring about the super-normal softening, deformation and fracturing of pieces of metal, for example spoons, forks, keys, etc. (as well as, occasionally, other materials such as plastic), either (a) by the simple act of gentle finger-stroking, or even (b) by the direct action of thought alone without any touching whatsoever. In thus reminding the reader of the topic for discussion, it may be brought into sharper focus through mention that, whatever the ultimate significance of the claim embraced under (a), it is the starkness of (b) which is clearly of most decisive interest in the current context. To this extent – and in full acceptance, right from the outset, of what may well be taken as the inherent improbability of such happenings – the concern in what follows will relate most expressly to the latter, with only implied or incidental reference to the less conceptually provocative, though more widely publicized, mode of the challenge embraced under (a).

To open with a number of delineatory details, there may be mention, first, that, although the claim to 'metal-bending' originated with Geller, it was not long before he was followed by others, mainly children, who also came to profess the same strange ability; and who, like him, came to offer themselves as subjects of investigation. The point has an importance which, like that of the distinction between (a) and (b) above, will be taken up more fully later. Secondly, there may be a highlighting of the fact that the debate over the phenomenon (and whatever its overtones) is to be seen as being specifically *scientific* in nature. That is to say, it is hardly to be regarded as centring on the unexamined claims of the 'benders' themselves, but rather on the pronouncements of trained figures of the scientific world who, following experimentation with Geller and/or others, came to express their conviction as to the *validation* of the happening. Thirdly, and in full deference to the many others throughout the world who also came to involve themselves in the debate, reference may be made to two personalities, in particular, for the prominence of the part which each, in his turn, played in the propagation and defence of the 'Geller-effect'. Both Chairholders of the University of London, their mention is vital for the course of what follows – John Taylor, Professor of Applied Mathematics at King's College, with his, popular, *Superminds: An Enquiry into the Paranormal;*[1] and J. B. Hasted, Professor of Experimental Physics at Birkbeck College, with his, more scholarly, *The Metal-Benders.*[2] Finally, but not least, there may be the reiteration of a point which, though obvious enough, in itself, is yet worth the price of emphasis. In short, that the debate over the effect is one which, in the sharpest possible way, turns on nothing less than the *scientific* assertion – in the full context of all the technology of the final quarter of the twentieth century – of the reality of the *miraculous* in the sense under discussion.

In turning to the wider circumstances of the controversy, immediate mention may be made of a feature of the affair which, as falling more under, what may be regarded as, the *sociology* of science than science as such, is directly reminiscent of the academic/scientific furore of a century earlier over the claims of Crookes. Thus, to quote Taylor:

> I hope that the evidence presented ... will go some way to convincing the general public that the Geller effect is genuine and that we *need* to understand it. [But] I hold no great hope of denting the scientific complacency of my brethren ... One distinguished scientist, a Nobel Prizewinner, told me that metal-bending was clearly done by fraud and his wife threw in for good measure that no scientist of repute would be caught dead investigating Geller. A scientific colleague with great research funds at his disposal would not hear of the effect being possible. In any case, investigations could not be supported financially: 'Suppose a question were asked about it in the House!'[3]

Further, the words of Hasted:

> Nearly all those who first investigated Uri Geller have been

subject to smear attack ... [of a kind] more familiar in party politics than in scientific investigation ... by people unwilling to consider the possibility of the existence of anything which is not materialistic or behaviouristic;[4]

And, in continuing:

Although Uri Geller has not been caught red-handed in faking a paranormal physical phenomenon, yet adverse circumstantial evidence about his public performances has been given wide publicity. This exercise has created an atmosphere in which not only Geller but also the researchers into metal-bending have come to be regarded as suspect by the scientific community. Colleagues have been polite, but blasts of icy wind have often reached me. (*MB*, p. 3)

With this, too, there is the point that the criticism of Geller, as indicated above, is to be seen as relating, most obviously, to his demonstrations of the touching/'stroking' mode of the phenomenon. Moreover, and following from this – as turning, purely and simply, on the charge of trickery/deception/fraud; that is, more specifically, on the charge that the effects in question are the product not of any super-normal ability as claimed, but merely of devices of 'magic', for example sleight of hand, the use of specially prepared (and weakened) materials, the surreptitious employment of some kind of 'softening agent'(!), diversionary 'patter', and so forth.

To the above must be added the full acknowledgement of another vital point. That is, the fact that the challenge to Geller (and whatever the degree of its circumstantiality) has been fuelled, not least, by the former's own frank, if reluctantly extracted, confession to the use of just such 'magic' during his early days as an entertainer in Israel. Thus, in his own, remorseful, words:

I finally gave in to the manager's pressure ... to add the magician's trick to the regular demonstration ... I felt it was wrong the minute I agreed. I didn't realize, though, how big a mistake I was making, one of the most crucial mistakes of my life. After all, the more I became known all over the country, the more controversy would grow as to whether what I did was real or phoney. I added the trick to the legitimate demonstrations and I hated myself every time I did it.[5]

To summarize, therefore, enough has been said to indicate not only the tangled complexity of the debate over the 'Geller-effect', but also the circumstances of the general cloud of suspicion surrounding the figure of Geller himself.

There may be pause at this point for the highlighting of two complicatory considerations, both of which, as arising from the above, the reader may already have in mind. First, the fact, as it has come to be widely accepted, of Geller (and, with this, the phenomenon with which his name is associated) being the subject of some kind of definitive/scientific *exposé*. Secondly, and on the face of things even more potentially serious, the fact, as again widely proclaimed, of Taylor's name being linked with some kind of public *retraction*. The two points, though seemingly supportive of each other, are, in fact, logically separate, with neither amounting to anything of substance for the main purpose. At the same time – though, to this extent, being peripheral to the central concern – they have a topicality which cannot be ignored. For this reason, their treatment must be seen by the reader as a brief, but necessary, diversion.

To begin with the former point, it is a matter whose substance has already been fully, if only implicitly, met in earlier comment on the exclusively circumstantial nature of the charges against Geller. Notwithstanding – and, not least, for the reason of the widespread misapprehension as to the true facts of the case – there may be the offer of a number of amplificatory considerations. To this end, there may be immediate emphasis on the highly relevant fact that the campaign against Geller, and, with this, the basis of all later talk of an *exposé*, originated, not from the investigations of scientists themselves, but from the writings of one of the former's fellow stage-performers – a personality described by Hasted as 'a fanatically sceptical conjuror, known as "The Amazing Randi"' (*MB*, p. 28).[6] In this connexion, too, it is not without interest to note the first-hand observations of Hasted regarding the latter's lack of credibility as a witness (*MB*, p. 29). So, also, the level of the quality of his writing as, for instance, in an *ad hominem* attack on Taylor:

Getting back to Professor John Taylor: He is rather unusual, to say the very least. There are not many leading British mathematicians who can lay claim to having been a consultant to *Forum* magazine, a British sex-advice publication. I would presume that his advice on this subject reflected an academic prowess, which is universally acknowledged as prodigious. At

King's College, London, he serves as Professor of Applied Mathematics and has several books to his credit. Nevertheless, one book, *Superminds*, has caused even his staunchest admirers to throw up their learned hands in dismay.[7]

And, again, in the tone of his call to a whole group of prominent physicists for a renunciation of their support of the 'Geller-effect':

> To the men such as Targ, Puthoff, Bastin, Hasted, Bohm, Taylor and others who have lent their scientific acceptance to a chimera, I suggest that it is time to call in their loans.[8]

In the same vein there is, again, the fact of the formation, in 1975, of an organization of conjurors and science-writers, mainly from the USA, for the express purpose of mounting a co-ordinated opposition to the publicity surrounding the claims of Geller (*MB*, pp. 14, 27) – a body, with Randi as a founding member, which was later to pursue its essentially propagandist function under the highly profiled, if hardly appropriate, title of the 'Committee for the Scientific Investigation of Claims of the Paranormal' ('CSICOP' or 'CSICP').

As against the above, it remains merely to add two further points. First, the part played by other conjurors/'magicians' in Hasted's early probing of the Randi–Geller confrontation – where, as he remarks, six of these (two from the USA, and one each from Denmark, Netherlands, France and Switzerland) came to '[state] publicly ... after [observing] Geller and other metal-benders ... that they could detect no fraud' (*MB*, p. 29). Secondly, Hasted's own cautious estimation of Geller's credibility as derived from personal attendance at the latter's public demonstrations:

> I have myself been present at only five performances, two in London and one each in Southampton, Longleat (near Bath) and Tokyo. Although I found no evidence of trickery, I was not personally responsible for the arrangements, so that the protocol was not always as I could have wished. It is worth mention that the softening of the large piece of heavy silver cutlery produced at Longleat was almost beyond dispute genuine. (*MB*, p. 29)

There can be no question, of course, of these assorted remarks being taken as offering anything in the way of positive support for

Geller. Indeed, their main import may be accepted as involving no more than a full endorsement of the caution expressed by Hasted in his remark that 'Geller's public performances represent a grey area into which the serious student should not venture' (*MB*, p. 29). At the same time, there is, no less, the point that they are entirely sufficient for the immediate purpose of demonstrating the complete untenability of the claim to a 'Geller-*exposé*' in any strong, 'once and for all', sense of this term. There is, in short, the conclusion that, in the last resort – and despite emotively generated presumptions to the contrary – the total force of all such talk amounts, at the very most, to not a whit more than a thoroughly prosaic verdict of 'not proven'.

As to the second point, it needs but a moment's reflection for a full realization that there must be an immediate retreat from what is suggested on the surface; that is from what, in effect, must be taken as a wholesale rejection by Taylor of the entire extent of all such strenuously assented claims as the following:

> The Geller effect cannot be lightly dismissed. People across the world can cause a range of objects, especially metallic ones, to bend into strange shapes and even to break, using a method which is apparently beyond our current scientific understanding ... I have myself directly observed the Geller effect in objects made of a range of metals: silver, lead, zinc, tin, copper, aluminium, iron (including various types of steel) and tungsten, with bending of up to 180°. Objects made of iron, copper and aluminium have been broken as well. The specimens tested had lengths varying from 5 centimetres to 30 centimetres, and thicknesses in cross-section varying from 0.1 millimetres for thin strips of copper or silver to rods of mild steel of 0.6 centimetres in diameter ... Plastic about 10 centimetres long and in cross-sectional area 0.1 to 0.5 square centimetres can also be caused to bend or break. Specimens of flexible plastic have been bent without breaking and brittle plastic strips have been fragmented.[9]

And, indeed, as the matter transpires, the true nature of the vaunted 'retraction'/'recantation' turns out to be much less innocuous than this, with its substance hinging more on convolutions in Taylor's thought than on any relation to fact. The full extent of the whole point – as it arises from remarks made by

Taylor in a book, *Science and the Supernatural*,[10] which followed his *Superminds* – may be delineated through the coalescing summaries of three, quite disparate, sources.

Thus, first, the words of Randi himself – significantly enough, in the context of upbraiding Taylor for *not* retracting in the above (main) sense:

> John Taylor, formerly Geller's most vocal and dedicated suppor-ter, has written a book, *Science and the Supernatural*, in which he does a 180-degree turn at high speed without academic whi-plash, reversing himself on the matter in a rather peculiar fashion. He tells us that since only the electromagnetic (EM) spectrum can explain Geller's feats – if they are genuine – and his research shows that EM forces are not involved, therefore the phenomena do not exist. What we look for in vain is a statement from Taylor admitting that he was fooled – completely, thor-oughly, and definitively.[11]

Secondly, the fuller portrayal of the matter as given by a more recent writer, the historian, Brian Inglis:

> Impressed by Uri Geller's performance on television, Taylor not merely abandoned his role as one of the media sceptics, but wrote a book, *Superminds*, presenting the case 'that for one modern 'miracle', the Geller effect, there *is* a rational, scientific explanation'. It appeared in 1975. Five years later, in his *Science and the Supernatural*, Taylor went into contortions to try to explain why he could not have witnessed what in *Superminds* he claimed he *had* witnessed, because he had been unable to find the (for him) 'rational, scientific explanation'. Taylor's excuse was that . . . because he had found that none of the known physical forces (gravity, radioactivity, electromagnetism and the force which holds the nuclear constituents together) could account for it . . . we must discard the notion 'if we wish to preserve the scientific viewpoint' . . . [i.e. the viewpoint] that all reality can be ex-plained 'by one aspect of it – the physical'.[12]

Thirdly, there is the appraisal of Hasted in his capacity as an experimental physicist:

> In Britain Geller made several successful television records of apparently paranormal bendings of cutlery, and many children

came forward and claimed, sometimes even demonstrated, similar happenings. Mathematical physicist John Taylor, who was present in the studio, started a programme of field-work and invited numbers of the children to his laboratory. He published accounts in a book entitled *Superminds*, and publicly affirmed that he believed paranormal metal-bending was a real effect. Later he was to announce something of a change of heart, brought about by his failure to detect the presence of electro-magnetic radiation during metal-bending. The reasoning was that bending must have been brought about by such radiation, and since none was observed, the bending may well have been produced normally, presumably by manual action previously undetected. This reasoning is difficult for physicists to under-stand. (*MB*, p. 28)

What may be seen, therefore, is that the issue is one which – like the substance of the, so-called, *exposé* – is related more to the realm of heuristic/cultural/sociological *presuppositions* than to what is of most importance for the main purpose, that is the methodology of (scientific) *discovery/validation*. More specifically, it is one which, through the very pressure of these presuppositions, derives its entire plausibility from what, in the last resort, amounts to no more than a painful confusion of two, quite separate, senses of the term *scientific*. In short, as already drawn – between the use of this term as it relates to *validation*, on the one hand, and *explanation*, on the other.

With this, there may be a return to the main discussion with the listing of a number of considerations that are geared more positive-ly to the side of Geller. To begin, and on grounds of simple fairness, there may be full acknowledgement of the latter's own uncompromising insistence on the genuineness of the phe-nomenon – and this, notwithstanding the complication noted earlier regarding his admittance to an, at least, limited, indulgence in 'magic'. Further, and as a counter to the vociferousness of the criticism centring on Geller's (paid) public performances, reference may be made to the careful recording by Hasted of his own first, private, introduction to the 'stroking effect'. The date of the event is given as 5 February 1974; the venue, Geller's room at a London hotel; and with Hasted's colleague at Birkbeck, the prominent theoretical physicist, David Bohm, being one of the three others present:

At length Geller said he would try, and asked for a hotel spoon. But I produced two latchkeys in polythene bags before he had a chance. I took them from the bags and laid them on the table ... Geller was quite happy with the keys, and at once took one in each hand, holding it lightly between the forefinger and thumb; I did not take my eyes off them once, not even for a moment. I can affirm that I did not see Geller's other fingers touch the keys (except at pick-up) and that he did not move them more than about an inch from the table surface; they were in my field of vision the whole time. Nothing happened for about forty seconds, and then Geller put the keys flat on the table about two inches apart and stroked them gently, one with each forefinger. All the time Geller was talking, but I never took my eyes off the two keys and I am certain they never left the table for a surreptitious bend to be performed. After one minute's stroking, the end of each key started to bend slightly upwards, one (the one he stroked by his right forefinger) distinctly more than the other. The angles were 11° and 8°, as measured afterwards ... This was my personal introduction to the metal-bending phenomenon, and whilst it is obviously not worth very much on its own, the conditions of the observation were sufficiently good for me to claim that a conjuror could not duplicate exactly what I reported. (*MB*, pp. 10, 12)[13]

Two other points of a more general nature may also be brought to the fore. They are given below.

In the first place, there is the fact that the circumstantiality of the criticism surrounding Geller's public performances must be set against the uniformly more favourable reporting of his ability arising from *experimental*, and professionally monitored, demonstrations at university laboratories throughout the world (*MB*, pp. 18, 28, 29).[14] Secondly – there is the, not inconsiderable, psychological consideration as to *why*, indeed, Geller should have wished to submit himself to detailed, and pecuniarily rewardless, scrutiny *without* a full belief in the genuineness of the effect. Overriding all the foregoing, however – and without detracting, in the least, from the importance of Geller in bringing the phenomenon to the glare of public attention – is a further vital consideration. The fact, in short, that the most powerful testimony to the reality of the 'Geller-effect' is to be seen as arising, not from the muddied circumstances surrounding the claims of Geller himself, but from

the so-called *induction effect* attaching to his television performances.

The matter is one whose substance is summarized by Hasted in
the following passage:

> In 1974 the 'induction effect' began to occupy attention. During
> Geller's television performances other people both in the studio
> and in their homes would find that a latchkey held gently in the
> hand would bend of its own accord. In most West European
> countries, as well as Japan, South Africa and others, the televi-
> sion companies received letters and telephone calls reporting
> cutlery bending of its own accord in viewers' homes. Hundreds
> of such cases have been followed up in West Germany, and in
> Britain by the Society for Psychical Research; investigations were
> made by mathematical physicist John Taylor, who wrote of his
> experience with children, the 'mini-Gellers' who could produce
> metal-bending effects on their own. In nearly all cases the effects
> began during or after the television performance. (*MB*, p. 14)

On this basis, therefore, there is, at once, the clear consideration of
a dimension to the 'metal-bending' debate which is logically
independent of the circumstances surrounding the probity of
Geller himself – one, indeed, which raises the possibility, as voiced
by Hasted, 'that a deliberately faked performance or account has
actually induced real paranormal metal-bending' (*MB*, p. 14).[15]
With this, again, are three other points. First, the fact of a division
between what may be respectively labelled as (a) the *immediate*, and
(b) the *mediate* modes of the ('induction') effect. Secondly, and
more substantially – the fact of both these modes (amounting, in
their instances, as Hasted notes, to *hundreds of cases*) being the
subject of investigation through the 'case-history' methodology
pioneered by the early Society for Psychical Research. Thirdly, and
most importantly – the fact of (b), in its opposition to (a), being
open, also, to further detailed scientific study through the demonstrations of those who followed in Geller's footsteps, that is the
so-called 'mini-Gellers' or, as in Italy, 'Gellerini' (*MB*, p. 29).

Pursuing this latter consideration further, there may be a delineation of its extent through the offer of three additional points –
all, again, as given by Hasted, with the minutiae of each contributing to the strength of the whole. First, and with regard to the global
nature of the academic/scientific interest in the phenomenon – his

listing, as of 1981, of nearly twenty centres of research spread through more than ten of the most industrially advanced countries of the world:

> We can now at least count the numbers of serious groups researching the subject in double figures: in the USA, the late Dr Wilbur Franklin at Kent State University, Dr Targ and Dr Puthoff at Stanford Research Institute, Eldon Byrd at the Office of Naval Research Laboratories, Washington, Dr Ronald Hawke at Livermore and Elizabeth Rauscher at Berkeley; in France, Dr Ducrocq, Dr Wolkowski and, more recently, scientists at the Pechiney Aluminium Company; in West Germany, the Freiburg University group, and also Dr Wälti in Switzerland. Professor Dierkens in Belgium, Dr Mattuck and Scott Hill in Copenhagen, Professor Ferdinando Bersani and Dr Aldo Martelli in Italy, Dr Charles Osbourne in Melbourne; the New Horizons Group in Toronto, and also Dr Bob Cantor; in Japan a number of different laboratories, from among which I would single out that of Professor Shigemi Sasaki in Tokyo; and finally there are reports of serious researches in China. (*MB*, p. 27)

Secondly, his identification of nearly twenty of the principal (non-British) subjects of this interest:

> Two of the Italians are Paride Giatti, who has been investigated by physicist Professor Bersani, and Orlando Bragante. The latter, investigated by Dr Aldo Martelli, is reliably reported to have bent cutlery in a sealed box. Other Italian metal-benders include Lucia Allegretti, Sandro Gasperini and Giovanni d'Emilio. In Israel, sixteen-year-old Ori Seboria has been investigated by Dr H. C. Berendt and others; when Ori visited Australia, scientists at the Caulfield Institute of Technology in Victoria also made observations, and other Australian children showed some powers. Sometimes, as in the case of Liza in Denmark and Bernard in Belgium, real names are not published in order to preserve privacy. In Switzerland, observations have been made with Edith Aufdermauer. In Japan, the most dedicated metal-bender is Masuaki Kiyota; but there are also Hirota Yamashita, Yasuchi Murasawa, Makoto Hirota, Toro Osaki, Jun Sekiguchi, Seiyuri Tanaka, Satoshi, Masao and Koji. (*MB*, pp. 29–30)

Thirdly, for the moment, his estimate of the specifically British experimentees as approximating to forty in number: 'Finally we come to the British metal-benders; John Taylor has compiled a list of at least thirty-eight. My own investigations have covered rather fewer' (*MB*, p. 30).

In drawing attention to the above, there is also the pressure of another critical point – that is, most particularly, the naming by Hasted of the primary subjects of his own researches:

> There are those who not only have strong 'powers' but who have had the patience to collaborate extensively with me; they include Nicholas W., Andrew G., Stephen North, Julie Knowles, Willie G. and Mark Henry. (*MB*, p. 30)

And further:

> There are also those who have successfully participated in at least one experiment with positive results. They include Belinda H., Graham P., Richard B., David and Stephen Nemeth, Susan Clarke, Clifford White, Alison Lloyd, Neil Howarth, Gill Costin, Kim Griffiths and Ian L. (*MB*, p. 30)

It is to the challenge arising from what Hasted says in this latter connexion that attention may be finally turned in bringing the discussion to a close.

By way of introduction, mention may be made, first, of the words of Hasted in summarizing, what he regards as, the more general significance of his interest in the 'metal-bending' effect. Thus, in reflecting themes that have already been brought to the fore:

> Psychic research is an underrated branch of science; it is likely to lead to a depth of understanding of reality greater than that which we already have; and the social consequences of such an understanding could be very great. Yet the number of serious scientists willing to devote time to it is at present small. And this has usually been the case throughout modern history; but there have nevertheless been times when the most far-sighted and competent scientists have seen fit to devote serious effort to it – one is reminded of Boyle, Faraday, Wallace, Weber, Crookes, Rayleigh, Langevin and others. There have been certain periods when interest has been aroused, usually as a result of publicity given to a psychic subject of remarkable power. In a matter of

years the interest subsided, only to revive when another set of social circumstances arose. Yet although many observations have been made and some valuable knowledge obtained about the patterns of psychic behaviour, there is next to nothing which could be described as physical theory by which the phenomena might be interpreted. (*MB*, p. 1)[16]

More for the main purpose, however, is the fact that, notwithstanding the attitude of sympathy towards the psychical expressed here, Hasted's own practical involvement with this latter arose only following the publicity surrounding Geller's demonstrations. Futher, and most particularly – from the specifically *physical* aspect of the effect's challenge. Thus, in his own words:

The subtlety and elusiveness of the psychic phenomena are very great, as great as any in the history of science ... But it must be admitted that when it comes to a choice of paranormal physical effects to investigate, the metal crystal lattice has several advantages. It is both stable against thermal and other normal external changes, and its own physical behaviour is well understood ... So although paranormal physical phenomena ... represent possibly the greatest challenge to physics at the present time, at least metal-bending can be said to be the easiest part of that challenge. (*MB*, pp. 1, 4, 5)

The point to be emphasized, therefore, is that Hasted's approach to the issue of the psychical is to be seen, as he makes plain, as that of a *physicist*, with the background of a lifetime's work in the field of *quantum* mechanics, rather than a para-psychologist in the tradition, for instance, of Rhine (*MB*, p. 2). In short – that the core of his study is to be viewed, as he, himself, describes it, as 'the detailed instrumental observation of the "metal-bending phenomenon" ... [i.e.] the observational proof of [the latter's] reality by many instrumentalists in agreement ... [with] orthodox techniques of physics [providing] the basis for this validation' (*MB*, p. 2).

With this, it must not go without mention that there is also a secondary dimension to Hasted's study as this relates to, what he modestly calls, his 'rash ... attempt to explore ... a minimum hypothesis ... for the interpretation of [the effect]' (*MB*, p. 2). Without entering into the details of what he has to say in this connexion, it is, yet, worth the trouble of noting two main points arising from it. First – and as reflecting a central theme of the discussion so far – his stress on the importance of the effect in providing 'evidence for what has been called a dualistic *mind–matter* interaction' (*MB*, p. 2, my italics). Secondly – and as anticipating a consideration to be taken up more fully later – his claim that *mind*, in its opposition to *matter*, possesses 'characteristics which are apparently *trans-spatial* and *trans-temporal*' (*MB*, p. 2, my italics). Returning, however to the main, *validational*, aspect of Hasted's work, there may be immediate acknowledgement that there is neither need nor intention in what follows to enter into a detailed survey of the whole scope of his researches, ranging, as they do, over the full list of the foregoing subjects and embracing both (a) the *touching* and (b) the *non-touching* modes of the phenomenon. The concern, rather – as indicated at the outset – will relate exclusively to the challenge of (b), leaving the cumulative impact of the whole as an extrapolation from this. More specifically, it will be the object to bring to the fore the strength of Hasted's claim to, what he summarizes as, 'the measurement, by means of sensitive equipment, of physical effects produced on metal specimens *which the metal-bender is not allowed to touch during the entire session*' (*MB*, p. 31, my italics).

Hasted's pioneering work in this latter regard, may be seen as having its inception in 'metal-bending' experiments conducted at City University, London, in 1975 – where, as he writes:

> It occurred to me at a very early stage . . . that very small elastic deformations might be of common occurrence in metal-bending sessions; they would be undetectable by eye, and would result in no permanent deformation; but they could possibly be detected by instruments. (*MB*, p. 50)[17]

His response to the above was one involving resort to a device known as the *resistive strain gauge*; that is, more specifically, an instrument with the capacity of detecting minute *strains* in attached metal specimens and which, in its electronic coupling with a *chart-recorder*, offered the possibility of a detailed instrumentation of the duration and intensity of these strains. On this basis, therefore – and deliberately putting aside the accompanying wealth of technical data (*cf. MB*, p. 50ff.) – the core of Hasted's approach to the matter in hand may be seen as being encapsulated in two main points. In short, and to reiterate: (a) the implanting of *strain gauges* in metal objects of the form, for example, and most particularly, of *latchkeys;*[18] and (b) the instrumental observation of *strains* in the latter – whether induced (i) *naturally*, that is mechanically/physically, or (ii) *super-normally* – through the analogue signals of a *chart-recorder*.

Turning to the results achieved by Hasted, it will be convenient to begin with his description of the instrumental happenings in the case of *manual* inducement:

> When the key is deformed elastically between the fingers and thumb, a deflection can be seen on the chart-record, with the paper moving typically at a speed of 1 inch every 5 seconds. A latchkey is difficult to deform permanently by finger pressure alone, so the chart-recorder trace returns to approximately its original level. (*MB*, p. 52)

With this, too, there may be a listing of certain of the experimental precautions taken by Hasted in the testing of his hypothesis.

> Of course the apparatus must be allowed to run 'quiet' for as long as possible (sometimes hours) before exposure to the metal-bender. No signal must appear when the metal-bender is not present. Battery operation is preferable, and precautions must be taken against inductively coupled mains artefacts and atmospheric artefacts (e.g. those arising from strong walkie-talkie radio sets). Dummy resistances, circuits and chart-records are used for this purpose, and any signal appearing also in the dummy channel must be rejected. (*MB*, pp. 53–4)[19]

Further – a noting of his procedures as these relate, most particularly, to his handling of subjects:

> The latchkey is suspended from its wires so as to minimize mechanical coupling; the child can point his fingers at the metal, at about six inches distance. We must watch carefully to see that there is no touching, but we should not appear to do so. If signals are still forthcoming the distance can be slowly increased. (*MB*, p. 54)

And, again, in supplementation:

The moment of truth for a metal-bender is when he realizes that similar signals [to those induced manually] appear when neither the fingers nor indeed any part of the body touches the latchkey. Sometimes I would place the latchkey on a plastic dish or in a glass bowl, and allow the metal-bender to stroke the glass beneath it. The best part of an hour was often necessary to produce the first paranormal signal, and it was almost as though the experimenter were coaxing it out of the metal-bender. The viewing of the chart-recorder is a form of biofeedback, and is best when the sensitivity is raised until the electrical noise shows as 'grass' on the trace; a tiny artefact is as much encouragement as the appearance of a tiny paranormal signal, and it does not matter if at first the two are confused. Larger signals are then to be expected. If they appeared when the key was resting in the glass bowl, I would then remove the bowl and allow the key to hang by its own electrical connections. The child would then just sit facing the key, possibly pointing his forefinger, or even stroking his fingers and thumb together. (*MB*, pp. 52–3)

Following from the above, however, and of most importance, are Hasted's experimental conclusions – in short that thirteen of the previously listed subjects obtained signals at about three feet; with three of these being successful at eight feet; and with one, Nicholas W., who will assume prominence in what follows, achieving the set objective whilst regularly working at a distance of fifteen feet (*cf. MB*, pp. 52, 54).[20]

In commenting on the above, there may be ready agreement to the 'table-top' elegance of Hasted's experiments, as, also, the meticulousness of his technical procedures. There may be acceptance, too – and no matter how reluctant or guarded – of the strength of his claim to the validation of what, within the present context, may certainly be regarded as falling under the label of the *super-normal*. At the same time, it must not pass unnoticed that, to this point, the claim itself is to be seen as relating more to, what Hasted refers to as, (a) the '[production] of *signals* without touch' (*MB*, p. 52, my italic), than that which, in the preceding discussion, has been taken as being of prime significance – that is (b) the 'non-touching' production of *physical*, if not directly observable, *strains/deformations* in discrete *metal pieces*. To make this point is not to deny the intrinsic importance of the possibilities arising from (a).

Nor, again, the natural – and, in the event, ultimately justifiable – (*scientific*) presumption to a *causal* connexion between the two. It *is*, however, to highlight the fact that – with both (a) and (b) ostensibly constituting modes of the *super-normal* – there is no *logical* necessity for the postulation of (b) as the *cause* of (a). The case might well be of (a) arising *sui generis*; and, with this, of (b) being logically beyond the realm of *any* (scientific/electronic) *validation*. Bringing the foregoing together, the conclusion to be emphasized is that, in so far as (b) is taken as being of primary relevance, then its physical relation to (a) is to be seen as being open to validation only through *super-normal*, as opposed to *natural/ scientific*, reference; that is, more fully – through appeal to the Humean criterion noted earlier of 'breaking' or 'transcending' a 'law of nature' in the sense of this latter which relates to *common/ ordinary* experience. In short, and with specific regard to the matter in hand – by appeal to the *super-normal* deformation and/or fracturing of metal specimens as this manifests itself at the level of *sensible/macro-physical* observation.

In the event, it is what Hasted has to say in this final connexion which constitutes the most challenging aspect of his whole work. The matter is one which relates, most particularly, though not exclusively, to experiments spread over some thirteen sessions in 1976; with the subject, Nicholas W. above, as the experimentee; and with the main results appearing in 1977 in a paper entitled 'Physical Aspects of Paranormal Metal Bending'.[21] Without, again, any attempt at being exhaustive, the substance of Hasted's achievements in this regard may be brought into focus through the offer of three key passages from his writings.

Thus, to begin – and in the light of what has already been said – there may be mention, first, of Hasted's own summary of his experiments as given in the aforementioned paper:

A strain gauge is mounted inside a latchkey and is connected in an electrical bridge circuit, whose off-balance signals are amplified and chart-recorded ... Two (and ultimately three) such latchkeys are hung by their flexible screened leads, thereby minimizing mechanical and electromagnetic coupling between the specimens. The subject remains seated in a chair remote from latchkeys, and he is usually occupied in building model aircraft. The subject is required to attempt remote bending action on the latchkeys. At certain sessions he has held other metal specimens in his hands, and some of these have bent. The amplifiers are allowed to reach steady conditions and the chart recorders are synchronized. Strain signals are recorded on either or both chart recorders, and occasionally a latchkey bends and ultimately fractures. In a violent bending event the latchkey can be seen to swing to and fro.[22]

Secondly, reference may be made to Hasted's account of what – in reproducing the chart-record of the entire proceedings – he describes as 'the first really impressive strain gauge session, which resulted in a *permanent deformation of the latchkey*' (*MB*, p. 54, my italics). It may be given in full:

Nicholas W. was seated by my side on the sofa in the lounge . . . whilst the key was hanging by its wire from the mantelpiece on the opposite wall. We had a long wait before the signals appeared, and I gave Nicholas cutlery which I asked him to bend. He twirled the pieces around, and in the course of time several displayed a 'curly bend'. My object in allowing him to handle cutlery was to encourage his possible 'power' to blossom and spill over onto the strain gauge specimen. Also his hands were occupied, so that any question of tampering with the strain gauge specimen was ruled out. During the session I changed the sensitivity of the chart-recorder amplifier at appropriate times. I shall never forget my increasing excitement as the small, doubtful signals increased in size, although I was completely confident of the reliability of my equipment, since prolonged tests had been made in Nicholas's absence, and there were no signals. Eventually the latchkey developed a permanent bend. (*MB*, p. 54, my italics)

Thirdly, and finally, there may be the listing of chronological fragments from a table given by Hasted of his original experimental records (*MB*, pp. 67–9). The selected extracts relate to the two most dramatic of his epigrammatic summaries:

9 Apr [1976] . . . Remarks . . . Brass screen on Key 1, which bent to 70°; Steel screen on Key 1, which bent to 135°; Steel screen on Key 2, which bent to 60°; *Key 1 fractures*; Key 2 bent at 60°; Key 2 bent to 80°; Key 2 bent to 85°; Key 2 partially fractured; *key 2 fractured* . . . (*MB*, p. 68, my italics)

And:

> 23 Apr [1976] . . . Remarks . . . 25° bend on Key 1, Failure of chart
> pen; 45° bend on Key 1, 25° bend on Key 2; Some misalignment
> of configuration; 35° bend on Key 1; 25° bend on Key 2; Some
> misalignment of configuration; 10° bend on Key 1; 45° on Key 2;
> . . . 135° bend on Key 1; 45° bend on Key 2; *Key 1 fractured* . . . (*MB*,
> p. 69, my italics)

Without resort to the accompanying mass of verbal, numerical and
visual data, enough has been said for the firm establishment of the
overwhelming strength of Hasted's case for the reality (with all its
inherent improbability) of the 'metal-bending' phenomenon. The
challenge is one which, as may well be seen, is only open to being
met through the extreme of an attack on the latter's probity, or,
indeed, sanity. Setting aside, however – as with Hume – one
improbability against another, there can be no doubt that, on any
fair assessment, the outcome must be seen as lying decisively on
the side of Hasted.

To summarize, therefore, the discussion of this chapter and
Chapters 6 and 7 may be brought to a close with a single main
point. Thus, as expressed by Broad, with especial regard to the
work of the Society for Psychical Research in its contemporary
standing as one of the oldest of all (specialized) Learned Bodies:

> Anyone who at the present day expresses confident opinions,
> whether positive or negative, on ostensibly para-normal phe-
> nomena, without first making himself thoroughly acquainted
> with the main methods and results of this careful and long-
> continued work, may be dismissed without further ceremony as
> a conceited ignoramus.[23]

With no personal offence intended by this remark, there may be a
return to more philosophically-oriented considerations.

9
The Challenge of the Super-normal

In returning to the central discussion, there may be a reminder that the entire argument of Chapters 6, 7 and 8 has had as its primary objective the establishment of a single, minimal, conclusion. That is, that the *evidence* for the *super/para-normal*, in the sense under consideration, is of so cumulatively strong a nature as to completely pre-empt any claim to rejection, and no matter how vociferously asserted, on the popular presupposition of so-called '*scientific* impossibility'. The end is one which has been more than met through the pursuit, most particularly, of three main points, each having a significance of its own though collectively relating to the sphere of, what may be characterized as, the *psychical*. First, the circumstances surrounding the eventual and triumphal validation of the profoundly provocative, if, currently, virtually ignored, phenomenon of *hypnotism*. Secondly, the strength of the case for the, nowadays, widely accepted, if still highly contentious, idea of *telepathy*. Thirdly, the stark indubitability of the challenge of contemporary testimony to the reality of the highly publicized effect known as *metal-bending*. To this extent, therefore – and as being all that is necessary for the chief purpose – enough has been said for the firm establishment of the (evidential) *legitimacy/ reasonableness* of regarding the *super/para-normal*, nebulous though it may be in its connotation, as a *mode* of the *real*.

It will be the concern in the present chapter to bring together a number of assorted points arising from what has been said as the basis for a more general advance in the course of that is to follow. They may be taken as falling under two main heads and as continuing to centre, in each case, on the idea of the *psychical*. First, the challenge presented by the latter to the position of Bultmann. Secondly, the views in this regard of one who has the distinction of being among the very first to grasp the full extent of the issue – that is, Schopenhauer. They may be considered in turn, beginning with the former.

The matter is one which may be approached through the dichotomy drawn by biblical scholars with respect to the key New Testament idea of 'works of *power/spirit*'. That is, between (a) *dynameis* on the one hand, and (b) *charismata*, on the other – where (a) would be regarded as relating primarily, if not exclusively, to the miracles performed by Jesus and the Apostles, and (b) to abnormal events of a lesser kind such as St Paul warns against taking too seriously in his Epistle to the Corinthians. It is marked by Bultmann himself:

> Certainly St. Paul shares the popular belief of his day that the Spirit manifests itself in miracles, and he attributes abnormal psychic phenomena to its agency.[1]

To draw this division, however, is also to raise the issue of Bultmann's puzzlingly anomalous response to its significance.

In this connexion, there is the point, at once, that, whilst the denial of (a) constitutes a core element of Bultmann's 'revolution', his outlook with regard to (b) is much less stringent. Indeed, as he is at pains to emphasize, a new dimension in biblical scholarship was opened up during the era of *spiritualistic/psychical* phenomena, in the 1880s, through precisely the realization that *spirit*, in the New Testament, is to be understood, not so much, as hitherto believed, in moral and intellectual terms, but rather more expansively, in those of 'a surprising amazing power which causes marvellous psychological phenomena such as glossolalia, prophesy, etc.'[2] This was, as he adds, a development which arose from the work of Hermann Gunkel and the, so-called, *religionsgeschichtliche Schule* which followed in his train.[3] Thus:

> While the earlier interpretation [of *spirit*] was guided by idealist conceptions, Gunkel's was guided by psychological conceptions. Psychological conceptions dominated the so-called *religionsgeschichtliche Schule* in general. Because these scholars were aware of psychological phenomena they recognized important thoughts in the New Testament which had hitherto been overlooked or undervalued.[4]

Granted this, however, there is, notwithstanding, the fact that (b), no less than (a), is to be seen as being ultimately excluded by Bultmann from his scheme of things. In the instance, however, not as with (a), through appeal to (*scientific*) *impossibility*, but rather on no more than a proclamation of (*theological/religious*) *irrelevance*. More specifically, – that 'the God of revelation is the God of judgement and forgiveness, not the Cause of abnormal phenomena.'[5] It may well be accepted that what Bultmann says here is as theologically obscurantist as it is philosophically naive. At the same time, the point that may be extracted is that, within the terms of his own framework, a vital *category* difference is to be drawn with regard to (a) and (b). There is, in short, the conclusion that, whereas it is central to his position to *deny* the very possibility of (a), his outlook with respect to (b) is merely one of implicit, if indifferent, *acceptance*.

What may be added is that it is, pre-eminently, Bultmann's position regarding (b) – or, reverting to more general terms, the *psychical* – which, most conspicuously, constitutes the 'Achilles' heel' of his whole stance. For, as has been fully argued, it is precisely the *evidential* strength of the latter which first came to stand as a challenge to the very view of *physical/common-sensical* reality embraced by Bultmann. Coupled with this comes the force of a further, more definitive, consequence; that is, as already indicated, the possibility of a decisive *logical* negation of Bultmann's – by any standard, already dubious – resort to the claimed necessity of Heideggerian existentialism.[6] For to accept, as above, the *philosophical* inadequacy of Bultmann's (once dominant) conception of *reality* as a closed and unbroken *causal* nexus is, at the same time, to raise the (*logical*) possibility of drastic *scientific* revision; and, recursively with this the (*possible*) outcome of a radically different alternative to the *secularist* ultimacy proposed by him. The alternative, indeed, of a new and deeper, specifically *religious*, synthesis based on just such a wider, *scientific*, view of things. These are considerations to which it will be necessary to return. In the meantime, the basis for this development may be laid by turning to the second main topic of the present concern – that is, the views of Schopenhauer.

To begin, there may be an immediate highlighting of his profound and early insight that the essence of 'magnetic'/mesmeric effects is to be seen as lying in 'a direct action of the *will* on others and at a distance';[7] or, more broadly, in the terms already noted – '*visio in distans et actio in distans* both as regards time and space' (*SS*, p. 266). With this, too, there may be a reiteration of his grasp of the issue's *philosophical* significance:

The phenomena we are discussing are, at any rate from the philosophical point of view, incomparably the most important of all the facts that are presented to us by the whole of experience. It is therefore the duty of every scholar and man of science to become thoroughly acquainted with them ... [Otherwise] materialism as physics ... [is] ... installed on the throne of metaphysics. (*SS*, p. 267)

More for the present, however, is another point. That is, his assertion of a relation between the foregoing and the *two-world* view proclaimed some seventy years earlier by Kant in his *Critique of Pure Reason*:

The phenomena that are here discussed, and were previously enumerated as the branches of one stem ... afford a confirmation as unexpected as it is certain and *factual* of Kant's fundamental doctrine of the contrast between the *phenomenon* and the *thing-in-itself* and of the antithesis between the laws of both. (*SS*, p. 266, my final italics)[8]

With mention that the topic of Kant's, self-styled, 'Copernican' revolution (*in philosophy*) will assume major prominence later, there may be pause, more immediately, for an anticipatory conspectus of the core of this teaching.

Three main points may be brought in the fore in this regard. First – that the parametrical concepts of *space*, *time*, and *causality* are to be conceived not as having any *objective/absolute* 'existence' in their own right, but as arising, rather, from the intrinsic nature of *perceiving/knowing* (human) *mind*. Secondly, and following from this – that *physical/common-sensical* reality, as instantiating the *ideality* of the preceding concepts, is to be seen as having the *philosophical* status, not of something ontologically 'existing' *in itself*, but of a *mind*-dependent, *perceptual*, reality. Thirdly, and in the varied terms of Kant's own technical vocabulary – that *physical/common-sensical* reality is to be viewed not as a *thing-in-itself*, but as *appearance/ representation/phenomenon*. On this basis, there may be a return to the views of Schopenhauer with three final considerations in supplementation of what has been said.

Thus, attention may be drawn, first, to his claim that the basis of intellectual opposition to the idea of the *super-normal* is to be seen as lying, most fundamentally, in a deep-seated and *psychologically* ingrained *realism* with regard to just the preceding concepts of *space, time* and *causality*:

> The positive incredulity with which every thinking man first learns the facts of ['magnetism'] which [are] only tardily yielding to our own experience or to the hundreds of cases of trustworthy evidence, is due to one and the same reason, to the fact that [such effects] run counter to the laws of *space, time* and *causality* which are known to us *a priori* and in their complex determine the course of events in possible experience. (*SS*, p. 300, my main italics)

Further, there may be mention of his testament to the *therapeutic* importance of Kant's Critical teaching as an intellectual counter to the philosophical *illegitimacy* of this *realist* presumption. Thus, in words from the second edition Preface of his most famous work, *The World as Will and Representation*:

> Kant's teaching produces a fundamental change in every mind that has grasped it. This change is so great that it may be regarded as an intellectual rebirth. It alone is capable of really removing the inborn *realism* [with regard to *space, time* and *causality*] which arises from the original disposition of the intellect ... In consequence of this, the mind undergoes a fundamental undeceiving and thereafter looks at all things in another light.[9]

Finally, reference may be made to his elaboration on the *explanatory* significance of this doctrine with regard to the issue in hand:

> The order and conformity to laws thereof which are based on *space, time* and *causality* (as brain functions), are to some extent set aside in ['magnetic' effects] ... Thus in consequence of the Kantian doctrine of the *ideality* of *space* and *time* [and following from this, *causality*], we see that the *thing-in-itself*, that which alone is the truly real in all phenomena as being free from these two forms of the intellect, knows no distinction between near and remote, between present, past, and future. Therefore the separations that are due to those forms of intuitive perception prove to be not absolute; on the contrary, they no longer offer any insuperable barriers to the [possibility of the effects] here

discussed. On the other hand, if *time* and *space* [and *causality*] were absolutely *real* and appertained to the *essence-in-itself of things* then [such effects] would certainly be an absolutely incomprehensible miracle. (*SS*, pp. 263–4, my italics)

To summarize, therefore, there is not only the fact of Schopenhauer's proclamation of the indubitable reality of the *super-normal*, but also the clarity of his vision with regard to its far-reaching significance for the vital issue of the ultimate *philosophical* status of the *physical/commonsensical* world.

The conclusion may be taken as the starting point of the argument of the final three chapters.

10

The Demise of Scientific Materialism

What may be seen from the preceding discussion is that the authority of no less a figure than Schopenhauer is to be added to the strength of the case already established for the *empirical* reality of the *super-normal*. Indeed, his aggressive words in this connexion, though written well over a century ago, are still worth the price of mention: 'Whoever at the present time doubts the facts of animal magnetism and its clairvoyance should be called not a sceptic but an ignoramus.'[1] More for the present, however, are the *conceptual* ramifications drawn by Schopenhauer in this regard.

Thus, to reiterate, there is, at once, his stress on the significance of the *super-normal* in highlighting the opposition between two, mutually exclusive, views of the nature of *physical/common-sensical* reality. That is, what may be characterized as (a) the (traditional) *scientific/materialistic* outlook with its ingrained *realistic* presuppositions regarding the parametrical concepts of *space*, *time* and *causality*; and (b) the more recently asserted, *two-world* standpoint of Kant, with its proclamation of the ultimate *ideality* of these concepts. With this, too, there is the fact, as seen by him, of the acuity of the challenge presented by the super-normal to the entrenched stance of (a), which is summarized in a passage that encapsulates the whole substance of the argument so far:

> And so in any account of the facts . . . [of 'magnetism'] . . . people say not merely 'it is not true', but 'it is not possible' (*a non posse ad non esse*); yet on the other hand, the retort is 'but it is so' (*ab esse ad posse*).[2]

Finally, and most importantly, there is his conclusion that the indubitability of the evidence in question is such as to entail a decisive rejection of (a) in favour of (b).

In drawing attention to the above, there may be the addition of two further points. First, that it is Schopenhauer's negation of (a) which has the most obvious immediate relevance. Secondly, that, from the viewpoint of the second half of the twentieth century, this rejection is open to decisive endorsement on grounds which, in themselves, have no direct link with the issue of *super-normality* itself. On this basis, the discussion may be continued with specific regard to the conceptual inadequacy of (a), leaving the strength of (b) for further development in Chapter 11.

To begin, there may be immediate reference to the conjunctive use of the terms 'scientific' and 'materialistic' in describing the position under review. For, as might be objected – and, as already indicated – contemporary developments in the domain of science itself have opened up a seemingly unbridgeable gap between the use of these terms. It is, of course, the exploitation of this rift which constitutes the chief objective of the present concern. In accepting this, however, there may still be insistence on the legitimacy of the coupling for the purpose in hand. Three main reasons may be cited. First, that it precisely represents the outlook, then approaching the zenith of its influence, which it was Schopenhauer's concern to reject. Secondly, that, despite its subsequent theoretical decline, it continues to constitute, what remains, in the popular mind, as the all-pervasive, *scientific* view of the physical world. Thirdly, that it pre-eminently embodies the standpoint from which the banner of so-called 'scientific *impossibility*' is still indiscriminately raised in its opposition to the challenge of the *super-normal*. In the light of the above, the position may be delineated more fully.

Whilst the figure of the 'incomparable Newton' must obviously be seen as crucial to this purpose, it will, yet, be convenient to approach the issue through the concept of *matter* proclaimed some two thousand years earlier by Democritus, the contemporary of Socrates, in his speculative notion of the *atom*. Three main propositions may be offered in capturing the position. Thus – (a) that, in the whole domain of 'entities', the *atoms* alone, as being contingently, beyond divisibility, are uncreated and imperishable; (b) that the objects of the macro-physical world, as subject to the conditions of generation, change and dissolution, are the product of *chance* conglomerations of the ever-changing interplay of these micro-physical and eternally 'existing' particles; and (c) that both the preceding macro and microphysical realms have their being in a common, *ontologically* 'existing', *space* and *time*. Following from the above, there may be mention, too, that, true to his thoroughgoing *materialism*, the whole sphere of the *mental* was pronounced by Democritus to be but a by-product of, or epi-phenomenon to, the chance and ephemeral massings of the (material) *atoms*. The further, *ethical*, aspect of this outlook, with its claim to providing a (*materialist*) refuge from the fears engendered by obscurantist *religion*, may be deliberately set apart for present purposes.[3] So, too, the fact that the whole position was pressed by Democritus in glorious disregard of the acute *logical* difficulties surrounding the notions of *space*, *time* and *change* which had been laid bare by his immediate forerunners, most particularly Parmenides and Zeno. The point to be stressed, rather, is the (*materialistic*) *realism* of the doctrine. That is, and whatever its inherent difficulties – that the *primal/ontological* 'existents' are to be seen as *space*, *time* and *matter* (in the form of the *atoms*).

Turning now to the significance of Newton, it hardly goes without saying that this is to be taken as centring on the monumental importance of his achievement in, first of all, setting aside the hitherto inviolate division between earthly and celestial bodies; and, then, in a single mighty act of mathematical synthesis, demonstrating both to be governed by the same physical laws – his *laws of motion*. With no attempt at comprehensiveness in the handling of the massive implications of this accomplishment, it will be sufficient for immediate purposes merely to indicate the close identification of the terms 'causal' and 'scientific' which came to follow from it. That is, the conjunction between (a) the idea of immutable *physical/causal* laws whose precise mathematical for-mulation opened up the prospect of ever-increasing and more detailed control over physical reality; and (b) that of their discovery through the methodology, in its association with mathematics, embraced in the key scientific procedures of observation, experi-mentation and validation. The enormity of the heuristic gap between the model of physical reality portrayed in this coupling and the purely speculative outlook of Democritus will be plain enough. At the same time, there is, also, a prominent feature of commonality. More specifically, that the dominant *causal/scientific* aspect of the position is itself to be seen as resting on the same foundation of *realism* with regard to *space* and *time* as the older *atomism*. Beyond this, however, is the fact that it is not the marvel of Newton's *mechanics* which is the intrinsic object of interest in the current regard. This, rather, is the standpoint of so-called 'causal' or 'scientific' *necessity/determinism* which arose, and took hold, as an *extrapolation* from the heuristic success of the former.

The position is to be seen as centring on the claim, no less, that there is nothing in the whole of reality which is not open to ultimate accommodation in the terms of the general theoretical scheme established by Newton in his *laws of motion*. Two immediate points may be made in setting the contention apart from the paradigmatically *scientific* aspects of Newton's achievements.

In the first place, there is the speculative extension of the latter's appeal from the world of (observable) macro-physical objects, earthly and celestial, to that of the Democritan idea of the (*material*) *atom*. The consideration has an importance which is summarized by Sir Edmund Whittaker in the following way:

> [It] was Pierre Gassendi (1592–1655), Professor at the Collège de France, in Paris, a follower of Copernicus and Galileo, who re-introduced the doctrine of the ancient atomists, namely that the universe is formed of material atoms, eternal and unchangeable, moving about in a space which except for them is empty. The most formidable objection to the new teaching was that in the Graeco-Roman world it had been associated with the moral and theological views of Epicurus and Lucretius. Gassendi, who was himself a priest, worked hard to show that it had no necessary connection with religious error, and that it could be accepted as a basis for physics by Christian men. After a sharp controversy with Descartes in 1641–6, he had such success that ... his doctrine was accepted not long afterwards by Newton, and in fact became the departure point for all subsequent natural philosophy.[4]

Secondly, and bound up with the above, there is the even more audacious move of the outlook in insinuating sovereignty over, not only the entire realm of the *physical*, but, in addition, that of the *mental*. Whilst drawing attention to the vast social impact of this latter – as, also, the consideration already noted regarding the significance of the 'Helmholtz' School of Medicine in its propagation – the concern for the present may be confined to the narrower, *physical*, dimension of the position. The aspect, in short, which is to be seen as turning on the postulation of (x) a micro-physical realm of absolutely permanent (Democritan) *atoms* as the underlying basis of macro-physical reality; and (y) Newtonian *causality* as the exclusive and altogether sufficient principle of governance of both these levels of (*material*) existence.

With this, enough has been said to complete the survey of the outlook which, at the time of the mid-nineteenth century, it was Schopenhauer's prescience to reject. It is a position which, as may be seen, is unabashedly both *realistic* and *materialistic* in its pretensions. Thus, as expressed in the (thoroughly *unscientific*) words of Newton himself:

> All these things being consider'd, it seems probable to me, that God in the Beginning form'd Matter in solid, massy, hard, impenetrable, moveable Particles, of such Sizes and Figures, and with such other Properties, and in such Proportion to Space, as most conduced to the End for which he form'd them; and that these primitive Particles being Solids are incomparably harder than any porous Bodies compounded of them; even so very hard, as never to wear or break in pieces; no ordinary Power being able to divide what God himself made one in the first Creation.[5]

It is, further, one whose entailing *determinism* had already received classical expression in the famous remark of Pierre de Laplace (1749–1827) that 'we may regard the present state of the universe as the effect of its past and the cause of its future.'[6] To this extent, and as may be fully accepted, it is plainly to be viewed as standing in stark opposition to any possibility of the *super-normal* in the sense in hand. At the time, there is the, no less, vital fact of the purely *speculative* nature of (x) and (y) above. Moreover, of this being a matter which came to be the subject of early *scientific* concern, most particularly, by Ernst Mach (1836–1916), following the rise of neo-Kantian positivism in Germany during the 1860s:

> Atoms cannot be perceived by the senses; like all substances they are things of thought. Furthermore, the atoms are invested with properties that absolutely contradict the attributes hitherto observed in bodies. However well fitted atomic theories may be to reproduce certain groups of facts, the physical inquirer [must] only admit those theories as *provisional* helps, and [must] strive to attain, in some more *natural* way, a satisfactory substitute.[7]

With a highlighting of the significance of this remark for the course of what is to follow, there may, more immediately, be a return to the *extension* of the outlook which arose from the *experimental* advances of the second half of the nineteenth century.

Again, with no pretension to being exhaustive, the consideration may be taken as centring on the scientifically towering figure of James Clerk Maxwell (1831–79). More specifically, on the triumph of (a) his *electro-magnetic* theory of *light*; and in necessary association with this his concept of (b) the *(electro-magnetic) field*. With regard, first, to (a), the mathematical synthesis achieved by Maxwell is of an order comparable to that attained by Newton respecting *massive* (macro-physical) bodies. Appearing in papers set forth between 1856–62, its substance may be summarized in terms of the following demonstrations. Namely – (l) that all that had been previously established regarding electricity and magnetism could be deduced from four equations, henceforth known as 'Maxwell's equations'; (m) that electro-magnetic energy was transmitted through space in the form of 'waves' having the same velocity as had already been actually measured in the case of light; and (n) that light itself, together with radiant heat, were but forms of electro-magnetic waves, differing only from other segments of this spectrum in wave-length/frequency. In adding that radio-waves, as well as other forms of *(immaterial) radiation*, were later to be accommodated within the foregoing scheme, enough has been said for a characterization, also, of the idea embraced under (b) above. There is, in short, the fact that the *(electro-magnetic) field*, as conceived by Maxwell, is to be understood as a system of *electro-magnetic* (energy) exchange in continuous distribution through a region of space as a whole; where the flux of amplitude changes at *points* within the system is recursively related to the contiguous (and continual) modification of the *system* itself.

Since the time of Maxwell, the *field* theoretical concept has increasingly come to dominate physical thinking, both with regard to *micro* as well as *macro* levels of research. In deliberately setting aside the technical details of this development, attention may be drawn to a number of more philosophically oriented considerations.

In this regard, there is, at once, the importance of the *field* concept in establishing a *qualitatively* different kind of *causality/ predictability* from that which, as promulgated by Newton in his *laws of motion*, had hitherto been taken as having universal and exclusive sway. Secondly, there is the fact of its significance in effectively expanding the traditional *Newtonian* conception of *space*.

In other words – in extending the connotation of the latter to include not only its function as the seat of (a) *massive* (energy) exchanges between discrete (macro/micro-physical) *bodies*, but also that of (b) *non-massive* (force) interactions between (*immaterial*) so-called *waves*. Finally, for the moment, and following from the above, there is the concept's challenge in bringing to the fore the vital issue of *how* the two preceding modes of *spatial* existence – the one *material*, the other *immaterial* – are to be conceived as being *ontologically* related to each other. The points, taken together, may be used as the basis for a delineation of the outlook which – as representing the culminating extension of the stance under review – came to be known as *classical* physics.

The position, which may be viewed as reaching the pinnacle of its theoretical interest at about the turn of the present century, is one that was generated, first and foremost, by the prevailing *realism/materialism* of the period. Further, by the terms of its original (Newtonian) *theological* determination. Thus, in this regard, there are (again, thoroughly *scientific*) the words of the no less (*scientifically*) progressive figure as Maxwell in addressing the British Association just a few years before his early death:

> An atom is a body which cannot be cut in two. A molecule is the smallest possible portion of a particular substance . . . No theory of evolution can be formed to account for the similarity of molecules, for evolution necessarily implies continuous change, and the molecule is incapable of growth or decay, of generation or destruction. None of the processes of Nature, since the time when Nature began, have produced the slightest difference in the properties of any molecule . . . But though in the course of ages catastrophes have occurred and may yet occur in the heavens, though ancient systems may be dissolved and new systems evolved out of their ruins, the molecules out of which these systems are built – the foundation stones of the material universe – remain unbroken and unworn.[8]

And, in concluding:

> They continue this day as they were created – perfect in number and measure and weight, and from the ineffaceable characters impressed on them we may learn that those aspirations after accuracy in measurement, truth in statement, and justice in

action, which we reckon among our noblest attributes as men, are ours because they are essential constituents of Him who in the beginning created, not only the heaven and the earth, but the materials of which heaven and earth consist.[9]

To summarize, therefore, there is the fact, as it was overwhelmingly taken for granted by both physicists and chemists of the day, that their grasp of the nature of *matter* was, to all intents, complete.

Pursuing the point further, the tools of the chemist, in particular, had triumphantly led to the listing of nearly a hundred different (chemical) elements, together with a host of (molecular) compounds of these. That such, in turn, were underlain by discrete and various (*micro-physical*) *atoms* as the ultimate (*material*) 'building-blocks' of the former, was assumed, virtually without demur, as being beyond question. To this extent, the resolution of the issue of (a) and (b) above was, within the context of the time, taken as little more than a formality – with the (*immaterial*) *fields* being regarded simply as *radiational* modifications of *ontologically* more basic (*macro/micro*) *material* transactions. In this connexion, too, there is the further point that the synthesis – with its recognition of *space* itself (even in its *astro-physical* dimensions) as a plenum of *causal* interchange – was, all too peremptorily, presumed as being but confirmatory of the already deeply entrenched standpoint of so-called 'causal' or *'scientific' necessity*. Returning, however, to the main concern, there is the conclusion that the outlook – and notwithstanding its embracement of *two* kinds of *causality* – is to be seen as resting, in the last resort, on no more and no less than the entailing (*materialistic*) *realism* of the Democritan doctrine of the *atom*.

The above may be taken as (*philosophically*) representing the full extent of the outlook on which Bultmann relies so heavily in his rejection of the idea of the miraculous. So, too, and more generally – that to which resort is still made in the urgency of contemporary claims to the *'scientific* impossibility' of the super-normal. At the same time, to reiterate, in this way, the continuing virulence of the position, is not to negate the fact of its inherent instability, most especially as this is to be seen as centring on the issue of *radiation*. It is a consideration which is summarized in the authoritative words of David Bohm:

Even during the period of the greatest triumphs of [classical] mechanism, physics began to develop in new directions, tending to lead away from the general conceptual framework that had been associated with the original form of mechanistic philosophy.[10]

What Bohm says here may be taken as turning on four developments, in particular, whose importance is delineated below.

Thus, and by way of mere listing, there are respectively: (1) the famous experiment conducted in 1887 by A. A. Michelson (1852–1931) and E. W. Morley (1838–1923) which led to the abandonment of the time-honoured idea of the *ether* as an all-pervasive 'substance' of super-fine *materiality* (and, with this, the 'medium' which, as was generally taken for granted, 'carried' the electro-magnetic *field*); (2) the *quantum* theory (of *energy*) set forth by Max Planck (1858–1947) in 1900; (3) the *photo-electric* (*photon*) theory of *light* of Albert Einstein (1878–1955) promulgated in 1905; and (4) the latter's *relativity* theories of 1915/1916 with their celebrated (*mathematical*) reformulations of the *common-sensical/realist* conception of *space* and *time* as a (*unified*) *space–time* continuum. With this, too, and of especial relevance for the course of what is to follow, are two further points, both relating to the work of Einstein. In the first place, there are the *theoretical* difficulties surrounding (c) whose general nature is summarized by the famed figure of Niels Bohr (1885–1962) in the following way:

> Notwithstanding its fertility, the idea of the photon implied a quite unforeseen dilemma, since any simple corpuscular picture of radiation would obviously be irreconcilable with interference effects, which present so essential an aspect of radiation phenomena, and which can be described only in terms of a wave picture.[11]

Secondly, there is the fact of (4), and despite its seemingly revolutionary nature, being (*philosophically*) but an amendment to the traditional (Democritan/Newtonian) view of the issue.[12] Returning, however, to the main concern, and as constituting the start of the second part of the discussion, there is the challenge to the *classical* outlook as it arose from the 'splitting' of the *atom* – an event dating from 1911, with the name of Ernest (later, Lord) Rutherford (1871–1937) immortalized in the happening.

The epic significance of the achievement is summarized by Sir Arthur Eddington in his Gifford Lectures for 1927:

In 1911 Rutherford introduced the greatest change in our idea of matter since the time of Democritus ... For the first time the main volume of the atom was entirely evacuated, and a 'solar system' type of atom was substituted for a substantial 'billiard ball'.[13]

Though needing *philosophical* qualification in the following chapter, two immediate points may be made in supplementation of what Eddington says here. First, there is the main substance of the theory as originally set forth by Rutherford. Thus, as this is to be seen as involving (a) the idea of a positively charged *nucleus*; and (b) that of one or more negatively charged *electrons* – with the latter conceived as being in regular orbit (at distance(s) of 'astronomical' proportions) around the former; and with the *mass* of the former (or the *number* of the latter) being determinant of the chemical nature of the atom as a whole. Secondly, there is the brilliance of the advance made in 1913 by Rutherford's assistant, the previously noted figure of Bohr, in his application to the foregoing of Planck's *quantum* theory (of *energy*). More specifically, his theory of the *electron*, namely, as: (x) existing, not in the *single* orbital path of Rutherford's model, but rather in a discrete *set* of such paths; (y) being like *light* in emitting *energy/radiation* in discrete 'packets' or *quanta*; and (z) releasing this energy only when in a state of *transition* between one orbital path and another. In thus delineating, what, in the course of time, came to be known as (the Rutherford–Bohr) *'old' quantum* theory, there may be a return to the views of Eddington with regard to another point.

Thus, his graphic elaboration on the *immaterialistic* determination of the foregoing in his famous characterization of a so-called 'scientific' table:

My scientific table is mostly emptiness. Sparsely scattered in that emptiness are numerous electric charges rushing about with great speed; but their combined bulk amounts to less than a billionth of the bulk of table itself ... There is nothing *substantial* about my [scientific] table. It is nearly all empty space – space pervaded, it is true, by fields of force, but these are assigned to the category of 'influences', not of 'things' [and] even in the minute part which is not empty we must not transfer the old notion of substance ... In dissecting matter into electric charges we have travelled far from the picture of it which first gave rise to our conception of substance, and the meaning of that conception – if it ever had any – has been lost by the way.[14]

With a highlighting of the especial relevance of the passage for the course of what is to follow, the discussion may be continued with a further pursuit of the Rutherford–Bohr theory as set within the context of what Whittaker refers to as, 'the gradual emergence of one of the greatest discoveries of the twentieth century . . . the connection of *mass* with *energy*.'[15]

Here, there may be pause for mention of two key points emerging from the above. Thus, there is, first, the fact that the theory is to be seen as taking its rise, not from any kind of *direct* insight into the atomic realm, but rather on the basis of (electronic) *signals* which are *presumed* as being, in some way, *analogues* of the latter. Secondly, and in the light of the earlier remark of Mach, that, despite the theory's *immaterialist* implications, it remains one that is rooted, in the last resort, in the *realist* terms of objectively 'existing' *particles*. Taken together, the considerations have a significance which is reflected in another vital fact. That is, the force of the claim – as it came to be asserted, most notably, through the mathematical demonstrations of Louis de Broglie (1892–1987) and, in particular, Erwin Schrödinger (1882–1970) – that the (electronic) data used in the later support of the Rutherford–Bohr theory was, in the event, more readily interpreted in terms of (*material*) *waves* than (*material*) *particles*. On this basis, reference may be made to a further remark by Eddington – this time from his Tarner Lectures for 1938:

> The question I am going to raise is – how much do we discover and how much do we manufacture by our experiments? When the late Lord Rutherford showed us the atomic nucleus, did he *find* it or did he *make* it? . . . Since most people are probably under the impression that Rutherford *found* the atomic nucleus, I will make myself advocate for the view that he *made* it.[16]

The deeper relevance of the passage may be pursued through attention to the circumstances which led, during the course of the 1920s, to the establishment and consolidation of, what came to be known as, *'new' quantum* theory or the 'Copenhagen Interpretation'.

The matter is to be seen as turning on the challenge that came to be voiced regarding the theoretical legitimacy of using either the term 'particle' or 'wave' in the elaboration of sub-atomic structures. In other words – of applying these (*empirical*) concepts to a 'realm' which, by its very nature, lay beyond the possibility of (human) *experience/observation*. In particular, in this connexion, is the historical fact of the pressure which came to be exerted, during the course of 1924–5, on the rapidly ascending *wave* theory of Schrödinger through the force of this objection. That is, more specifically – the charge, as it came to be asserted, that, despite the mathematical sophistication of the theory, it was, yet, subject to the fatal *philosophical* flaw of using the key concept of 'wave' in a way which completely transcended the conditions of its *meaningful/empirical* employment. The consideration may be taken as the backdrop to developments of a most crucial nature which unfolded in quick succession over the period 1925–7.

With necessary simplification, the events may be seen as centring on two figures: in particular, Max Born (1882–1970) and Werner Heisenberg (1901–76), with the latter being, initially, research assistant to Born at Göttingen, and later researcher/lecturer under Bohr at Copenhagen. Thus, in this regard, there is the immediate fact of the far-reaching importance of Born in his bold acceptance of the meaninglessness of any (*realist*) talk of '*matter* waves' in the context of Schrödinger's prevailing *wave* theory of the *atom*. Further, his proclamation, instead, of the purely *heuristic* idea of, what he called, '*probability* waves' – 'waves' in their frankly acknowledged and strictly limited function as *tools* for the mathematical expression of (electronic) *quantum* data. In intimate relation with this is the, no less, vital inspiration of Heisenberg. First, in his outright rejection of the possibility of any (*realist*) *description* of the sub-atomic 'realm'. Secondly, in his concomitant proclamation of the 'new' *quantum* approach of, what came to be known as, *matrix mechanics*; that is, an outlook dedicated, in the true scientific spirit, to an experimental base of no more than what is actually *observable* – in the instance, (electronic) *signals/magnitudes* in their purely *heuristic* determinations as 'waves' and 'particles'. To this extent, there is the clear point of the wholesale and necessary abandonment by the 'new' physics of the last vestiges of the *realist* presuppositions regarding *space, time* and *matter* which had dominated physical science from the time of Newton right down to, and beyond, the turn of the present century.

The conclusion, epic in its implications, is unequivocally summarized by Born in following the earlier lead of Mach:

> The ultimate origin of the difficulty [of *quantum* theory] lies in the fact (or philosophical principle) that we are compelled to use the words of common language when we wish to describe a phenomenon, not by logical or mathematical analysis, but by a picture appealing to the imagination. Common language has grown by everyday experience and can never surpass these limits. Classical physics has restricted itself to the use of concepts of this kind; by analysing visible motions it has developed two ways of representing them by elementary processes; moving particles and waves. There is no other way of giving a pictorial description of motions – we have to apply it even in the region of atomic processes, where classical physics breaks down.[17]

So, too, by Heisenberg:

> The mathematically formulated laws of quantum theory show clearly that our ordinary intuitive concepts cannot be unambiguously applied to the smallest particles. All the words or concepts we use to describe ordinary physical objects such as position, velocity, color, size and so on, become indefinite and problematic if we try to use them of elementary particles.[18]

What must be added is the, no less dramatic, shattering of the idea of universal *causation* which came, in 1927, with the enunciation by Heisenberg of his renowned *uncertainty/indeterminacy* principle. More specifically, his demonstration of the impossibility of ever measuring, with exact precision, the simultaneous *position/momentum* of any moving 'particle' – and, following from this, the corollary of these latter, as *signals*, being open only to *probablistic/statistical*, as opposed to *causal*, analysis. To summarize, therefore, there is the conclusion – as voiced by Bohr in his capacity as spiritual leader of the *'new' quantum* school – that the 'Copenhagen Interpretation' is to be seen as entailing 'the necessity of a final renunciation of the classical ideal of *causality* . . . [together with] . . . a radical revision of our attitude toward the problem of *physical reality*'.[19]

In commenting on the above, there is the point, at once, that the course of time has brought about the firm establishment of the

'Copenhagen Interpretation', not simply as the first fully coherent approach to atomic data, but also as the *single* such theory, with no hint of a competitor. It is this fact which brings to the fore the provocativeness of the claim of Eddington noted earlier regarding the epistemological status of *quantum* propositions – that is that they are to be conceived as being more in the nature of *constructions* than *descriptions*. Beyond this, again, is the consideration that the triumph of the outlook has been due, not least, to the extraordinary success of its working methodology – with this leading to the identification of what (if only *heuristically* conceived as the 'build-ing-blocks' of *physical* reality) currently amount to more than a hundred different 'particles' of ever-increasing degrees of be-havioural elusiveness. This said, the concern in what follows must be seen as lying with the outlook's *theoretical* legitimacy. It is to this – and its significance for the stand of Schopenhauer – that attention may be finally turned.

The discussion may be opened with the fact that, although by no means the only opponent of the 'Copenhagen Interpretation', it was the famed figure of Einstein who, right up until the time of his death, held the mantle of being the theory's most implacable critic. The consideration is one that is the subject of an interesting perspective by Heisenberg:

Einstein refused point-blank to accept the uncertainty principle, and tried to think up cases in which the principle would not hold. Once again it was driven home to me how terribly difficult it is to give up an attitude on which one's entire scientific approach and career have been based. Einstein had devoted his life to probing that objective world of physical processes which runs its course in space and time, independent of us, according to firm laws. The mathematical symbols of theoretical physics were also symbols of this objective world and as such enabled physicists to make statements about its future behavior. And now it was being asserted that, on the atomic scale, this objective world of space and time did not even exist and that the mathematical symbols of theoretical physics referred to possibili-ties rather than to facts. Einstein was not prepared to let us do what, to him, amounted to pulling the ground from under his feet;[20]

And further:

> Later in his life, also, when quantum theory had long since become an integral part of modern physics, Einstein was unable to change his attitude – at best, he was prepared to accept the existence of quantum theory as a temporary expedient. 'God does not throw dice' was his unshakeable principle, one that he would not allow anybody to challenge. To which Bohr could only counter with: 'Nor is it our business to prescribe to God how He should run the world.'[21]

More for the main purpose, however, is the fact that the basis of this opposition is to be seen as resting on the strength of Einstein's conviction in the reality of, what came to be known as *hidden* (*local/causal*) *variables*. That is, more fully – his claim that the (*statistically* based) *probability* pronouncements of the 'Copenhagen' outlook were to be regarded not as having any final validity in their own right, but rather as being no more than provisional formulations of deeper (and, yet to be discovered) *causal* laws. The consideration may be viewed as a necessary propaedeutic to another main point. That is, the bolt to the heart of the 'new' physics which came, in 1935, with the publication by Einstein – in association with two younger colleagues, Boris Podolsky and Nathan Rosen – of a paper under the title 'Can Quantum-Mechanical Description of Physical Reality be Considered Complete?'[22]

Of seminal importance for the future course of theoretical physics, its wider setting may be drawn through the preliminary of a fuller expression of Heisenberg's *uncertainty/indeterminacy* principle, namely as this is to be seen as entailing that the very act of measuring the *position/momentum* of a moving 'particle', necessarily involves a 'disturbance' of the measuring/observing apparatus; and, following from this – the impossibility of ever conducting a *simultaneous* measurement of the correlate. On this basis, the substance of the Einstein/Podolsky/Rosen paper – 'EPR', as it came to be called – may be portrayed in terms of three main objectives. First, the postulation of a 'thought-experiment' designed to negate the preceding presupposition. Secondly, and bound up with this – the demonstration of the incompleteness of the *probability* descriptions of the 'new' physics. Thirdly, and by implication – the justification of the reality of *hidden* (*causal*) *variables*. As to the experiment itself, it may be briefly summarized as one involving the idea of two interacting, but spatially separated, (*quantum*) measuring/observing systems; where, as a result of measurements obtained from one of the systems, an observer is able to predict with complete certainty (that is with probability equal to unity) the values of correlates in the, spatially removed, second system. Though necessarily inadequate from a technical standpoint, the delineation is, notwithstanding, sufficient to bring out what was taken by 'EPR' as the fatal weakness of the 'Copenhagen' outlook; that is, of supposing that the fluctuations described by the *uncertainty/indeterminacy* principle must *necessarily* be ascribed to some kind of 'disturbance' of the measuring/observing apparatus. The point may be taken as the basis for a closer consideration of the theoretical foundations of 'EPR'.

The matter may be approached through the *synopsis* of the paper given by the authors themselves:

> In a complete theory there is an element corresponding to each element of reality. A sufficient condition for the reality of a physical quantity is the possibility of predicting it with certainty, without disturbing the system. In quantum mechanics in the case of two physical quantities described by non-commuting operators, the knowledge of one precludes the knowledge of the other. Then either (1) the description of reality given by the wave function in quantum mechanics is not complete or (2) these two quantities cannot have simultaneous reality. Consideration of the problem of making predictions concerning a system on the basis of measurements made on another system that had previously interacted with it leads to the result that if (1) is false then (2) is also false. One is thus led to conclude that the description of reality as given by a wave function is not complete.[23]

In amplification of the above there is the immediate point that the whole claim is to be seen as resting squarely on the principle known as *local causes* or *separability*. That is, the postulate that a *measuring/observing* apparatus, in any one region of space, cannot *affect/disturb* the experimental data of another, *spatially separated* system – or, more generally, that there is no such thing as *action-at-a-distance*. To this extent, the wider aim of the passage may be seen as that of asserting that *quantum–mechanical* predictions made by *measuring/observing* apparatus 'A' regarding a second system 'B' are only to be explained on the basis of appeal to the reality of *hidden (causal) variables*.

In noting the inherent *realism* of the stand, attention must also be drawn to the fulsome, and startling, acknowledgement by 'EPR' of the *conceptual* challenge to its validity presented by the idea which may be characterized as *simultaneity*. That is, the concept – and, no matter how far removed from the *realist/common-sensical* view of things – that the experimental data of one *measuring/observing* system might, indeed, be *simultaneously* (*non-temporally/causally*) related to the experimental situation in a second, *spatially removed*, system. In other words, and with specific regard to the 'EPR' *gedankenexperiment* – that the predictions made by system 'A' respecting the second system 'B' are to be seen as arising, not from the reality of *hidden variables*, but, from the *simultaneity* of the influence exerted on 'B' by the experimental situation in 'A'. Thus, 'EPR' in *rejecting* this possibility:

> One could object to . . . [the 'EPR'] . . . conclusion on the grounds that our criterion of reality is not sufficiently restrictive. Indeed, one would not arrive at our conclusion if one insisted that two or more physical quantities can be regarded as simultaneous elements of reality *only when they can be simultaneously measured or predicted* . . . This makes the reality of . . . [the quantities P and Q] . . . depend upon the process of measurement carried out in the first system, which does not disturb the second system in any way. No reasonable definition of reality could be expected to permit this.[24]

To summarize, therefore, there is the point that the 'EPR' argument for the reality of *hidden (causal) variables* is to be seen as resting on (a) the *assertion* of the principle of *local causes/separability*, on the one hand; and (b) the *denial* of the idea of *simultaneity/action-at-a-distance*, on the other.

'EPR' may be taken as Einstein's greatest, if inadvertent, contribution to the cause of *quantum* theory, as well as the Pandora Box of modern physics. For, in the event, whilst it was the clear objective of the paper to argue for the time-honoured cause of *realism*, the message accepted by the 'Copenhagen' school was, effectively, that the principle of *local causes* must be abandoned in favour of (some form of) the idea of *simultaneity*. The 'official' response, coming from Bohr in the later course of 1935, is one which may be summarized, for immediate purposes, in three bare points.[25] First, that the interacting systems of the 'EPR' *gedankenexperiment* are to be conceived not *realistically* as *locally separate*, but *phenomenally* as a *single* apparatus in a relation of *unity* with the (*perceiving/experimenting*) *observer* and the *observed* (*phenomenal*) *apparatus*. Secondly, that the fluctuations of the *quantum* correlates are to be regarded, not, *realistically*, as arising from some kind of *physical* disturbance of the apparatus, but, *phenomenally*, as a necessary, *conceptual*, feature of the act of *measuring*. Thirdly, that the fact of (*quantum*) predictive *certainty* is to be explained, not *realistically*, by appeal to *hidden* (*causal*) *variables*, but, *phenomenally*, through conditions of *interaction* between the (*perceiving/experimenting*) *observer* and the *observed* (*phenomenal*) *apparatus*. The point that may be brought to the fore, therefore, is that the position adopted by Bohr in defending the 'Copenhagen Interpretation' against the *realist* challenge of 'EPR' is one involving a radical and decisive shift in specifically *scientific* thinking. It is, in effect, one entailing full acceptance of a thoroughgoing (*philosophical*) *idealism* – with *physical/common-sensical* reality being conceived, not as an ontologically 'existing' *thing-in-itself*, but, as a function, in some sense, of perceiving (*human*) *mind/consciousness*.

In reaching this conclusion, the various strands of the preceding survey may be brought together in two main points. First, that the year 1935, with 'EPR' as the lightning-rod, saw the battle lines drawn, by *science* itself, with regard to two, mutually exclusive, *philosophical* views of the nature of *physical/common-sensical* reality. Namely, (a) *realism* and (b) *idealism*. Secondly, that the dispositions, in each case, are to be seen as turning on the opposition between two specifically *scientific* concepts; that is, as delineated above, (x) *local causes/separability*, on the one hand; and (y) *simultaneity/action-at-a-distance*, on the other. With mention, once more, of the relevance of these considerations for the claims of Schopenhauer, there is, also, another point – in short, the massiveness of the further support to his position which arose from subsequent theoretical advances regarding precisely the foregoing issues of (x) and (y).

With necessarily limited space for discussion, the developments may be seen as having their beginning in a paper by John S. Bell which appeared in 1964 under the title 'On the Einstein Podolsky Rosen Paradox'.[26] Mathematical in conception, its substance, as reworked and consolidated, has come to be known as *Bell's*

Theorem with an acquired status rivalling that of 'EPR'. Having its inception in the same puzzling connectedness between *quantum* correlates/'particles' which had led 'EPR' to the proclamation of *hidden variables*, it is to be seen as embracing two vital advances over the former. First, and following a lead given by Bohm in 1951, there is the centrepiece of a *gedankenexperiment* which, though the conceptual equivalent of 'EPR', possesses the advantage of being open to much simpler mathematical expression.[27] Secondly, and again following the lead of Bohm, there is the refinement of a formula based on, and covering, the various historical forms of the *realist* idea of *locality/separability*. With these preliminaries, the theorem itself may be portrayed in a way which is, at least, adequate for present purposes; that is, more specifically, as proclaiming that the mutually exclusive opposition between (a) the *validity* of the *predictions of quantum mechanics*, and (b) the *reality* of *hidden (causal) variables*, is open to decisive testing in a single experimental procedure satisfying a simple and comprehensive formulation of the idea of *locality/separability*. In short, and without equivocation – that either (a) or (b) must be false.

With this, it remains merely to add three final points in bringing the survey to a close. Thus, there is, first, the fact of the series of crucial experiments which – as beginning at the outset of the 1970s and culminating in the highly publicized papers of Alain Aspect in the early 1980s – has gone to give decisive support to (a) above, in its opposition to (b).[28] Secondly, mention may be made of the rise in recent years of a marked *speculative* strain in physical science having a direct relation to the demise of (b) – as where the traditional bounds of the discipline have been burst by appeal to such scientifically esoteric concepts as *consciousness, mind, God*,[29] *superliminal* (faster-than-light) *communication*, and even by actual use of the term *telepathy*. In deliberate avoidance of detail, the point may be characterized by reference to a single compelling extract from the work of the renowned figure of John Archibald Wheeler, the foremost exponent of the famous 'Many Worlds' development of *quantum* theory:

Far from being brought into its present condition by 'reprocessing' from earlier cycles, may the universe in some strange sense be 'brought into being' by the participation of those who participate? On this view the concept of 'cycles' would even seem to be altogether wrong. Instead the vital act is the act of participation.[30]

And, in continuing:

'Participator' is the incontrovertible new concept given by quantum mechanics; it strikes down the term 'observer' of classical theory, the man who stands behind the thick glass wall and watches what goes on without taking part. It can't be done, quantum mechanics says. Even with the lowly electron one must participate before one can give any meaning whatsoever to its position or its momentum. Is this firmly established result the tiny tip of a giant iceberg? Does the universe also derive its meaning from 'participation'?[31]

Finally, and most directly, there may be a highlighting of the words of two other leading physicists, John Clauser and Abner Shimony, as drawn in their comprehensive survey of the 'world-making' significance of *Bell's Theorem*.[32]

Thus, there is, first, their *abstract*:

Bell's theorem represents a significant advance in understanding the conceptual foundations of quantum mechanics. The theorem shows that essentially all local theories of natural phenomena that are formulated within the framework of realism may be tested using a single experimental arrangement. Moreover, the predictions by these theories must significantly differ from those by quantum mechanics. Experimental results evidently refute the theorem's predictions for these theories and favour those of quantum mechanics. The conclusions are philosophically startling: either one must totally abandon the realistic philosophy of most working scientists, or dramatically revise our concept of space-time.[33]

Secondly, there is their *conclusion*:

Because of the evidence in favour of quantum mechanics from the experiments based upon Bell's theorem, we are forced either to abandon the strong version of EPR's criterion of reality – which is tantamount to abandoning a realistic view of the physical world (perhaps an unheard tree falling in the forest makes no sound after all) – or else to accept some kind of action-at-a-distance. Either option is radical, and a comprehensive study of the philosophical consequences remains to be made.[34]

With the final comment of the above, like the earlier noted remark of Eddington, being subject to the reservation of what is to follow, there is, more immediately, not only the clear fact of the abandonment by modern physics of its time-honoured attachment to the tradition of (Democritan/Newtonian) *realism/materialism*, but also its fulsome recognition of the hitherto eschewed idea of *actio in distans*, with all the vast implications arising therefrom.

It remains merely to reiterate that it forms no part of the present intention to draw from the above any conclusion regarding the *empirical* reality of the super-normal. Though clear enough from what has been said, the consideration has a relevance in view of certain, recently expressed, *scientific* concern in this regard.[35] This said, there is, notwithstanding, the fact of its significance in another vital respect – in short, that of its function in establishing the complete intellectual vacuousness of claims to the *'scientific* impossibility' of such happenings as voiced (and no matter how professionally distinguished the authority) from the historically venerable, but now completely outmoded, stance of (*materialistic*) *realism*.

11

Physical Reality and Philosophical Ideality

In continuing the preceding discussion, reference is made here to a passage from Schrödinger that describes the underlying presupposition of the whole scientific enterprise as traditionally conceived – his account of what he calls, the 'principle of *objectivation*' as set out in his Tarner Lectures for 1956:

> By this I mean the thing that is also frequently called the 'hypothesis of the real world' around us. I maintain that it amounts to a certain simplification which we adopt in order to master the infinitely intricate problem of nature. Without being aware of it and without being rigorously systematic about it, we exclude the Subject of Cognizance from the domain of nature that we endeavour to understand. We step with our own person back into the part of an onlooker who does not belong to the world, which by this very procedure becomes an objective world.[1]

What has been seen is that, due, not least, to the efforts of Schrödinger himself, the presupposition, together with the associated stance of *realism/materialism* from which it takes its rise, is one whose final (*scientific*) nemesis has come through the culminating triumph of the *quantum* outlook. On this basis – and reverting to the earlier claim of Schopenhauer – the present concern must be seen as lying with a delineation of the strength of the alternative, *idealistic*, interpretation of *physical/common-sensical* reality.

It is a matter which may be approached through the fact that the same era of the second half of the seventeenth century which set the stamp of Newton's *physical* speculations on the future course of Western thought was also the period which saw the rise of another vital strain of this tradition; that is, the postulation of the antithetical idea of *mind* as something ontologically existing in its own right – a vision which, as originally set forth in the sceptical reflections of

René Descartes, was subsequently to attain full maturity in the massive synthesis achieved by Immanuel Kant in his *Critique of Pure Reason*. With the sole aim of establishing the foregoing objective, the sweep of the matter may be covered through the convenience of a division of the discussion into four separate, but interrelated, parts.

I

To begin with Descartes (1596–1650), as the progenitor of the movement, his position – as set forth in his two main philosophical writings, the *Discours de la méthode/Discourse on Method* (1637) and the, more concentrated, *Meditationes de Prima Philosophia/Meditations on First Philosophy* (1641) – is one which may be seen as turning on his new-found tool of, what, in the course of time, came to be known as, 'Cartesian'/'Methodic'/'Hyperbolic' *doubt*. More specifically, the procedure whereby, as a necessary condition of his search for indubitable *truth/knowledge*, he took upon himself the task of questioning the *truth/validity/reality* of everything capable of being *doubted*. Thus, taking, first, the issue of scepticism regarding the *senses*, Descartes raises the instance of his state of being awake and sitting, clothed in his dressing gown, before the fire of his room. Is this an experience that can be doubted? Yes, says Descartes, for it might be no more than a vivid dream; with the true state of affairs being that he was really asleep, *sans* dressing gown, in the fastness of his bed. In a similar way, the experience might conceivably be the powerful hallucination of a deranged mind such as sometimes occurs in conditions of madness. Beyond this, the *reality/status* of the *physical/common-sensical* world is also open to question. Even, indeed, the *truth/validity* of the propositions of (pure) *mathematics*. For, the latter, like the former in which they are instantiated, might (conceivably) arise through the agency of a powerful but malignant demon whose delight and purpose it is to cause deception. Putting aside the widely-debated topic of the validity, as well as meaningfulness, of the assorted, and often sketchy, arguments deployed by Descartes in the preceding regard, attention may be confined to the conclusion which he draws from them. This is, put simply, that *thought* alone escapes the net of his 'methodic' doubt. It might well be that the *physical/common-sensical* world is, in some sense, illusory. So, too, that, in the ultimate scheme of things, I have no 'real' body. But the bare fact of my *doubting* entails a crucial and incontrovertible fact; that is, no less – the indubitability of my *existence* as a *thinking* being. In short, in Descartes' own epic words: *Cogito ergo sum* – 'I think, therefore I am'.

Whatever the difficulties arising from the foregoing usages of 'I' and 'exist', there is the clear fact that the term *thinking*, as employed by Descartes, is to be seen as covering a whole spectrum of 'states' which, as he acknowledges, are not always easy to distinguish – doubting, understanding, conceiving, affirming, denying, willing, imagining, feeling, dreaming. Further, and most especially – that it is to be conceived exclusively in terms of *awareness/consciousness*, even as extended to the case of dreams.[2] In this connexion, too, mention may be made of the revolutionary significance of Descartes' achievement in switching the very meaning of the critical term *idea* away from its traditional Platonic/ Scholastic connotation, that is as metaphysical *Forms/Ideas*, to the modern sense of relating to, what may be roughly characterized as, 'contents' of *mind*.[3] These are considerations to which it will be necessary to return. More for the present is the way in which Descartes resumes his probing of the nature of 'material' substance through his phenomenological analysis of a piece of *wax*.

Famous in the history of philosophy, it is an account that is given entirely in terms of (*mental*) *qualities*, or, more broadly, *ideas* in the preceding sense. Thus, as he remarks, the wax, taken from the honeycomb, smells of flowers and tastes of honey. It has a certain colour, shape and size; it is hard and cold; and, when struck, emits a sound. This same piece of wax, however, on the occasion of being set before the fire, acquires a completely different set of such characteristics. The smell, taste and colour change. So do the shape and size. It becomes soft and warm – and gives off no sound if struck. Whence, then, the *idea* of the wax *per se*? Certainly not, as he holds, from anything *sensibly* 'material'. Hence, and necessarily – in some way, from *mind*. With this, therefore, there is, once more, Descartes' affirmation of the ontological primacy of the *mental* over the 'material'. So, also, the ground of the distinction which he draws between (a) *mind*, on the one hand; and (b) 'matter'/'body', on the other – with the latter conceived as being, in some sense, a *mode* of the former.

Following from the above, and to complete the immediate conspetus, attention may be drawn to two further tenets of the

Cartesian scheme. First, Descartes' tripartite classification of the various kinds of *ideas* – (p) those that appear to be 'given' from 'without'; (q) those that are (imaginatively) 'invented' on the basis of the former; and (r) those that are *innate* in the sense of arising *sui generis* from *mind*. Secondly, and more in his standing as a man of his time – his appeal to the *Benevolence/Omnipotence* of *God* as the ultimate ground of the 'external'/'objective', that is *physical/ common-sensical* world, represented by (p). In this latter connexion too, mention may be made of another point which, though of great *historical/cultural* relevance, is, yet, to be seen as being in plain contradiction with the depth of the strictly *philosophical* insight of the preceding conclusion. More specifically – Descartes' proclamation of his famous, and, in the event, highly treacherous, duality of (x) *thinking* and (y) *extended* 'substance'; with (y), no less than (x), conceived as having *ontological* status. In merely noting this wider *theologically* grounded, aspect of the Cartesian outlook, there is, more immediately, the main conclusion – in short, the clear fact of the innovative and uncompromising *idealism* of the 'negative'/ *sceptical* strain of Descartes' thought.

II

In turning, next, to the potent new stance of the British *empiricist* school, the discussion may be opened with a delineation of the position of John Locke (1632–1704) as the originator of the movement.

Pivotal to the present purpose, it is an outlook which, as promulgated in his famous *Essay Concerning Human Understanding* (1690), is to be seen as turning on two key propositions, namely (a) the denial of the Cartesian idea of *innateness*; and, reciprocally, (b) the assertion that *all* knowledge arises, in the last resort, from the 'given-ness' of (*perceptual*) *experience*. Thus, in his own famous words:

> Let us then suppose the Mind to be, as we say, white Paper, void of all Characters, without any Ideas; how comes it to be furnished? Whence comes it by that vast store, which the busy and boundless Fancy of man has painted on it, with an almost endless variety? Whence has it all the materials of Reason and Knowledge? To this I answer, in one word, from *Experience*: In

that, all our Knowledge is founded; and from that it ultimately derives itself. (II, i, 2)

In leaving the main significance of (a) for later remark, there is need, for the moment, merely to mention that the innovativeness of Locke in this regard is to be viewed as extending well beyond the specialism of his attack on Cartesianism. More specifically – it embraces, also, an assault on the whole earlier tradition of Western thought where, as stemming, most principally, from Plato, it was accepted as being virtually beyond question that *soul/mind* was open to a whole host of influences – intellectual, moral, aesthetic, demonic, divine – in addition to *(empirical) perception*.[4] This said, there may be the offer of two points in supplementation of (b).

In the first place, there is Locke's full and unqualified endorsement of the incontrovertibility of Descartes' claim regarding the epistemological primacy of the term *idea*:

> Since the *Mind*, in all its Thoughts and Reasonings, hath no Other immediate object but its own *Ideas*, which it alone does or can contemplate, it is evident that our Knowledge is only conversant about them. (*IV*, i, 1)

Secondly, and notwithstanding his heartsearchings over consistency, there is the uncompromising nature of his *(personal)* conviction regarding the ultimate basis of the 'given-ness'/'externality'/ 'objectivity' of the foregoing *ideality*. In particular, that this is to be explained, not simply, as with Descartes, by appeal to Divine Agency, but rather *realistically* through the acceptance of, what, for him, as a self-proclaimed 'under-labourer' in the cause of *science*, was the indubitable existence of micro-physical *material/corpuscular* 'entities', that is *atoms*. To summarize, therefore, there is the point that the 'new' *empiricism* of Locke is to be viewed as an amalgam of two disparate and, in the event, quite irreconcilable elements. First – (x) the (incipient) *idealism* of the 'new' *philosophy* of Descartes; secondly – (y) the (speculative) *realism* of the 'new' *physics* of Newton.

The conclusion may be amplified through the distinction made famous, if not invented, by Locke between (a) *primary*, and (b) *secondary* qualities, namely where (a) – which he takes as being, in some way, *necessarily* associated with the notion of *body* – are listed as, shape, solidity, extension, number, motion, rest; and (b) as colours, sounds, tastes, odours. Postulated on the basis of, what he himself describes as, a 'little Excursion into Natural Philosophy' (II, viii, 22), it is a division which manifestly portrays his unabashed commitment to the strain of (y) above. Thus, as he holds, the *primary* qualities 'do really exist in the Bodies themselves' (II, viii, 15); and the corresponding *ideas* are *causally* generated (mental) *representations/resemblances* of these. On the other hand, the *secondary* qualities, though *causally* arising from 'powers' in the ontologically 'existing' *primary* qualities, are, yet, 'nothing in the Objects themselves' (II, viii, 14). They have merely *subjective/relational* existence; that is, purely and simply, as *ideas*. With this, and in deliberate avoidance of difficulties, enough has been said for the establishment of a single main point regarding, what, in the course of time, came to be known as, Locke's *representative* theory of *perception*. In short, that, for Locke, (*perceptual*) *experience*, is to be conceived as being in the nature of a (*mental*) *representation* of 'underlying' (ontologically 'existing', but *non-perceptible*) *material* 'transactions' from which it *causally* takes its rise.

In commenting on the above, there is the immediate fact of the way in which this latter has come to be ingrained into the very fabric of the Western way of thinking. Thus, there is the clear interrelation of the theory with the 'principle of *objectivation*' delineated at the outset by Schrödinger. With this, too, is its easy recognizability as the framework assumed in the popular (*realist*) identification of the physical scientist as one whose business it is to probe behind the veil of *perceptual/common-sensical* experience to the ultimate (*imperceptible*) nature of *material* ontology; so, also, its significance as the presuppositional setting of the climactic triumphs of the great era of 'classical' physics – as exemplified, for instance, in Maxwell's unification of the *electro-magnetic* spectrum and the Rutherford–Bohr theory of the *atom*. As to *truth*, however, there is the consideration, at once – as seen from the perspective of Chapter 10 – that it is pre-eminently the *rejection* of this (Lockean) sense of *representation* which constitutes the crux of the move from the Rutherford–Bohr '*old*' *quantum* theory to the '*new*' *quantum* position of the 'Copenhagen Interpretation'; and with this, the knell of *science* itself to the ancient tradition of *realism/materialism*. This said, there may be a return to the main concern with the force of another point. The fact, namely, that despite the long (and continuing) prevalence of the outlook, it is, notwithstanding, to be seen as having already met an early and decisive *philosophical* negation at the hands of Locke's *empiricist* successor, George Berkeley (1685–1753).

It might be accepted that there is a sense in which the latter – an ordinand of the Church of England who culminated a life of philanthropic endeavours as Bishop of Cloyne in Ireland – may be taken, merely, as bringing to a final head the incipience of Descartes' own earlier position regarding the *ideality* of *physical/ common-sensical* experience. At the same time, the clarity and vigour, as well as elegance of style, with which he does this – most particularly, in his early writings, *A Treatise Concerning the Principles of Human Nature* (1710) and *Three Dialogues between Hylas and Philonous* (1713) – are altogether sufficient, of themselves, to establish for him an especial place in philosophical annals as the bearer of a vitally new and incontrovertible truth. Thus, the words of Schopenhauer in expressing the degree of his own indebtedness to Berkeley:

> The world is my representation: this is a truth valid with reference to every living and knowing being ... The truth is by no means new. It was to be found already in the sceptical reflections from which Descartes started. But Berkeley was the first to enunciate it positively, and he has thus rendered an immortal service to philosophy.[5]

So, also, from another perspective, the endorsement of Clifford:

> The doctrine of Berkeley, in its positive aspect, is a distinct and most important step in philosophy; it established in a security that has never yielded to attack the subjective character of the world of phenomena, that the world which I perceive *is* my perceptions and nothing more.[6]

With these preliminaries, the terms of the position – styled by Berkeley himself as *immaterialism* – may be drawn more fully.

Thus, there may be reference, first, to his negation of the (Lockean) doctrine of *primary* qualities. More specifically – his demonstration that the latter, no less than the *secondary* qualities, are to be regarded as having a purely *mental* status (*Cf.* 10, 14).[7] With this, further, is his rejection of the *materialistic/atomic* under- pinning of Locke's *representative* theory as lying beyond the possibility of verification; that is, as being a postulate having no more than *obscurantist* standing (*Cf.* 18, 86). Most particularly, however – and as embracing the above – is his claim to the complete *incomprehensibility* of all talk of (either *macro* or *micro-physical*) *materiality*. 'What is meant', as he challenges the reader, 'by the term *exist* when applied to sensible things [?]' (3). The question itself contains its own reply. *Necessarily* nothing beyond the measure of *mind*-dependent *qualities*:

> The table I write on, I say, exists, that is, I see and feel it; and if I were out of my study I should say it existed, meaning thereby that if I was in my study I might perceive it, or that some other … actually does perceive it. There was an odour, that is, it was smelled; there was a sound, that is to say, it was heard; a colour or figure, and it was perceived by sight or touch. This is all that I can understand by these and the like expressions. For as to what is said of the absolute existence of unthinking things without any relation to their being perceived, that seems perfectly unintelligible. (3)

To summarize, therefore, there is not only the starkness of the challenge raised by Berkeley regarding the *meaningfulness* of the Newtonian/Lockean doctrine of the (*material*) *atom*, but also the potency of the more positive aspect of his position; that is, the thrust of his claim that the *existence* of (*physical/common-sensical*) *things/objects* is *analytically/logically* related to the conditions of their being *perceived*. In short, in his own epigrammatic words – that 'their *esse* is *percipi*' (3).

Widely misunderstood in the context of its time, the significance of the proclamation may be amplified in the light of the (Kantian) distinction which constitutes the title of the present chapter. Thus, as may be emphasized, it is certainly not – nor could it be – Berkeley's intention to deny the *empirical* reality of the *physical/common-sensical* world. Rather, and fully accepting the latter – the intention is merely to assert, at a different logical level of discourse, the complementarity of its *philosophical* standing. In other words – its *ultimate* 'immateriality'/'ideality', as opposed to 'materiality':

> By the principles premised, we are not deprived of any one thing in Nature. Whatever we see, feel, hear, or any wise conceive or understand, remains as secure as ever, and is as real as ever.

There is a *rerum natura*, and the distinction between realities and
chimeras retains its full force . . . That the things I see with mine
eyes and touch with my hands do exist, really exist, I make not
the least question. The only thing whose existence we deny, is
that which philosophers call matter or corporeal substance. And
in doing of this, there is no damage done to the rest of mankind,
who, I dare say, will never miss it. (34, 35)

The point may be supplemented by two further considerations
regarding the wider ramifications of the Berkeleyan scheme.

In the first place, there is the fact of Berkeley's postulation of *God*
as the *Cause* and *Sustainer* of the 'given'/'objective' (*perceptual*) order
– with the latter conceived as being, in some way, the *sensible*
expression of the *Thought/Will* of the former. It is a point which is
open to amusing illustration through the wit of Ronald Knox.
Thus, in a comic, but not inaccurate portrayal of Berkeley's
position made famous by Bertrand Russell:

> There was a young man who said, 'God
> Must think it exceedingly odd
> > If he finds that this tree
> > Continues to be
> When there's no one about in the Quad.'

> *Reply*

> Dear Sir:
> > Your astonishment's odd:
> I am always about in the Quad.
> > And that's why the tree
> > Will continue to be
> Since observed by
> > *Yours faithfully,*
> > GOD.[8]

Secondly, and following from the above, there is the far-reaching
epistemological point of the propositions of *science* being, for Berkeley, necessarily *correlational/descriptive*, as against *causal/
explanatory*, in nature. With mention that both considerations will
be the subject of later remark, there may be pause for a consolidation of the main substance of what has been said.

In this regard, there is, at once, the extent of the move made by Berkeley away from the *materialistic/atomic* base of Locke's *representative* theory to a position which may be characterized as *'direct perception'*. Further, the vital fact of this Berkeleyan step effectively constituting the foundation of the 'new' *quantum* outlook of the 'Copenhagen Interpretation'. With this, too, may be mention of the strength of Berkeley's *positivistic* influence on the key (*scientific*) figure of Mach – as manifested, most especially, in the vigour of the latter's rejection, during the high period of the 'classical' era, of the entrenched and virulent doctrine of the (*material*) atom. And, again – that it is precisely the provocativeness of the *immaterialism* in hand which is reflected in the parenthetical possibility raised by Clauser and Shimony in their crucially important conclusion of the preceding chapter. On the preceding basis, attention may be turned to the culminating position of the tradition under discussion as represented in the thought of one who has already been the subject of extensive remark; that is, Hume (1711–76) – in the brilliance of his early *A Treatise of Human Nature* (1739), as supplemented by the later, and more popularly geared, *An Enquiry concerning the Human Understanding* (1748).[9]

In delineating the main parameters of the position, attention may be drawn, first, to the measure of Hume's terminological advance over his predecessors with regard to the critical notion of *idea*. In particular, and as postulated at the outset of the *Treatise*, his use of (a) *impression*, as against *idea*, to relate to the 'given-ness'/ 'objectivity' of (*perceptual*) *experience*; and (b) *perception* as a 'blanket' term to embrace both arms of the ensuing *impression–idea* dichotomy. To accept the dogmatic confidence exhibited by Hume in asserting this development is not to belie the difficulties experienced by him or his followers in the complexities of its subsequent application. With this, again, as a point to which it will be necessary to return, there is, more immediately, a consideration which connects with the preceding discussion of Berkeley; that is, the uninhibited *idealism* of this opening and far-reaching stand. Closely intertwined with this is a second point; namely, the uncompromising extent of Hume's commitment to the foundational tenets of Locke's *empiricism*. Thus, in the terms of his revised vocabulary:

Since nothing is ever present to the mind but *perceptions*, and since all *ideas* are deriv'd from something antecedently present to the mind; it follows that 'tis impossible for us so much as to conceive or form an *idea* of any thing specifically different from *ideas* and *impressions*. Let us fix our attention out of ourselves as much as possible: Let us chace our imagination to the heavens, or the utmost limits of the universe; we never really advance a step beyond ourselves, nor can conceive any kind of existence, but those *perceptions*, which have appear'd in that narrow compass.[10]

To this, again, may be added a third element of the Humean stance which – with all its vast impact on the subsequent course of Western thought – has come to be known as *phenomenalism*.

It is a strain which, in one of its aspects, may be viewed as a final flowering of the original spirit of Cartesian *scepticism*; and in another, as arising from the constraints of Locke's *empiricism*; and yet further, as a logical extension of Berkeleyan *positivism*. Most particularly, however – and certainly for present purposes – it is a matter which may be approached through the circumstances surrounding the wholesale rejection by Hume of, what is, in effect, the central presupposition of Berkeley; that is, his postulation of *God* as the underlying source of the rule-governed/coherent/ordered world presented in *perception*. 'From what impression', as Hume generically demands, '*is . . .* [*this*] *. . . supposed idea derived?*'[11] There is none. To this extent, it is a claim which, like that of Locke regarding the (*material*) *atom*, must be relegated to the status of the (*philosophically/scientifically*) *meaningless*. How, then, is the fact in hand to be explained? No 'high' doctrine is necessary. The most that can be said is that there is 'a gentle force, which commonly prevails'.[12] Beyond this, the question itself – as, also, that relating to the ultimate basis of *self-perception/consciousness* – is, by its very nature, such as to (*logically*) transcend the possibility of answer:

> As to . . . *impressions* . . . their ultimate cause is . . . perfectly inexplicable by human reason, and 'twill always be impossible to decide with certainty, whether they arise immediately from the object, or are produc'd by the creative power of the mind, or are deriv'd from the author of our being.[13]

With this, therefore, are the twin heads of Hume's *phenomenalism*. On the one hand, (a) the full-blown *idealism* of his *impression-idea* division; on the other hand, (b) an absolute and necessary *agnostic-*

ism regarding the ultimate basis of this dichotomy.

It remains to complete the segment with a highlighting of three key consequences of the Humean position. In the first place, there is the fact of his revolutionary new doctrine of *causation*. Again, as he asks – from what *impression* is this *idea* derived? And, again, the answer – None! What is yielded by (*perceptual/phenomenal*) *experience* is no more than *contiguity* and *succession*; not *necessary connexion*. How, then, is the *idea* to be explained? Purely and simply as a function of (*psychological*) *association* on the basis of *constant conjunction*:

> We remember to have seen that species of object we call *flame*, and to have felt that species of sensation we call *heat*. We likewise call to mind their *constant conjunction* in all past instances. Without any further ceremony, we call the one *cause* and the other *effect*, and infer the existence of the one from that of the other.[14]

Following from this, there is, secondly, the *epistemological* conclusion already noted in the case of Berkeley, namely, though for different metaphysical reasons – that the propositions of *science* are to be viewed as being necessarily and exclusively *correlational/inductive/probablistic*, as opposed to *causal/explanatory*, in nature. Thirdly, and finally, there is the provocativeness of his challenge to both *philosophy* and *religion* alike – as this has been taken up in the present century through the influence of the *logical positivist* movement, namely, that such *empirical* (*inductive/probablistic*) generalizations in association (most particularly) with the *deductive* relations of *arithmetic/geometry/algebra* are to be viewed as constituting an *exhaustive* dichotomy of *all* (significant) claims to *knowledge*.[15] Thus, in the dare of the concluding words of the *Enquiry*:

> When we run over libraries, persuaded of these principles, what havoc must we make? If we take in our hand any volume; of divinity or school metaphysics, for instance; let us ask, *Does it contain any abstract reasoning concerning quantity or number?* No. *Does it contain any experimental reasoning concerning matter of fact and existence?* No. Commit it then to the flames, for it can contain nothing but sophistry and illusion.

With this, and leaving the far-reaching ramifications of this dichotomy for later remark, enough has been said for the firm establishment of all that is necessary for the central purpose. There is, in short, not only the fact of the glorious tradition of British *empiricism* culminating in the *phenomenalistic idealism* of Hume; but also the clear reflection of the strength of the latter in the move from 'old' to 'new' *quantum* theory.

It remains merely to add that the vast impact which Hume has come to exert on contemporary culture, contrasts sharply with the way in with his ideas were received in the context of his time. Thus, in the poignancy of some of his last written words:

> But it will happen to me as to so many other Writers. Though I have reached a considerable Age, I shall not live to see any Justice done to me. It is not impossible, however, that my Self-conceit and Prepossessions may lead me into this way of thinking.[16]

More fully, there is the fact, as given by Hume himself, that the *Treatise* 'fell *deadborn from the Press*',[17] while the *Enquiry*, too, met but very limited success. Indeed, the first to recognize the massiveness of his achievement – as this is to be seen as turning, most particularly, on his analysis of the *causal* issue – was Kant, writing seven years after Hume's death and more than forty years following the appearance of the *Treatise*:

> Hume suffered the usual misfortune of metaphysicians, of not being understood. It is positively painful to see how utterly his opponents . . . missed the point of the problem; for . . . they were ever taking for granted that which he doubted, and demonstrating with zeal and often impudence that which he never thought of doubting.[18]

With this, however, is the reciprocity of another point. That is, the extent to which the *realist/materialist* presuppositions of Newton regarding *space, time, causality* and the *atom* had come to dominate the thought of the age. The consideration – already sufficiently emphasized – may be taken as the back-drop to developments falling within the purview of the third main segment of the present concern; namely, those associated with the universal genius of Gottfried Wilhelm Leibniz (1646–1716).

III

Discoverer, independently of Newton, of the differential calculus and inventor of one of the world's first calculating machines, Leibniz – with his life of unrelenting political, religious, legal and academic activity – is to be seen, also, as among the most prolific writers of all time, leaving a mass of papers and letters which remain, even to this day, defiant of anything like final collation. There may be mention, too, that, unlike Hume, his efforts were to establish for him a standing, in his own time, as an intellectual pillar of the age. Thereafter, too, his ideas, as diffused through the teachings of Christian Wolff (1679–1754), the 'school-master of Germany', came to dominate the thought of German universities and constitute the tradition in which Kant himself was raised. At the same time, there is also the fact that the circumstances of these triumphs must be set against the sadness of his end. Left behind in Hanover when his patron, the Duke of Brunswick, became George I of Britain, he was buried, in the words of an eye-witness, 'more like a robber than, what he really was, the ornament of his country'.[19] Because of his lack of attachment to any church, his funeral went unofficiated by the clergy; he was accompanied to his grave only by his secretary; and his death went unnoticed, not only by his royal patrons, but also by the Berlin Academy of which he was founder and life-president.

Turning to his thought, there may be immediate mention that the only full-scale philosophical work of Leibniz to appear in his lifetime was the *theologically* oriented *Theodicy*. That is, his celebrated attempt to reconcile the Judæo-Christian (*theistic*) conception of *God* as *Omnipotent/All-Benevolent* with the contingent reality of *evil*, on the one hand, and the idea of (moral) *freedom*, on the other.[20] Though, in itself, peripheral to the main purpose, there is, notwithstanding, the fact of its symptomatic relevance. More specifically, there is the consideration that, despite the stamp of his end as *parcus deorem cultor et infrequens*, the overriding thrust of Leibniz's whole philosophical endeavour is one which, like that of Berkeley, is essentially *religious/theological* in inspiration. With this, however, must go the fact that, as seen by Leibniz, the greatest impediment to his overall scheme was that set by the *realist/materialist* presuppositions of Newton and Locke, together with the incipience of these in the Cartesian doctrine of '*extended* substance'. Further, and most particularly – that, in the process of meeting this challenge, Leibniz came to proclaim ideas that were to forever change the faces of both *philosophy* and *science*.

With the preceding preliminaries over, attention may be turned to the main terms of his reconstruction as embraced, respectively, under the interrelated heads of (A) *space* and *time;* (B) the *atom;* and (C) *innate* ideas. With (C) being left for the culminating discussion of the segment, the concern, more immediately, may be seen as lying in the task of relating (A) and (B) to the central course of what has been said.

With regard, first, to (A), Leibniz's most definitive statement of his position is that given in the so-called *Leibniz–Clarke Correspondence* – an exchange of papers (five from each side) between Leibniz and the English divine and philosopher Samuel Clarke (1675–1725) conducted over the period 1715–6, and published by Clarke in 1717, just following Leibniz's death.[21] With Clarke as the protagonist for Newtonian ideas – and with the argument, on both sides, involving a mêlée of *theological/scientific/philosophical* considerations[22] – the work is to be seen as representing the culminating phase of a running engagement between Leibniz and the followers of Newton that went back to the early years of the century. One, too, whose wider *cultural/historical* significance is also worthy of note:

> The exchange of papers between Leibniz and Clarke is the most frequently cited of all eighteenth-century philosophical controversies. For their contemporaries it was the final confrontation of 'the mathematical philosophy', represented by Newton and his champion Clarke, and 'the metaphysical philosophy'. To many modern observers it appears to mark one of the final stages in that temporary emancipation of the natural sciences from philosophy and theology, which made possible the progress of science in the succeeding two centuries.[23]

As to the debate itself, there is neither need nor intent to pursue the multiplicity of its strains. Instead, the main purpose may be served with the offer of, what would be generally regarded as, the most telling aspect of Leibniz's attack. In the event, it is an argument that was originally deployed by Zeno of Elea, the disciple of Parmenides and older contemporary of Democritus. Thus, and with merely implicative reference to *time* – that (a) there is a *category* difference between *space* and *things/objects* (in *space*);

and (b) to ascribe the status of the latter to the former is to entail the *paradox* (and *logical* regress) of a *space* of *space*.[24] Beyond this, however, and most importantly, is Leibniz's conclusion; namely that *space* and *time* are not *substantial* in their own right, but rather are *derivative* – from the logically prior notion of *things/objects*. In other words, they are *relational/adjectival*.

The wider ramifications of this conclusion, with its re-assertion of the deep-rooted and long-sustained Aristotelian/Scholastic teaching regarding *space* and *time*, may be pursued through attention to Leibniz's position regarding (B) above. Promulgated in a stream of papers which, beginning about 1696, continued right up to his last years, it is a matter whose fullest synoptic treatment is contained in his famous *Monadology*, a work which, though written in 1714, did not see the light of day until 1840.[25] In drawing on these writings, there may be a delineation of the main features of the position which Broad, in his own appraisal, describes as, 'one of the most elaborate and all-embracing systems of constructive metaphysics that exist'.[26]

A start may be made with the fact of Leibniz's outright rejection of the central Cartesian postulate of '*extended* substance'. This is, as he maintains, a totally inadequate conception – one wholly lacking the capacity to relate the *geometrical-kinematic* components of its denotation. As such, it must be redefined, in particular in terms of *force* – with force conceived as involving a duality of modes, namely (x) 'primitive *passive*' force as the ground of a body's *impenetrability/elasticity/inertia* (and, hence, of its *shape/size*); and (y) 'primitive *active*' force as that of its *movement*. In deliberately setting aside (y), the point to be emphasized is that Leibniz's stand regarding (x) is mirrored *mutatis mutandis* in his rebuttal of the Newtonian claim to the reality of the (*material*) *atom*. With this, too, must go the strength of his response to an associated aspect of this doctrine – that of the *atom* being *contingently* beyond the possibility of further *divisibility*. This, as Leibniz proclaims, is an entirely arbitrary ascription which flies in the face of the *logical* challenge (and *regress*) of *infinite* divisibility.[27] To this extent, again, it is an idea which must be seen as giving way to that of *force*, and more specifically, as he argues – to his own conception of a 'monad' as the *unextended* centre of such energy. On the foregoing basis, therefore – and in conscious avoidance of difficulties – there is the challenge of Leibniz's key contention. In short, that the *monads* are 'the true atoms of nature; in a word ... the elements of things'.[28]

What may be seen from the above is the *immaterialism* of the Leibnizian position. To this must be added the fact of its *idealism* – though with this viewed as having a far more esoteric foundation than that of the *epistemologically* oriented tradition considered so far. Thus, in writing in direct opposition to both Cartesians and Newtonians/Lockeans, it is Leibniz's clear claim that the primary (*ontological*) *existent* is to be found, purely and simply, in, what he (*technically*) calls *perception*:

> Perception and what depends on it are *inexplicable by mechanical reasons*, that is, by figures and motions . . . This is the only thing – namely, perceptions and their changes – that can be found in simple substance. It is in this alone that the *internal actions* of simple substances can consist.[29]

With note that 'perception' in the ordinary sense, that is as it relates to human/animal intelligence, is taken by Leibniz as but a *mode* of the foregoing, there is, more urgently, the claim of another point. That is, that the *monads* – as conceived on the Leibnizian view as 'simple substance' and 'the true atoms of nature' – are in no way to be regarded as centres of merely *physical* energy; but rather, and whatever the difficulties – as 'units' of 'perceptual' activity; *mentalistic* 'entities' after the analogy of 'souls'.

The conclusion may be supplemented by mention of Leibniz's postulation of an ascending hierarchy of three classes of *monads*: (a) those of the 'bare' kind; (b) animal souls; and (c) rational souls/ spirits. Further, and with (a) to the fore – his theory of the *objects/things* of the *physical/common-sensical* world being constituted of 'aggregates' of *monads* of this rudimentary variety. With this, too – and in the light of the *theological* import of the previously noted *Theodicy* – there may be reference to the doctrine of each and every *monad* being an entelechy, *pre-ordained* by God at the miracle of Creation, with a two-fold capacity, namely (x) *perception* and (y) *appetition* – with (x) conceived as the ability to manifest a particular kind of 'perception' and (y) that of adjusting the *degree/intensity* of this potentiality to the constantly changing (and, once more, *preordained*) complexity of *monadic* interplay in *toto*. And, again, on the basis of such *pre-ordination* – his idea of 'every monad . . . [being] . . . a mirror of the universe in its own way'.[30] More fully – his claim to the whole course of *physical/common-sensical* reality being open, in principle, to complete *predictability* from the 'point of view' of any particular *monad*:

> Every body responds to everything which happens in the universe, so that he who sees all could read in each everything that happens everywhere, and, indeed, even what has happened and will happen, observing in the present all that is removed from it, whether in space or in time.[31]

Beyond these details, however, and more for the course of what is to follow, are a number of considerations relating, more specifically, to the terms of Leibniz's *epistemology*.

In this regard, there is the point, first, of his conception of 'bare' *monadic* interchange in the preceding sense as falling under, what he calls, *obscure/confused*, as opposed to, *clear/distinct*, 'perception'. That is, activity which, though *mental*, is, yet, to be regarded as taking place below the level of *consciousness/awareness* – and, to this extent, and in some way, as constituting the 'material' of the *physical/common-sensical* world. Secondly, there may be a highlighting of the *psychological* determination of the above as this is developed by Leibniz through the vocabulary of his *understanding–sensibility* dichotomy, namely with the former conceived as the 'faculty' of *clear/distinct* 'representation' – that is *concepts*; and the latter that of *obscure/confused* 'representation' – that is (*sensible*) *intuition*. Finally, and of most especial relevance for the later discussion of Kant, there may be reference to the Leibnizian teaching regarding (a) *space* and *time*, on the one hand, and (b) *causality*, together with such other *universal/structural* concepts as *substance, necessity*, etc., on the other. Thus, with respect to (a) – that these are to be seen as *concepts/constructs* derived by *understanding* through the (*logically* prior) apprehension of *things/objects*. And (b) – that these, as constituting the *formal/logical/defining* characteristics of *reality* as such, are to be conceived as having the quite distinctive status of, what he calls, *pure/intellectual* concepts. With the foregoing as grist, attention may be turned to more critically geared comment.

To begin, there is the fact that, despite the undoubted brilliance of the foregoing theory of the (*immaterial*) *monad*, the overall basis of the 'constructive'/*speculative* aspect of Leibniz's *idealism* is still to be seen as being exclusively *religious/theological* in determination;

that is, as lying, purely and simply, in what may be characterized as 'the *mental* activity of *God*'. As such, a clear parallel may be drawn with the outlook which, as has been seen, was later developed by Berkeley. To accept this overriding commonality, however, is not to overlook certain vital points of difference. For Berkeley – with his view of *God* as *Sustainer*, as well as *Creator/Cause* of the 'given'/objective (*perceptual*) order – there is the, already noted, consequence of the statements of *science* having a necessarily *descriptive/correlational* standing. In contrast, the Leibnizian stance – with its grounding in the idea of *Pre-established Harmony* – is one in which the whole course of nature is to be seen as representing a completely closed system of (*pre-ordained*) *causal/deductive* interrelations. With this, again, is the fact of the Berkeleyan position being forever open to the possibility of *miracles*; whereas, for Leibniz, there is, and can only be, the single great miracle of *Creation*.[32] At the same time – and, again, in the light of what has been said – the details of these remarks may be set against the significance of a broader consideration; namely the power of Hume's *scepticism/positivism* in its implicative rejection, not only of the Leibnizian conception of *God*, but, also, its entailing *determinism*. As a consequence, a deliberate circumscription may be imposed on the wider dimensions of the position in hand for the purpose of bringing into focus what is really of most importance for the main concern; that is, the strength of the 'minimal'/*critical* strain of Leibniz's thought in its (implicative) postulation – before the time of both Berkeley and Hume – of a thorough-going *phenomenalism*. In short, and arising from his negation of the *realism/materialism* of the Newtonian/Lockean outlook – it is the starkness of his claim to the ultimate status of the *physical/commonsensical* world being, in his own, frequently expressed, words, *phenomenon bene fundatum*.

With its obvious relevance, the conclusion may be supplemented by a number of considerations which relate, more specifically, to the epistemological legitimacy of Leibniz's associated (and *speculative*) theory of the (*immaterial*) *monad*. In full acceptance that it is an issue which, in a more extensive setting – and, as associated, most particularly, with the rise of the *logical positivist* movement – has come to assume central contemporary prominence, the object must be with remarks which, though not without interest for the wider debate, are more directly related to the main course of the present concern.[33]

Here, there is the point, at once, that strange though this conception might appear when set against the seeming simplicity of the Newtonian stance, it is certainly not such as to be open to any merely peremptory rejection. Thus, to the (*logical positivist*) charge of its deficiency in being purely *speculative* – and, to this extent, as lying beyond the possibility of (*empirical*) *validation* – there may be the immediate, if oblique, reply that so, no less, is the now 'household' and virtually unquestioned idea of the (*material*) *atom*. With this, too, is the fact of the Leibnizian position being asserted in clear recognition of the long-established *logical* incoherence of the latter. Further – it is in full deployment of the most advanced *theological/mathematical/scientific/philosophical* thought of the day. At the same time – and in complete acknowledgement of the theory's intellectual richness – there might still be the objection that, with its *religious/theological* grounding, it remains a vision which rises little above the *theologically* dominated age which saw its inception. One which, as belonging to, what might be taken as, 'old style' *metaphysical* thinking, has come to be entirely superseded by the relentless advance and heuristic success of the '*mathematical* philosophy' of Newton.

Broad in its scope, it is a consideration which may be countered, first – and, again, if only obliquely – with a point already made.[34] Namely that the acceptance by Newton of the Democritan idea of the (*material*) *atom* is hardly to be seen as being tied to any embracement by him of the anti-religious implications traditionally conjoined with this ancient doctrine; but rather, and uncompromisingly, to the strength of his (*personal*) conviction that it was a concept which could be assimilated to the needs of *religious* (Christian) orthodoxy, and in particular to the biblical story of *Creation*.[35] Indeed, as may be emphasized, the image of the Judæo-Christian God indulging his Will in the fabrication of the *physical/common-sensical* world is as fundamental to Newton as it is to Leibniz, with the real contention between the two being over the nature of the 'material' used in this Divine process. To this, moreover, may be added the fact of the role played by this thoroughly *unscientific* presupposition in the development of the Newtonian, no less than Leibnizian, concept of *universal necessity* – and, with this, the hotch-potch of presumptions which has come to usurp the thought of the modern world under the label of 'classical' (*scientific*) *realism/materialism*.[36]

Beyond the above, however – and as relating, more positively, to the *heuristic* importance of the *monadic* theory – are two final points which, in their elaboration, connect, full-circle, with the claim made at the outset regarding the doctrine's abiding significance for both *science* and *philosophy*.

In the first place there is the fact that, though originally set forth on *religious/philosophical* grounds, the Leibnizian conception of the (*immaterial*) *monad* has the status of effectively constituting the basis of modern (*physical*) *field* theory. The issue is one which, in its development, may be taken as turning, most decisively, on the work of the philosopher/mathematician/scientist, Roger Joseph Boscovich (1711–87), and the fame of his *mathematical* demonstration of a system of (*physical*) *immaterialism* in place of the crude *realism/materialism* of the Newtonian outlook. This said, it must not go without mention that Kant, too, has a position of prominence in the pioneering of this radically new conception of 'matter', as did the English astronomer and geologist, John Michell (1724–93); as well as the names of Giambattista Vico (1668–1744) and Emanuel Swedenborg (1688–1772). Thus, by way of perspective, in the words of L. L. Whyte:

> It is instructive to observe in retrospect that this revolution in thinking was not an arbitrary flash in a single mind, but an apparently inescapable step which thinkers of varied kinds were being compelled to take during the eighteenth century as the most natural advance from the naive atomism ... of, Democritus, Epicurus, Lucretius, Gassendi, Boyle, Newton ... A sequence of six thinkers: Vico, Leibniz, Swedenborg, Boscovich, Michell, Kant were all moving in parallel.[37]

In restricting the discussion to the main figures of Boscovich and Kant, the significance of the latter may be left for later remark, with the concern for the moment being exclusively with the more fully worked out position of the former. More specifically, concern will centre on the so-called *kinematic* theory of the 'atom' which, as promulgated by Boscovich in his widely acclaimed *Theoria Philosophiae Naturalis* (1758), came to exert a crucial influence on the mind of Michael Faraday (1791–1867), and, hence, on that of Maxwell.[38]

It is a theory which, though largely forgotten in the twentieth century pre-occupation with experimental advance, remains, to this day, the most sustained of all attempts to offer a comprehensive delineation of the structure of 'atomic' reality. It is one, moreover, which, in itself, brings to the fore the *quantum* paradox of even venturing on the use of the terms 'atom'/'particle'/'entity' in this regard. For, whilst, on the one hand, giving unequivocal endorsement to the Newtonian postulation of an imperceptible *micro-physical* 'realm', Boscovich, notwithstanding, follows Leibniz in dismissing the notion of the (*material*) *atom* as nonsensical. At the same time – and in giving a *physical* twist to the Leibnizian doctrine of the (*immaterial*) *monad* – he proclaims, instead, the (*mathematical*) conception of, what he himself calls, a *punctum*, or, what, in present-day terms, would be labelled a '*point*-particle'; namely, that of a (*logically* indivisible) *punctiform* 'entity' possessing the (*physical*) characteristics of spatial position, mobility, inertia and various inherent forces of attraction and repulsion, but, no (*spatial*) *extension*. Leaving aside the vexed (*quantum*) question of whether such *puncta* – or, again, what Boscovich calls, *prima elementa* – may truly be regarded as *physical*, there is, more immediality, the broader dimension of the Boscovichian scheme.[39] That is – his (*mathematical*) portrayal of the *macro-physical* world as being, in some sense, the product of shimmering configurations of constantly interacting and continuously interrelated '*point*-centres' of *micro-physical* energy. Indispensable to modern physics, it is a conception which brings to the fore, also, the fact that, for Boscovich, no less than for Leibniz – and as against the Newtonian outlook – *space* and *time* are to be seen as being *relational* in nature. Further – that , in its ultimate standing, the *physical/common-sensical* world is to be viewed as being *phenomenal/ideal*. Overriding these details, however, is the main conclusion which, is that, as arising from the rejection by Leibniz of the *realism/materialism* of Newton, a clear line of development may be drawn from his theory of the (*immaterial*) *monad*, through Boscovich, to the revolutionary *quantum* advances of the present century.

With this – and turning to the second point – there is the no less important fact of the theory having a place of landmark significance in the discovery of the epoch-making, if, still, nebulous idea of the *unconscious*. It is a matter which, in its association with the remaining topic of (C) above, that is *innateness*, may be approached through prefactory, but, necessary, attention to the wider circumstances of its setting.

Of vital consequence for the terms of the present endeavour, it is a conception whose cultural impact is nowhere better summarized than by the preceding writer, Whyte, in another of his works:

> The European and Western ideal of the self-aware individual confronting destiny with his own indomitable will and sceptical reason as the only factors on which he can rely is perhaps the noblest aim which has yet been accepted by any community. This conception of the self-conscious person gave ancient ideals a new, characteristically European *élan* and, through its myriad expressions has been the greatest single influence molding thought and behaviour during the last three hundred years. Exact science is one of its expressions;[40]

And, in continuing:

> But it has become evident that this ideal was a moral mistake and an intellectual error, for it exaggerates the ethical, philosophical and scientific importance of the *awareness* of the *individual*. And one of the main factors exposing this inadequate ideal was the discovery of *unconscious* mind. That is why the idea of the *unconscious* is the supreme revolutionary conception of the modern age: it undermines the traditional foundations of Europe and the West ... For, in a historical sense, the idea is anti-Classical, anti-European and anti-Enlightenment.[41]

The point, with all its immense implications, may be amplified by a number of further remarks.

In this regard, enough has been said for immediate retreat from any attachment to the, still, widely prevalent, presumption of the discovery having its roots in the *clinical* studies of Freud. What must be accepted, rather, is that this famed achievement, with its close identification of the *unconscious* with *sexuality*, is itself to be seen as but a specialized outcome of more than a century's earlier effort in the *practical* and, often, seemingly *thaumaturgical*, exploration/exploitation of *mind* as an 'entity' in its own right; that is, endeavours which, as falling, most especially, under the labels of 'mesmeric' and 'spiritualistic', came to attain, albeit, reluctant, *scientific* attention through the climactic events of the Charcot–Bernheim controversy, on the one hand, and the establishment of the Society for Psychical Research, on the other. At the same time, there is, also, the scope of the *theoretical* evolution of the idea.

Three main points may be offered in this regard, with each,

again, resting on the authority of Whyte. First – his assessment of the chronological span of the foregoing development:

> The discovery of the unconscious by self-conscious man occupied some two centuries, roughly from 1700 to 1900 . . . *The idea of unconscious mental processes was, in many of its aspects, conceivable around 1700, topical around 1800, and became effective around 1900,* thanks to the imaginative efforts of a large number of individuals of varied interests in many lands.[42]

Secondly – the perspicacity of his insight into the immense, if unwitting, contribution of Descartes to this process:

> Until an attempt had been made . . . to choose *awareness* as the defining characteristic of an independent mode of being called mind, there was no occasion to invent the idea of *unconscious* mind as a provisional correction of that choice. It is only after Descartes that we find first, the idea and then the term, 'unconscious mind' entering European thought . . . It was the prestige of Cartesian ideas that created the 'problem of the unconscious' . . . Descartes, by his definition of *mind* as *awareness*, may be said to have provoked, as reaction, the European discovery of the *unconscious* mind.[43]

Thirdly – his conclusion respecting the emergence of the actual term 'unconscious':

> The available surveys suggest that *Unbewusstsein* and *bewusstlos* (in meanings close to those now current) were first used by E. Platner in 1776, and these or similar terms were made popular by Goethe, Schiller and Schelling between 1780 and 1820. The word 'unconscious' as an adjective (with the same meaning) appears in English in 1751, and more frequently after 1800, for example, in the writings of Wordsworth and Coleridge. By 1850 both adjective and noun were extensively used in Germany and were moderately common in England.[44]

With a highlighting of the period 1700–80 for the idea's gestation, as, also, the overwhelmingly German setting of its birth, there may be a return to the main point of the wider strains of Leibniz's parentage.

Here there may be reference to two developments of the second quarter of the eighteenth century arising from the circumstances surrounding the dissemination of the *monadic* theory. First, the fact, as it transpired, of the establishment of a German/Wolffian school of so-called *faculty* psychology, centring on the claim that the newly discovered (mental) 'realm' was open to eventual and exhaustive understanding through no more than an extension of *empirical/causal* reasoning. Secondly, the fact, as it followed, of the emergence of an opposing school led by the now little known but then prominent theologian/philosopher C. A. Crusius (1715–75), with his challenge that the idea was to be seen as entailing an unanalysable *vitalism/spontaneity*, or 'Grundkraft'; and, to this extent, as lying beyond the bounds of *scientific* methodology.[45] With this, too, there may be emphasis on the vigour of the debate. Thus, as indicated in the firmness of Kant's own early grasp of the issue:

> The field of our *obscure* ideas is immeasurable, while our clear ideas are only the infinitesimally few points on this map that lie open to consciousness: our mind is like an immense *map* with only a few places *illuminated*. This fact can inspire us with admiration for our own being.[46]

Further – in the intensity of its continuation into the 1770s with the famed figures of J. G. Hamann (1730–88), the 'Magus of the North', and Kant's most brilliant student, J. G. Herder (1744–1803) championing the cause of Crusius; and the *faculty* school of Wolff reaching a peak in 1777 with the publication by the philosopher/ psychologist, N. N. Tetens (1736?–1807), of his celebrated *Philosophische Versuche*.[47] With this latter consideration, in particular, of foremost concern, there is the reflexivity of the point of main intent. More specifically – the fact of this new impetus to the idea in hand arising from an event which, over and above the influence of the *monadic* theory itself, is, again, to be seen as turning on the name of Leibniz; in short, the publication in 1765, sixty years after it was written, and half a century after the author's death, of Leibniz's first full-scale philosophical work – his *New Essays on the Human Understanding*.[48]

Originally conceived as a point-by-point response to Locke's own renowned *Essay* and, then, graciously set aside by Leibniz on the occasion of the former's death in 1704, it is a work whose philosophical freshness – as set against the obscurities of the

Wolffian interpretation of his ideas – brought to the world of the German Enlightenment the burst of 'a minor Leibniz renaissance'.[49] One, moreover, whose precision of attack on the ambiguities in Locke's use of the term *idea* came to exert a profound influence on the eclectic mind of Kant during the 'silent decade' of 1770–80 when, to the exclusion of virtually all else, he was engaged in the task of writing the *Critique*.[50] With the above in mind, it remains merely to bring to the fore the work's relevance in, what, certainly, for present purposes, may be seen as its two most basic respects.

First – the fact of it containing the, generally agreed, première *scientific* expression of the idea under discussion, namely as given in the crude, but still *quantitative*, terms of *'petites (minute) perceptions'*:

> To give a clearer idea of these minute perceptions which we are unable to pick out from the crowd, I like to use the example of the roaring noise of the sea which impresses itself on us when we are standing on the shore. To hear this noise as we do, we must hear the parts which make up this whole, that is the noise of each wave, although each of these little noises makes itself known only when combined confusedly with all the others, and would not be noticed if the wave which made it were by itself. We must be affected slightly by the notion of this wave, and have some perception of each of these noises, however faint they may be; otherwise there would be no perception of a hundred thousand waves, since a hundred thousand nothings cannot make something.[51]

Secondly – and in returning to the topic of *innateness* – the leap of the work in using precisely this idea as the basis for a division between two radically different conceptions of (virginal) *mind*.

Thus, there is the ring of the words of Leibniz as a voice from the past in countering Locke's own peremptory but long prevailing dismissal of the preceding notion:

> Our disagreements concern points of some importance. There is the question whether the soul in itself is completely blank like a writing tablet on which nothing has yet been written – *a tabula rasa* – as Aristotle and the author of the *Essay* maintain, and whether everything which is inscribed there comes solely from

the senses and experience; or whether the soul inherently contains the sources of various notions and doctrines which external objects merely rouse up on suitable occasions, as I believe and as do Plato and even the Schoolmen;[52]

And, further, in projecting his opposing vision of the matter:

I have used the analogy of a veined block of marble, as opposed to an entirely *homogeneous* block of marble, or to a *blank* tablet – what the philosophers call a *tabula rasa*. For if the soul were like such a blank tablet then truths would be in us as the shape of Hercules is in the piece of marble when the marble is entirely neutral as to whether it assumes this shape or some other. However, if there were veins in the block which marked out the shape of Hercules rather than other shapes, then that block would be more determined to that shape and Hercules would be *innate* in it, in a way, *even though labour would be required to expose the veins and polish them into clarity, removing everything that prevents their being seen.*[53]

With its intimation of *mind* itself being the source of such *universal/ pure/structural* concepts as *substance, causality, necessity*, and so on – or, what, with Kant, was to become established as the (*philosophical*) *a priori* – the point is one which may be conveniently left for continuation in the following and concluding segment. More for the present is the fact that entirely enough has been said for a full demonstration, not only of (a) the thoroughness of Leibniz's thought in its rejection of the *realist/materialist* presumptions of Newton/Locke; but, also, and in going beyond both Berkeley and Hume, (b) the massiveness of its contribution to, what is, perhaps, the most momentous discovery in the whole evolution of the race – the (*empirical*) *reality* of *mind*.

IV

With the circumstances of the contemporary *quantum* debate still to the fore, attention may be turned, finally, to the culminating significance of the self-styled 'revolution' in *philosophy* wrought by Kant (1724–1804) in his monumental *Critique of Pure Reason* (1781, 1787).[54] It is a matter which, for present purposes – and, again, with necessary simplification – may be developed through an amplification of the vital distinction already noted between *appearances/representations/phenomena* and *things-in-themselves*.

By way of approach, there may be reference to the influences which, as Kant himself came to recall, led him away from his early adherence to the *realism/materialism* of Newton/Locke to the 'Copernican-style' scale of his (Critical) rejection of this outlook. There is, first, the fulsomeness of his tribute to the importance, in this respect, of Hume's treatment of the *causal* issue, namely in the famous words of the *Prolegomena*:

> I openly confess my recollection of David Hume was the very thing which many years ago first interrupted my dogmatic slumber and gave my investigations in the field of speculative philosophy a quite new direction.[55]

At the same time, there must also be mention that this is not the only reference by Kant to factors which he took as being antipathetical to his 'dogmatic slumber'. For there is the testament, too, that his awakening came through, what he calls, the '*antinomy/antinomies* of pure reason'. That is, a singular, and culturally crucial set of four pairs of *mutually exclusive*, but, in each case, *unverifiable* propositions deriving ultimately from the paradoxical nature of the concepts of *space* and *time*.[56] Thus, in a late letter to his long-time correspondent, Christian Garve (1742–98):

> It was the *antinomy of pure reason* – 'the world has a beginning, it has no beginning, and so on,' right up to the 4th . . . that is what first aroused me from my dogmatic slumber and drove me to the critique of reason itself.[57]

There is no contradiction in these statements. What must be accepted, rather, is that the former is to be seen as being already embraced by the latter. Moreover – that, in the sequence of their chronological impact, they are to be viewed as anticipating the same line of development later followed by Born and Heisenberg in their move to the 'Copenhagen Interpretation'. It is a consideration which may be demonstrated more fully.

There may be remark, at once, that Kant's discovery of the *antinomies* – or, more specifically, the two relating, most directly, to *space* and *time* (that is the two which, in the *Critique*, he came to call the *mathematical*, as opposed to the *dynamical*)[58] – took place in 1769, a year which, as he himself later recalls, 'gave me a great light'.[59] Further – that this discovery was bound up with the renewal of interest in Leibniz which followed the posthumous publication, in 1765, of his *New Essays*. With this, too, is the fact of this influence constituting the crux of the solution to the above which Kant came to proclaim in his *Inaugural Dissertation* of 1770 on the occasion of his appointment to the Chair at Königsberg.[60]

The matter is one which, in its broader dimensions, may be seen as turning on, no more and no less than, the already noted, vastness of Leibniz's contribution to the idea of *mind* as an 'entity' in itself. More specifically, however, is the fact of its basis lying in a drastic revision by Kant of the Leibnizian teaching regarding *understanding/sensibility*. Thus, as Kant came to enunciate, this division is, in no way to be taken, with Leibniz, as being simply one of *degree*, namely as in the terms of the (*epistemological*) dichotomy between: (a) *clear/distinct* and (b) *obscure/confused* 'representations', but rather, in the (*psychological*) terms of *kind* – with (x) *understanding* conceived as *activity/spontaneity* in the *generation* of *concepts*; and (y) *sensibility* as *passivity* in the *reception* of (*sensible*) *intuition*. To this was added a radically new view of *space* and *time* – more specifically, that these are to be regarded, not, following Leibniz, as ('clear') *concepts/constructs* arising from *understanding*, but instead as invariant characteristics of (*sensible*) *intuition* deriving from *sensibility*, that is, in the terms of his later vocabulary, as *forms of sensibility*. To this extent, as Kant came to conclude, the (*mathematical*) *antinomies* were open to being seen in a completely new light. Far from being contradictions in the ordinary (*logical*) sense, they were, in their true determination, *inherently* irreconcilable statements having their origin in the *intrinsic* nature of *mind/sensibility* as such.

At the same time, there is, also, another aspect of the *Dissertation* which needs to be brought to the fore. For, whilst, on the one hand, asserting his revolutionary teaching with respect to *space* and *time*, Kant – significantly enough in the current context – continued to subscribe, in all essential respects, to a *realist* view of *objects/things*. In particular, in this connexion, is the strength of his adherence to the position of Leibniz regarding the so-called *pure/intellectual* concepts – that is *substance, causality, necessity*, and so on. More specifically, that these *structural/limiting* characteristics of *objectivity* are to be seen as being (l) *constitutive* of the whole reach of *supersensible*, no less than, *sensible, reality*; and (m) *knowable* through the function of *understanding*. The consideration may be taken as bringing into view the second figure of the present concern, Hume, and in particular the *anti-metaphysical* stance of the *Enquiry* – a work which Kant had come to know through a German translation of the mid-1750s; and which, as all the evidence suggests, was the sole, if, still, important, Humean influence on him up to the time in hand. With the foregoing in mind, though with the details of subsidiary intent, there may be a highlighting of the duality of claims made by Kant in the *Dissertation*. On the one hand – that the problem of the (*mathematical*) *antinomies* was solved through his teaching of the *ideality* of *space* and *time*; on the other hand – that the traditional pretension of *philosophy* to the search for 'real' (*metaphysical*) *knowledge* was retained through the Leibnizian doctrine of the *pure/intellectual* concepts.

The inherent instability of these two contentions was to be exposed in little more than a year through the second wave of the influence of Hume as represented in the power of his *causal* theory. As to the circumstances of this impact there is the quite uncontroversial point of these arising in the first quarter of 1772 through Kant's reading, in translation, of a popular writing by the Scottish philosopher James Beattie (1735–1803).[61] It was a work which, in the event – and in denigration of Hume – contained precisely the passages from the early and 'dead-born' *Treatise* that were necessary for an appreciation of the true extent of his *causal* challenge.[62] As to scale – this, too, may be the subject of easy remark. For whereas, only weeks earlier, Kant had made the confident prediction that he was now ready 'to bring out a "Critique of Pure Reason"' and that he 'should be in a position to publish it within three months',[63] the eventual appearance of this work was to cost him the span of nearly a decade's further labour. To summarize, therefore – and in supplementation of a point already made – there is the position as given by Norman Kemp Smith: 'Thus, at last, by a circuitous path, through the quotations of an adversary, Hume awakened philosophy from its dogmatic slumber, and won for his argument the appreciation which, despite its cogency it had for thirty years so vainly demanded.'[64]

Turning to the outcome of the above, as reflected in the argument of the *Critique*, there is the immediate fact of Kant's uncompromising endorsement of the main thrust of Hume's teaching – his outright rejection of the *causal* principle, 'every *event* has a *cause*', as having any *realist/materialist* standing. With this, too, is the no less important consideration of his uncompromising acceptance of the force of this contention in demolishing one of the main pillars of his last published work, the *Dissertation*, namely his claim to the *pure/intellectual* concepts (with *causality* prominent among them) constituting the key to 'real' *metaphysical/supersensible* knowledge. At the same time – and as against Hume – there is, notwithstanding, the clarity of his insight that there remained the problem of the *phenomenal* 'reality' of the concept. It is, as he came to maintain, a challenge which, at its most dramatic, is demonstrated in the incomparable glory of the Newtonian system, with its spectacular deployment of, what, from the contemporary point of view, would be called, the *hypothetico-deductive* method, as opposed to that of simple *induction*. More definitively, however, is the strength of his appeal to the 'existence'/'knowability' of the principle as one of the *pure/intellectual* concepts – or, as they now come to be called, following Aristotle, *categories*.

Thus, as Kant argues, the idea is one which, in its ultimate starkness, is to be seen as a *formal/limiting/structural conditions* of the most ontologically basic of all (human) conceptions, namely that of an *object/thing* as such. Further, and following from this – of (*physical/common-sensical*) *experience*; of *discursive* (*linguistic*) *representation*; and, indeed, of (*human*) *thought/reason* itself. With this, too, is the press of his claim that the implicative extent of Hume's treatment of the *causal* issue is such as to embrace, also, the other *categories*. For, as *conjointly* constitutive of the skeletal (*logical*) structure of *objectivity*, they are to be viewed as being *analytically/ necessarily* interrelated with each other. Finally, for the moment, and most importantly, is the point, as seen by Kant, that neither individually nor collectively are the *categories* to be conceived as having any *meaning/significance* in their own right, but instead, only in necessary relation to the conditions of *space* and *time*.

With this, therefore – and as set against the position of the *Dissertation* – there is the culminating and two-fold step made by Kant in the *Critique*. First, his postulation that (a) the *categories*, or *pure concepts of understanding*, no less than, (b) the *forms* of *sensibility*, that is *space* and *time*, are to be regarded as functions of (specifically *human*) *mind*. Secondly, his conclusion that *physical/common-sensical* experience, as arising from a *conceptual/reflexive* duality of (a)/(b), is to be conceived as being, in its ultimate (*philosophical*) nature, *relational/perceptual/ideal* – in short, as *appearance/representation/ phenomenon*, as opposed to, what, with the Democritan/Newtonian model in mind, may be, figuratively, called, *thing-in-itself*.

With a return, in this way, to the vital significance of the concept of *appearance* for the Critical position, there may be the immediate supplement of a consideration already sufficiently emphasized in the earlier discussion of Berkeley, namely that the term, as used by Kant, is in no sense to be construed as, in any way, casting doubt on the *empirical* reality of the *physical/common-sensical* world; but rather, and only, as asserting, at a different (*logical*) level of discourse, the *complementarity* of its *philosophical* ideality. Beyond this, however, and more for the course of what is to follow, is the pivotal function of the idea – in its equation with (*perceptual*) *experience* – as a link between (x) Kant's theory of (*unconscious*) *mind*, or 'transcendental' philosophy and (y) his theory of *knowledge*. Thus, as cryptically conveyed in the opening words of the *Critique*:

> There can be no doubt that all our *knowledge* begins with *experience* ... In the order of time, therefore, we have no *knowledge* antecedent to *experience*, and with *experience* all our *knowledge* begins. But though all our *knowledge* begins with *experience*, it does not follow that it all arises out of *experience*. (*BI*, my italics)

The implications of the passage may be developed more fully with the terms of (x) and (y) being considered in turn.

To begin, there may be an amplificatory note on the *categories*. Thus, that, as constituting the issue which, as Kant says, cost him his 'greatest labour', these are to be seen as being honed by him into a list of twelve, equally divided under the four heads of (i) *number*, (ii) *degree*, (iii) *relations* and (iv) *modes*. Moreover, and with an importance which will be taken up later – into a further dichotomy of (a) the *mathematical*, and (b) the *dynamical*; with (i) and (ii) falling under (a), and (iii) and (iv) under (b).[65] With this, too – and, again, as a matter for later remark – there is a point relating to *sensibility* in its previously mentioned function as the (*unconscious/transcendental*) *receptor* of an undifferentiated 'content' of so-called (*sensible*) *intuition*; that is, the fact of this entailing a decisive rejection by Kant of any suggestion of (human) *mind*, as it were, '[producing] its objects in so far as *existence* is concerned' (A92 B125). More broadly, however, there is the scope of the theory itself.

Here, there is the consideration, at once, of this being most prominently instantiated in Kant's famous doctrine of *inner sense*. More specifically, his pioneering model of the generative activity of *(unconscious/transcendental) mind* as this is unabashedly, and consciously/necessarily, drawn by him in the *causal/faculty* terms of, what was identified earlier as, Wolffian/Tetensian *psychology*, with the original *understanding–sensibility* base being supplemented by (x) the postulation of the mediating function of a third faculty, that is *imagination*; and (y) a delineation of the complexity of *intuition/ category/spatio-temporality* interchange under the title of *schematism*. In deliberately setting aside the detailed intricacy, not to say, inherent elegance, of the model, the concern must be with two points made by Kant in juxtaposing the extent of its challenge against the claims, in the same regard, of his noted contemporary, Tetens. First, that, as developed throughout, on the basis of *conceptual* principles, it is to be seen as having *objective*, as opposed to merely *speculative*, validity (A xvi–xvii).[66] Secondly, and notwithstanding – that, as elaborated, purely and simply in the *causal* terms of *faculty* psychology, it is, yet, to be regarded as being *inherently/necessarily* inadequate to the task of capturing the ultimate essence of *(human) consciousness/awareness* as such; that is, and no matter to what degree of sophistication it might be carried – as ineluctably giving way, in the last resort, to the postulation, at a different *logical* level, of what, in the earlier reference to Crusius/ Hamann/Herder, was characterized as, an unanalysable *spontaneity/vitalism*, or, what Kant himself calls, *(transcendental) apperception*. To the foregoing extent, therefore, there is Kant's summary of the overriding features of his theory of *(unconscious/transcendental) mind* as expressed in his clear, if oblique, response to the position of Tetens: '[Whereas] in systems of psychology *inner sense* is ... commonly regarded as being identical with the faculty of *apperception* ... we have carefully distinguished [between the two]' (B 153).[67]

The conclusion is one which, as already noted, is effectively echoed in the present-century debate between Freud and Jung over the *unconscious*, with the exclusively *causal* approach of the former being met by the latter's appeal, also, to wider, *non-causal/ acausal* considerations. With this, too – and as instantiating the insight that the problem of *consciousness/awareness* as such is to be seen as being of a different *order* from those arising *within the context* of this reality – there is the vividness of its portrayal in the contemporary words of Schrödinger:

[Physical experience] is a marvel – than which only one is greater; one that, if intimately connected with it, yet lies on a different plane. I mean the fact that we, whose total being is entirely based on a marvellous interplay of this very kind, yet possess the power of acquiring considerable knowledge about it. I think it is possible that this knowledge may advance to little short of a complete understanding – of the first marvel. The second may well be beyond human understanding.[68]

Returning, however, to the main discussion, there may be a switch of attention to the reflexivity of its significance for Kant's theory of *knowledge*.

To reiterate a point already made, there may be remark that Kant, like Plato, two millennia earlier, postulates, what may be characterized as, a 'two-world' view. That is to say, a duality of a *sensible* (*perceptual*) world, on the one hand, and a *supersensible* 'reality' on the other; with the latter conceived as being, in some sense, the ground of the former. At the same time – and with a reiteration of the Kantian position being associated with the vital new discovery of the *unconscious* – there must, also, be a highlighting of a radical *epistemological* difference between the two outlooks. For Plato, with his time-honoured stance, the sole 'objects' of ('real') *knowledge* are to be seen as belonging to the *supersensible* 'realm' of the *Forms* or *Ideas*. For Kant, in contrast, *knowledge* is to be viewed as being necessarily restricted to the sphere of *appearances*; with the rider that 'nothing whatsoever can be asserted of the *thing in itself*, which may underlie these *appearances*' (A49 B66, my italics).

With this – and in accepting the need to develop the remainder of the discussion in relation to the challenge of Hume – there is the immediate point of the Kantian position, no less than the Humean, entailing a thoroughgoing *empiricism*; that is to say, the claim that *all* knowledge is to be seen as arising, in the last resort, from the 'given' world of *spatio-temporally* interrelated *objects* and *events*. So, also, a radical *positivism* with regard to *meaning*:

If knowledge is to have objective reality, that is, to relate to an object, and is to acquire meaning and significance in respect to it, the object must be capable of being in some manner given. Otherwise the concepts are empty; through them we have indeed thought, but in this thinking we have really known nothing; we have merely played with representations. (A155–6 B194–5)

To this, again, may be added the fact that the idea of (*transcendental*) *apperception* is to be seen as entailing, as in the case of Hume, an absolute and necessary *agnosticism/scepticism* with regard to the *ultimate* basis of human *experience/existence*. Going beyond these similarities, however – and as relating, more specifically, to Kant's theory of *inner sense* – there is another consideration. In short, that, on the basis of this, still exemplary, analysis, Kant offers, what, in the event, amounts to a much more exhaustive classification of *knowledge* than that set forth, thirty years earlier, by Hume in the terms of his bare dichotomy between *relations of ideas* and *matters of fact*.

Falling as it does under the famed title of the *analytic-synthetic* distinction, the issue is one which – not least for the scale of its bearing on the *quantum* debate – has come to exert a dominating influence over whole fields of twentieth century thought. To this extent, it is a matter which is clearly open to most fruitful pursuit through the circumstances of its present-day setting. With this, however, must go two ancillary considerations. First, that, though originally drawn in conscious opposition to the claim of Hume, the division is, yet, to be seen as being the subject of subsequent and virulent counter-thrust by the latter, through the fact of its adoption, for certain set and limited purposes, as a central tenet of the modern *logical positivist* school. Secondly, that, in this *logical positivist* re-assertion of the Humean dichotomy, there is, notwithstanding, the consideration that the vocabulary which came to be used was, not that of Hume, but, of Kant. This said, and as representing, what may well be regarded as, the most far-reaching of all contemporary philosophical concerns, the discussion may be brought to a close through a highlighting of its significance in the current regard.

With the details, again, of subsidiary intent, there may, to open, be the offer of Kant's own delineation of his use of the terms *analytic* and *synthetic*. Thus, as given in the context of his insight that all *knowledge* claims are reducible, in the last resort, to the logical structure of *categorical*, that is *subject-predicate*, assertions, he states:

In all judgments in which the relation of a subject to the

predicate is thought (I take into consideration affirmative judgments only, the subsequent application to negative judgments being easily made), this relation is possible in two different ways. Either the predicate B belongs to the subject A, as something which is (covertly) contained in this concept A; or B lies outside the concept A, although it does indeed stand in connection with it. In the one case I entitle the judgment *analytic*, in the other *synthetic*. *Analytic* judgments (affirmative) are therefore those in which the connection of the predicate with the subject is thought through *identity*; those in which this connection is thought *without identity* should be entitled *synthetic*. (A6 B10–A7 B11, my italics)[69]

On this basis, there is, what – certainly, *prima facie* – amounts to a clear point of connexion with the earlier dichotomy of Hume, namely (a) that an *analytic* proposition, no less than a (Humean) *relation of ideas*, is to be conceived as being *a priori* in the sense of asserting a *necessary/logical* relation between the subject and predicate terms; and, hence, one whose *truth* or *falsity* is determinable by appeal to the *principle of contradiction* alone. Concomitantly – (b) that a *synthetic* proposition, just as a (Humean) *matter of fact*, is a statement asserting a *non-analytic* relation between its terms; and following from this, one whose *truth* value is determinable only by appeal to the *facts* of the case. At the same time, and more immediately, there is, also, the *logical positivist* formulation of the same division, namely that (x) an *analytic* proposition is one whose negation involves a *contradiction in terms*; and (y) a *synthetic* proposition, one which is always open to *falsification* through the circumstances of *(factual) experience*.

Pursuing the consideration, further, and with regard, first, to (y), there may be mention of a point which will be obvious enough from what has been said. Thus, that, as with Hume's *matters of fact*, these are to be seen as falling exclusively under the label of *empirical* generalizations. That is, statements of the form 'All swans are white'. In other words, propositions whose mode of derivation is, purely and simply, that of *inductive* enumeration and whose *epistemological* standing no more than that of *probability* claims. Beyond this, however, and, again, as being fully consonant with the earlier position of Hume, is the *logical positivist* stance regarding (x). More specifically, that these are to be conceived as being *definitional* in nature and, to this extent, as being reducible, one and all, to the conditions of (*discursive*) *language*. Further, as belonging, most particularly, to one or other of two main, and, seemingly, radically diverse, classes. On the one hand, and quite uncontroversially, *tautologies* – as represented by such 'trivialities' as 'All bachelors are unmarried males'. On the other, and much more contentiously, the *axiomatic* foundations of *mathematics* – as instantiated, most basically, in the *arithmetical* assertion '1 + 1 = 2' (or '1 + 2 = 3', and so on) and the (Euclidean) *geometrical* postulates, for example, 'The shortest distance between two points is a straight line'/'Any three points must be seen as lying in a plane'.[70] With this, therefore, and as being of most direct relevance for the course of what is to follow, are the two key *knowledge* tenets of the modern *logical positivist* school. On the one hand: (a) that the whole vast range of the propositions of *science* are to be seen as being encompassed by the single *epistemological* type of *empirical/probability* generalisations. On the other hand: (b) that *mathematics*, as resting on *axioms*, is to be viewed as being, in its final determination, but a mode, like the former, of *discursive/linguistic* expression.

In turning to the way in which these, essentially Humean, claims are met by Kant, there is the point, at once, of his outright rejection of (b) – not, however, through any denial of *arithmetic* and (Euclidean) *geometry* being *axiomatic*; nor, of both disciplines being *deductively* developed from the latter in accordance with the *principle of contradiction*. But rather through the fact, as seen by him, of the *axioms*, in each case, being, not merely *verbal*, but, *synthetic*. More specifically – of the *axioms* arising from an incontrovertible, if minimal, content or subject matter which, in a unique and highly distinctive manner is open to display and inspection through the medium of, what he calls, *pure intuition*; or, what, for present purposes, may be characterized as 'imagination' or the 'mind's eye', namely, as in the case of *arithmetic* – the *mental* portrayal of a dot (or, even, a bare sensation, for example a pin-prick) as successively replicated in (*mental*) *time*; and, as with (Euclidean) *geometry* – the *mental* representation of a line or lines as *statically* extended in (*mental*) *space*. To this extent, the point that may be brought to the fore is that, for Kant – and in opposition to the stance of Hume and the *logical positivists* – the *axioms/definitions* of (pure) *mathematics* are to be conceived as arising from *mentally* 'picturable' entities, that is dots, lines, which are *intuitions* in their own right, and not simply representations *of*, or derivations *from*, physical things.[71] In other words – as constituting a content which is *pure* in the sense of being *logically* independent of the conditions of *physical/common-sensical* experience.[72]

At the same time, and whilst being taken as *synthetic* in this sense, there is, notwithstanding, the fact that such *axioms* are also conceived by Kant as being *a priori*; that is, as being, like *analytic* propositions, beyond the possibility of *falsification*. This, however, is not, as with the latter, through any necessary relation to the demands of (*discursive/public*) *language*; but instead, and more basically, for the reason of the *concepts* through which they are expressed being *co-extensive in intension* with the (*pure*) *intuitions* from which they take their rise; as for instance, the fact of the assertion '$1 + 1 = 3$ (i.e. $1 + 1 + 1$)' being negated by what is *universally* and *necessarily* 'picturable' in the 'mind's eye', or *pure intuition*, as '$1 + 1 = 2$ (i.e. $1 + 1$)'.[73] To summarize, therefore, there is the conclusion that, on the view in hand, the *axioms* of (pure) *mathematics* are to be seen as being both *synthetic* and *a priori*; in short, that they fall under the distinctively Kantian head of the 'synthetic *a priori*'.

With Kant, in this respect, being the forerunner of the contemporary *intuitionist* school of the discipline, attention may be turned to the broader dimensions of his formulation of the *analytic–synthetic* distinction. That is, his classification of *knowledge* as this is conceived in its more general mode of relating, not only to (a) the conditions of (*physical/common-sensical*) *experience*, but also to (b), those of (*discursive/public*) *language*.

Thus, and with regard to *analytic* propositions, there is the immediate fact of these being taken by Kant as extending well beyond the range of mere *tautologies* to embrace, also, assertions of the kind 'All bodies are extended' (A7 B11); that is statements which, though *analytic* in the sense of the subject term already instantiating that of the predicate, are, yet, to be regarded as genuinely *explicative*. Indeed, following from this, and vital to the extension of *knowledge*: 'A great, perhaps, the greatest, part of the business of our reason consists in *analysis* of the *concepts* which we already have of *objects*' (A5 B9, my italics).[74] Beyond this, and with regard to the ontologically more fundamental range of propositions which are *ampliative*, that is *synthetic*, in nature, there is – and quite uncontentiously – Kant's full and necessary acceptance of the class of the *empirical*; or, what he himself, alternatively, calls the 'synthetic *a posteriori*'. Moreover – of the illustration which he gives of such propositions being one whose *falsification* has come to be the subject of dramatic public demonstration through the circumstances of television portrayals of current space technology; namely (and as set against the *analytic* proposition 'All bodies are extended') the *inductive* generalisation 'All bodies are heavy' (A7 B11). At the same time, and in going beyond the Humean/*logical positivist* position, there is, also, the claim of Kant to another division of the (*discursive*) *synthetic*, namely the 'synthetic *a priori*'. In other words, *discursive* propositions which, though *synthetic* in the sense of being derived from the (*factual*) conditions of *physical/common-sensical* experience, are, yet, to be viewed as being beyond the possibility of (*empirical*) *falsification*.

With bare mention of such propositions, for Kant, being rooted in, and expressive of, the *formal/limiting/structural* functions of (*unconscious/transcendental*) *mind*, there is, more immediately, the interrelation of two other considerations. First, the fact of their classification under the heads of (x) the *philosophical* and (b) the *scientific* (cf. A712–35 B740–66). Secondly – of those falling under (x) being conceived as being exclusively *discursive* in nature;[75] and those under (y), in necessary relation, also, to the *quantitative* terms of (pure) *mathematics*.[76] Thus, for instance, and with regard to (x) – 'Everything which happens has its cause' (A9 B13); and with respect to (y) – the principles of Newtonian physics, for example, 'In all changes of the material world, the quantity of matter remains unchanged'/'In all communication of motion, the action and reaction must always be equal' (B17). To this, again, and by way of minimal amplification, there may be the addition of two other points made by Kant in separating the class from that of the *empirical*.

In this regard, there is, first, the consideration that the *concepts* of such (*synthetic a priori*) propositions are to be seen as being of a *logically* higher order than those of *empirical* statements. More specifically, as being derived, not, as with the latter, *directly* from *factual* experience, but rather *mediately* through *analysis* of the *formal/limiting/structural* characteristics of such 'first order', that is, *empirical*, concepts. Thus, by way of illustration, there may be appeal to the words of Kant with regard to the derivation of the ('higher' level) concept of *cause*:

With the concept of cause I do really go beyond the empirical concept of an event (something happening), yet I do not pass to the intuition which exhibits the concept of cause *in concreto*, but to the time-conditions in general, which in experience may be found to be in accord with this concept. *I therefore proceed merely in accordance with concepts.* (A722 B750 note. My main italics.)

Secondly, and as drawn in opposition to the (purely) *inductive* derivation of *empirical* generalisations, there may be reference to Kant's portrayal of the imaginative creativity involved in the *construction* of (*synthetic*) relations between *concepts* which are 'higher'/*a priori* in the preceding sense:

A light broke upon all students of nature [when] they learned that reason has insight only into that which it produces after a plan of its own, and that it must not allow itself to be kept, as it were, in nature's leading-strings, but must itself show the way with principles of judgment based upon fixed laws, constraining nature to give answer to questions of reason's own determining. (B xiii)

And, in continuing:

Accidental observations, made in obedience to no previously thought-out plan, can never be made to yield a necessary law, which alone reason is concerned to discover. Reason, holding in one hand its principles, according to which alone concordant appearances can be admitted as equivalent to laws, and, in the other hand the experiment which it has devised in conformity with these principles, must approach nature in order to be taught by it. It must not, however, do so in the character of a pupil who listens to everything that the teacher chooses to say, but of an appointed judge who compels the witnesses to answer questions which he has himself formulated. (B xiii)

To summarize, therefore, and as being entirely adequate for the present purpose, there is the conclusion that (*discursive*) *synthetic a priori* propositions, for Kant, are statements (as expressed through *language*) whose *proof/justification/validation* is to be seen as deriving from the *universality* of their applicability to the observational data from which, in the last resort, they take their rise. In short, statements which, though *synthetic*, are, yet, to be viewed as being beyond *falsification* by *physical/common-sensical* experience for the reason that their denial entails a negation of this very *experience*.[77]

With this, and returning to the main discussion, there is the point that, notwithstanding the vociferousness with which the *logical positivist* position has come to take its modern hold, it remains a stance which, in merely reiterating that of Hume, continues to be under siege through the Kantian idea of the *synthetic a priori*. Moreover, the theory of (*unconscious/transcendental*) *mind* whose own *validation*, as Kant triumphantly proclaims, is, itself, most decisively to be found in its *explanatory* power with regard to precisely the foregoing – namely 'How is pure mathematics possible?'/'How is pure science of nature possible?'/'How is metaphysics, as science, possible?' (B20–3).[78] On this basis – *and leaving the respective strengths of the two positions entirely for the judgement of the reader* – the conspectus may be closed with a consolidation of its significance with regard to the *quantum* issue.

Here, there must be immediate withdrawal from any suggestion of the debate being intertwined with the question of *hidden variables*, as, for instance, of the *logical positivist* outlook deriving some sort of vindication from the *probability* contentions of the 'Copenhagen Interpretation'. Or of the latter, in its turn, deriving support from the uncompromising extent of the former's identification of the *synthetic* with the *probablistic*. Or, again, of the Kantian position, with its insistence on the reality of the *causal* principle, in some way, lending itself to the claims of Einstein. These, and notwithstanding the fact of their voicing, are confusions so gross as to be beyond the worth of comment. Cutting through the tangle of such presuppositions, however, the consideration for emphasis is one which will be perfectly plain, namely that the debate – with all the vastness of its ramifications with regard to *mind* and *meaning*[79] – is to be seen as turning on no more than a single *empirical/phenomenological/logical* point; that is, and as fully delineated – whether, indeed, as with the *logical positivist* view, the whole immense reach of human (*ampliative*) *knowledge* is really, that is as a *matter of fact*, reducible to the unitary class of the exclusively *inductive/probablistic*. Or, alternatively – whether, following Kant, recognition must be accorded, in addition, to a logically higher range of propositions which, as in the instances of (pure) *mathematics* (Newtonian) *physics* and (critical) *philosophy*, are to be conceived as being in the nature of (*mental*) *constructions*.

At the same time, and going beyond the above, there is, also, the fact that, though logically separated from the (*scientific*) controversy over *hidden variables*, the debate is still to be regarded as being in vital relation to the circumstances surrounding the (*philosophical*) move from 'old' to 'new' *quantum* theory. For, as hardly goes with saying, the virulence of the *logical positivist* assault on the citadel of Kantian *idealism* is in no way to be taken as offering succour to the *realist/materialist* cause of Newton/Locke/Einstein. Rather, and whatever its implications with regard to *meaning* – the very reverse is the case, namely with the presuppositional base of the position being, in full reflection of that of Hume, no more and no less than a thoroughgoing *phenomenalism*. What may be extracted, therefore, is a crucial point of connexion with the earlier conclusion of Clauser and Shimony. More specifically, and as representing the twentieth-century culmination of the epoch-making tradition of eighteenth-century *metaphysical* thought – that the *analytic–synthetic* debate is one whose importance is to be seen, not least, in its overriding and anticipatory embracement of the key (*philosophical*) aspects of the 'Copenhagen Interpretation': on the one hand, the completeness of its discounting of all vestiges of the stance of (*scientific*) *realism/materialism*; and on the other hand, the firmness of its grounding in, what, in either of its Humean or Kantian modes, is to be viewed as an uncompromising *idealism*.

With the minimality of the above being all that is necessary for the main purpose, it remains merely to add a number of points in final supplementation of what has been said.

There may, first – and in amplification of Kant's *intuitionist* theory of (pure) *mathematics* – be expansion on the previously noted classification of the *categories* under the heads of (a) the *mathematical* and (b) the *dynamical*. In particular, in this regard, is the fact of both (a) and (b) being necessary for explaining the *dynamical* interrelations of (*physical/common-sensical*) *experience*; whereas (a) alone being sufficient for the *static* demonstrations (through dots and lines) of *pure intuition*. To this extent, there is, if only sketchily, Kant's solution to the problem of 'the application of *mathematics* to *appearances*' (A178 B221, my italics); thus that the logical conditions of the former are themselves to be seen as already *constitutive* of those of the latter. In addition, however, is another consideration which, with all its significance for the *quantum* debate, is to be set in opposition to the time-honoured and quasi-mystical Pythagorean/Platonic vision of the discipline, namely that, on the view in hand – as, also, on the Humean/*logical positivist* outlook – the *axiomatic* foundations of *arithmetic* and

(Euclidean) *geometry* are, in no sense to be conceived as transcending the parameters of (*physical/common-sensical*) *experience*. Rather, and fully in common with the broader dimensions of *discursive/linguistic* representation, they are to be seen as being grounded in no more than conditions of *objectivity* deriving from specifically *human* understanding.[80]

Secondly, there may be a return to the claim made, if only fleetingly, in the *Critique* that it forms no part of the intention of the work to hold that *mind* 'produces its objects in so far as *existence* is concerned' (A92 B125). Pursuing the consideration further, there is the fact that towards the end of his life, in sketches that were later to be published in the *Opus Postumum*,[81] Kant offers the speculation that it is 'moving forces in space' such as 'heat, light, magnetic stuff, electricity'[82] which are to be taken as constituting the *physical* basis of (*perceptual/common-sensical*) *experience*. In this, and, again, as previously indicated, he was following a direction which he had first laid down in 1786 in his *Metaphysical Foundations of Natural Science*; and which, as inspired by the *kinematic* 'atomic' theory of Boscovich, he had originally envisaged in 1765.[83] With the details of this little considered aspect of Kant's thought being beyond the scope of the present purpose, there may, more urgently, be the sufficiency of two bare points arising from it. First – Kant's insistence, throughout the *Opus Postumum* sketches that the *immaterialist* ideas which he is advancing are altogether compatible with the *idealism* of the *Critique*.[84] Secondly – his fear, as expressed in the late, and already noted, letter to Garve, that his Critical philosophy would remain incomplete unless he could make clear the importance of these *physical/immaterialist* projections:

> I am as it were mentally paralyzed even though physically I am reasonably well. I see before me the unpaid bill of my uncompleted philosophy, even while I am aware that philosophy, both as regards its means and its ends, is capable of completion. It is a pain like that of Tantalus though not a hopeless pain. The project on which I am now working concerns the 'Transition from the metaphysical foundations of natural science to physics'. It must be completed, or else a gap will remain in the critical philosophy.[85]

In easy acceptance of the relevance of the above for the development of contemporary *field* theory, there is, in addition, the fact of both standing in the long shadow of the thought of Plato. More specifically – the image, as expressed in the *Timaeus* (34Bff.), of the *physical/common-sensical* order being, in its true nature, a function of *soul* in its relation to the (Pythagorean) *numbers*.[86]

Finally, but, not least, there may be remark on Kant's claim to the complete *unknowability* of, what he (metaphorically) calls *things-in-themselves*; or, more generally, and less contentiously, *noumena/noumenon*.[87] Thus, in its relation to his doctrine of *appearances*:

> The transcendental concept of appearances in space ... is a critical reminder that nothing intuited in space is a thing in itself, that space is not a form inhering in things in themselves as their intrinsic property, that objects in themselves are quite unknown to us, and that what we call outer objects are nothing but representations of our sensibility, the form of which is space. The true correlate of sensibility, the thing in itself, is not known and cannot be known, through these representations; and in experience no question is ever asked in regard to it. (A30 B45)

On this, there is the point that, though undoubtedly embracing a heuristic caution against *indiscriminate* speculation, the idea is certainly not to be taken, following the terms of the *logical positivist* outlook, as negating the legitimacy of *speculative* (*causal*) thinking *per se*. Rather, and with Kant's own (*projective/transcendental*) theory of (*immaterial*) 'moving forces' as a measure – as entailing something much more directly related to the *quantum* issue. Namely that, no matter to what degree such theorising might be carried, it is still to be conceived purely and simply as thought *about*, or deriving *from*, *appearances*; with no advance whatsoever to the nature of *ontologically* 'existing' reality. In other words, and as set against the *realist/materialist* view of *knowledge* – as no more than an extension of the *matrix* of human (*perceptual*) *experience*:

> Through observation and analysis of appearances we penetrate to nature's inner recesses, and no one can say how far this knowledge may in time extend. But with all this knowledge, and even if the whole of nature were revealed to us, we should still never be able to answer those transcendental questions which go beyond nature. (A278 B334)

To summarize, therefore, there is the conclusion that, through his *appearance/thing-in-itself* distinction, Kant not only draws the bounds of (human) *knowledge*, but also exhaustively demonstrates that this, in itself, generates a problem to which the only response, *in the final 'transcendental', analysis*, is one of absolute and necessary *agnosticism*.

With note of this constituting the ground of Kant's *ethical* and *religious* philosophy, there are, more immediately, two other points arising from what has been said. First, and as fully drawn – the clear fact of the Kantian outlook completely cradling the conclusion of Clauser and Shimony of the preceding chapter. Secondly, and bound up with this – the possibility of *Bell's Theorem*, and notwithstanding the sophistication of its formulation and validation, being, not *synthetic*, but *analytic*. Most particularly, however, is the overriding outcome of the foregoing – in short that the central stream of the whole course of the Western tradition in *philosophy* is to be seen as coalescing with the demands of the contemporary revolution in *physics* in entailing a decisive and irrevocable negation of the pernicious and entirely gratuitous doctrine embraced under the crusading banner of (*scientific*) *realism/materialism*.

12

Knowledge, Super-normality and Faith

'"The world is my representation" is, like the axioms of Euclid, a proposition which everyone must recognize as true as soon as he understands it, although it is not a proposition that everyone understands as soon as he hears it.'[1] With these words of Schopenhauer encapsulating the culminating head of Western philosophical thought, their power may be amplified. Thus, in another passage by the same thinker:

[It was] . . . only after men had tried their hand for thousands of years at merely *objective* philosophizing did they discover that, among the many things that make the world so puzzling and precarious, the first and foremost is that, however immeasurable and massive it may be, its existence hangs nevertheless on a single thread; and this thread is the actual consciousness in which it exists. This condition, with which the existence of the world is irrevocably encumbered, marks it with the stamp of *ideality* . . . and consequently with the stamp of mere *phenomenon*.[2]

Further, by Schrödinger, in quoting Jung:

All science . . . is a function of the soul, in which all knowledge is rooted. The soul is the greatest of all cosmic miracles, it is the *conditio sine qua non* of the world as an object.[3]

And, in continuing:

It is exceedingly astonishing that the Western world (apart from very rare exceptions) seems to have so little appreciation of this being so. The flood of external objects of cognizance has made the subject of all cognizance withdraw to the background, often to apparent non-existence.[4]

With its shades of the deepest traditions of the East as well as the 'Copenhagen Interpretation', the truth is one which may be taken as the focal point of concluding remark.[5]

In this regard, and as already sufficiently emphasized, there is the consideration that this is certainly not to deny the *empirical* reality of the *physical/common-sensical* world. Merely and simply, to correct a deep-rooted and totally erroneous presumption about its (*philosophical*) *status*. Nor is it, in any way, to question the legitimacy of the *scientific* endeavour in the marvel of its success in understanding and controlling this order – but rather and only, to destroy a *myth*; one which, as deriving from an early and primitive association with the demands of Judæo-Christian *orthodoxy*, has come to dominate the thought of the modern world through no more than the *heuristic* triumph of the former. That is, and as fully drawn – the shibboleth of (*scientific*) *realism/materialism*.[6] To this extent, the exercise of 'discovering' new 'particles' may continue as ever – perhaps, in a manner limited only by the patience and resources of investigators to pursue it; so, also, speculative probing into the 'origin' of the universe, as, again, into that of 'life'. What is at stake is not the *experimental* expertise of the practising scientist, but the wholly spurious *dogma* that the fruits of such effort are to be interpreted as being, in some way, and to some degree, *descriptive/reductive* of an ontologically 'existing' *material* reality. As against this – and whatever the extent of the *technological* advance involved – must be set the indubitability of the view of *scientific* knowledge entailed in the above. In short – that it is to be conceived exclusively in terms of an ever-expanding *matrix* set upon, and arising from, the screen of (specifically *human*) *consciousness/awareness/understanding*.

With mention of the *ethical* dimension to this view of *knowledge* as drawn against the moral ambivalence of that instantiated in the (*realist*) conception of attaining a 'God's eye' view of things, there is, too, a complete exposure of the grand illusion of so-called '*scientific* impossibility'. For *science*, in its true and abiding nature is, but – and gloriously so – a *methodology*, standing for no fixed beliefs. And, for this same discipline to proclaim *a priori* the *impossibility* of certain happenings is, not only to contradict itself, but also manifest the degree to which it has become contaminated by the foregoing (*philosophical*) virus of (*materialistic*) realism. Thus, not unfairly, the comment of Arthur Koestler:

The materialistic philosophy in which the average modern scientist was reared has retained its dogmatic power over his mind, though matter itself has evaporated; and he reacts to phenomena which do not fit into it much in the same manner as his scholastic forebears reacted to the suggestion that new stars might appear in the immutable eighth sphere.[7]

The consideration is one which stands as a monument to the perspicacity of the already noted remark of Lecky regarding human *credulity*, that people of *all* periods – of the modern (*scientific*) age, no less than of ancient times – 'are always prepared to accept on very slight evidence what they believe to be exceedingly probable'.[8] More particularly, however, is the fact of the above as it relates to the idea which has constituted the central topic of the present concern; that is, the *super-normal*.

Here, there is the point, at once, that, notwithstanding the claim to '*scientific* impossibility', it was, indeed, the pressure of this latter which, as in the hands of Schopenhauer, nearly a century before the 'Copenhagen Interpretation', first came to stand as an *empirical* challenge to the, then, all-pervasive power of the (Newtonian) *realist/materialist* view of the world. Further – that, with the circumstances of the current *scientific* rejection of this outlook capping those of its earlier *philosophical* negation, there is removed, and at a stroke, what, over the centuries, has come to exert its (*cultural*) tyranny as a complete and virtually unquestioned *theoretical* panacea to the foregoing. At the same time, there is, also, the importance of another consideration. More specifically, the fact of the alternative *idealistic* view of *physical/common-sensical* reality constituting a framework in which the *super-normal* – as represented, for instance, in the urgency of such, now, well-attested effects as those falling under the far-reaching idea of *telepathy* – is open to full accommodation. Thus, the scope of the Kantian model as portrayed, once more, in the pioneering terms of Schopenhauer:

The true conception of *actio in distans* [/*visio in distans*] is that the space between the causative and the caused, whether full or empty, has absolutely no influence on the effect, but it is quite immaterial whether it amounts to an inch or a billion times the orbit of Uranus ... Accordingly, it must be thought of as a communication that is independent of the phenomenon and of the laws thereof, as something that occurs in the thing-in-itself and is afterwards perceivable in the phenomenon, such thing-in-itself, as the inner essence of things, being everywhere the root of their phenomenal appearance.[9]

With no attempt at embellishing this necessarily sketchy vision, there is, more immediately, the point of main intent. In short – that, in the relation of contradiction between (a) the doctrine of (*scientific*) *realism/materialism* and (b) the idea of the *super-normal/ mentalistic/psychical*, it is (a), rather than (b), which, in the event, and as the West approaches its twenty-first century, has come to be, not only the arm of 'give', but also drastic abnegation.

In full acceptance of the strength of the above, there may, as hardly goes with saying, be peremptory rejection of any attempt to interpret its significance as being, in any way, invitative to a new era of *superstition/supernaturalism*, as against which both *science* and *philosophy*, in ancient Greece, as well as the cycle of more recent times, originally came to take their rise. The call, rather, is simply and entirely legitimately to an *expanded* sense of (the *methodological* indispensability of) the *scientific/philosophical* endeavour. Namely, one which, as going beyond the terms of the merely *physical*, is to be seen as embracing, further, the, now irrevocably established, *ontological* primacy of *mind*. Thus, the point as it is expressed in the visionary projection of Schopenhauer:

> A time will come when *philosophy, animal magnetism* [the *psychical*] and *natural science* . . . will shed so bright a light on one another that truths will be discovered at which we could not otherwise hope to arrive.[10]

This said, there may, to conclude, be a return to the topic of original concern as this is to be seen as turning on the so-called 'revolution in *theology*' associated with the name of Bultmann.

As firmly underscored by the discussion of Chapters 10 and 11, there is, at once, the undoubted strength of Bultmann's assertion of the *mythological* character of whole swathes of the biblical narratives. Further, and following from this, there is his implicative negation of the entire substance of the *traditional/fundamentalist* conception of (Christian) *faith*. More specifically, the claim, as formulated, most definitively, by Augustine (354–430), Bishop of Hippo, at the time of the final collapse of the Roman Empire, as the

West entered the 'thousand year sleep' of its (*theologically* dominated) Dark Age, that the New Testament writings, in their conjunction with those of the Old Testament, are to be viewed as representing a unique and superior, that is *revelationary*, body of 'knowledge'. Indeed, and, no less – the *Word* of the One and Only (Old Testament) *God*. With note of the entailing *realism* of a doctrine which, in itself, and notwithstanding the continuing power of its hold, is only open to interpretation as an *incoherent* (and specifically *theological*) *myth*, the concern must be with the broader and more startling aspects of Bultmann's position.[11] That is, (a) the uninhibited extent of his embracement of the cause of (*scientific*) *realism/materialism*; (b) the dramatic excess of his abandonment of any form whatsoever of (*religious*) *super-naturalism*; and (c) the extravagance of his leap to the *secularist* ultimacy of Heideggerian *existentialism*.

With the reciprocity between (a) and (b) already the subject of decisive negation, the stance of Bultmann in this regard must be set against the strength of two considerations. First, the contemporary challenge of the *psychical* as a mode (with the *miraculous*) of the *super-normal*. Secondly, the incontrovertibility of the *idealist/ phenomenalist* conception of (*human*) *existence* proclaimed at the outset by Schopenhauer. To this extent, the end consequence of Bultmann's famed exercise in *demythologizing* the New Testament message is to be seen as something far removed from the *spiritual/ religious* nihilism of (c). What emerges, rather, is the need for a radically new *religious/super-naturalistic* interpretation of the Christian faith, most especially, the core doctrine of the Resurrection. More specifically, one which, with the *psychical* as an *empirical* template, is cast, not in the crude (*realist*) language of everyday experience, but in the framework of the foregoing and hard-won *idealist/phenomenalist* view of the *physical/common-sensical* order. There is, in short, the vital significance of the epigrammatic (*theological*) conclusion of Kant in the *Critique*: 'I found it necessary to deny [religious/Augustinian] *knowledge*, in order to make room for [real/rational] *faith*' (B xxx).[12]

It remains to bring the discussion to a close with a number of assorted supplementary considerations.

Thus, there may, to begin, be a highlighting of the crude *realism/materialism* entailed in the traditional, and still standard, interpretation of the *Resurrection*. That is, the *dogma*, as endorsed in the Creeds, if not the Epistles and Gospels, that the latter, as prototypical of the reward awaiting all true believers, is to be conceived as being uninhibitedly *physical/material* in character; one of 'flesh and blood' and the eventual 'repossession' by each and every member of the faithful of his/her own original/personal 'atoms'. More definitively, however, and on a note of topicality, there is the contemporary virulence of the doctrine as vividly conveyed in the recent and highly publicized furore over a television comment by David Jenkins, Bishop of Durham. Thus, the remark, and nothing more, though as it brought forth demands from high and low for his resignation, that 'I don't think it means a physical resurrection; it means a spiritual resurrection, a transforming resurrection, a real resurrection'.[13] With the issue a dramatic confirmation of the need, as detailed above, for an *idealist/phenomenalist* portrayal of the event in hand, there is, concomitantly, the urgency of another consideration; namely, the importance of the task, pre-eminently and rightfully that of the clergy, of *educating* an ever more critical laity to the far-reaching *religious* ramifications of the foregoing, and *philosophically/ scientifically* established, *truth*. It is a challenge which is, certainly, to be seen as involving a much extended curriculum for clerical training beyond that of traditional Apologetics. At the same time, it is, also, such as to offer the possibility of a vital new impetus to the *theoretical* development of the Christian faith.

Secondly, and as set against the zealous cruelty with which the *super-normal/mentalistic/psychical* was, in bygone centuries, persecuted by both Roman and Protestant Churches alike, there may be a highlighting of, what would appear to be, the clear emergence of a new clerical attitude towards its significance. Thus, the words of Michael Perry, Archdeacon of Durham, in an article in *The Times* under the title 'The psychic and the spiritual':

Religion dismisses the psychic aspects of life at its peril. It poses special pastoral and theological questions to the churches, which have wide ramifications.[14]

Further, in indicating definitive, if, unofficial, progress in the field:

As usual, private enterprise runs ahead of official cognisance. The Churches' Fellowship for Psychical and Spiritual Studies ['CFPSS'] was founded in 1953 and its quarterly, *The Christian Parapsychologist*, aims to promote awareness of the psychic dimension within Christian thinking and a discriminating discussion of the whole subject, including its implications within theology.[15]

And, again, in concluding:

After one hundred years of the Society for Psychical Research and [at the time] nearly thirty of the CFPSS there is still much work to be done. Thinking Christians would do well to be better informed of the work of the parapsychologists.[16]

The remarks are to be seen in the context of two other points made by Perry, both of relevance for the current concern. On the one hand, the fact of a (sharply divided) report on the religious significance of the *psychical*, originally presented to the Archbishop of Canterbury in 1939, receiving eventual if belated publication forty years later, in 1979.[17] On the other hand, that of a sympathetic and balanced assessment of the same issue being received and published by the Church of Scotland in 1976.[18]

Thirdly, there may be remark on the relation of *necessity/ reflexivity* which, as on the (*traditional/fundamentalist*) Augustinian outlook (and as instantiated in the *dogma* of the *Trinity*) is to be seen as pertaining between the twin pillars of its key contentions, namely (a) the doctrine of the *Resurrection* and (b) the idea of a One and Only, All-Powerful/All-Benevolent (*anthropomorphic/theistic-Male*) *God*. As against this, the point for emphasis is that of a radical *category* difference between the two claims. Thus, of (a) having the (putative) status of a *factual/historical/phenomenological* assertion; one, moreover, deriving *empirical* support from the contemporary challenge of the *psychical*. And, (b) being such as to be hopelessly and irretrievably mired, *logically/epistemologically/anthropologically*, as well as *theologically*, in the slough of the purely *mythological*.

To make this point is, once more, not to question the vastness of the contribution of (b) to the *political/cultural/economic* development of Christendom; and, hence, the modern industrialized world. Nor, further, is it to raise any doubt about the immensity of the *psychological/spiritual* succour which it has undoubtedly accorded over the centuries to countless millions of struggling humanity in the fragility of their earthly existence. The object is merely and simply to highlight the fact of its (*epistemological*) standing as being, like that of the (*material*) *atom*, no more than a *myth*. What must go with this, too, is the ramification, as in the instance of the latter, of there being a more sinister side to the circumstances of its hold. More specifically, of it being, also, the source of immeasurable suffering, *psychological/physical/economic*, not least, but certainly not exclusively, to innocents in far places who, until the stroke of its impact, never knew its name.[19] Returning, however, to the main concern, there is the consideration, not only of (a) being in merely *contingent* association with (b), but also of the former, in its relation of *opposition* to the latter, constituting the sole (legitimate) arm of specifically Christian *indispensability*.[20]

Finally, there is the point that to accept the *theoretical* inadequacy of the foregoing (*theistic*) conception of *God*, is not to entail the abandonment of any sense whatsoever of the term's meaningfulness; but, rather, to highlight the alternative of, what may be characterized as, its *deistic* connotation. More specifically, the idea, as developed, most fully, by Kant, in the *Critique*, of the *Godhead* representing, not a *Thing/Object/Person*, but, and *necessarily*, a 'Problem', 'Principle' or bare 'Incomprehensibility'. One whose very *Ineffability* is to be seen as constituting the sole possible mark of its appeal.[21] Thus, and in the light of what has been said, the consideration as captured in the contemporary terms of Whyte:

> Today faith, if it bears any relation to the natural world, implies faith in the unconscious. If there is a God, he must speak there; if there is a healing power, it must operate there; if there is a principle of ordering in the organic realm, its most powerful manifestation must be found there.[22]

To summarize, therefore, there is the force of two main extractions. First, the fact of the core *super-normalism* of the *kerygma* being open to free *literal* accommodation within the terms of the preceding *idealism/phenomenalism*. Secondly, that of the scythe of Bultmann's famed exercise in *demythologizing* the New Testament message, reaping a harvest of no more than merely secondary (*theological*) accretions to the central (*religious*) standing of the *Resurrection* itself.

With this, and to end on a whimsy, the question may be raised as to what Hume's own position on the *miraculous/super-normal* might have been had he lived a century later. Thoroughly open-minded as he was, he might well have been, like Schopenhauer, among the first to realize the far-reaching extent of its significance. Certainly, his philosophy is such as to pre-eminently find a ready place for its acceptance.

Notes

Introduction

1. Hume, 'Of Miracles', Sect. X of *An Enquiry concerning the Human Understanding* (1748), L. A. Selby-Bigge (ed.) *Enquiries concerning Human Understanding and concerning the Principles of Morals* (Oxford: Clarendon, 1902) 3rd edn., 1975, pp. 109–31, p. 115 note.

Chapter 1:   THE CRISIS IN MODERN THEOLOGY

1. Later published in *Kerygma und Mythos: Ein theologisches Gespräch*, H. W. Bartsch (ed.) (Hamburg: Reich, 1947), 2 vols., I, pp. 15–48. The quotations which follow are given to the English translation of this work by R. H. Fuller, *Kerygma and Myth: A Theological Debate, with contributions by Rudolf Bultmann, Ernst Lohmeyer, Julius Schniewind, Friedrich Schumann, Helmut Thielicke and Austin Farrer* (London: S.P.C.K., 1953) 2 vols., I, pp. 1–44. These, together with wider references, will be given in the text under the prefix '*KM*'.
2. Bonhoeffer, *Letters and Papers from Prison*, translated from *Widerstand und Ergebung: Briefe und Aufzeichnungen aus der Haft* by R. H. Fuller, P. Clarke and others (London: SCM, 1953); enlarged edition, ed. E. Bethge (London: SCM, 1971) p. 285. The German edition, as may be noted, appeared in 1970.
3. Robinson (London: SCM, 1963). Further references to this work will be given in the text under the prefix '*HG*'.
4. Robinson, 'The Debate Continues', D. L. Edwards (ed.), *The Honest to God Debate: Some reactions to the book 'Honest to God' with a new chapter by its author John A. T. Robinson* (London: SCM, 1963) pp. 232–75, p. 262. Further references to this work will be given in the text under the prefix '*HGD*'.
5. Paul Tillich, *The Shaking of the Foundations* (New York: Scribner, 1948) p. 57.
6. The *logical* difficulties raised here will be the subject of later remark. See chap. 12 of this volume.
7. Anonymous, *The Times* (London, 4 April 1963). The comment, of course, was originally made of Auguste Comte.
8. Bultmann, *Jesus Christ and Mythology*, Yale and Vanderbilt Lectures, 1951 (New York: Scribner, 1958) pp. 16, 37.

Chapter 2:   THE IDEA OF THE MIRACULOUS

1. Jaspers, Bultmann/Jaspers, *Myth and Christianity: An Inquiry into the Possibility of Religion Without Myth* (New York: Noonday, 1958) pp. 3–4.
2. Cf. the well-known contribution of H. and H. A. Frankfort to this

211

topic in the collection of essays. H. and H. A. Frankfort (eds), *The Intellectual Adventure of Ancient Man* (Chicago: Chicago University Press, 1946); reprinted under the title *Before Philosophy* (London: Pelican, 1949).

3. Bultmann, *Jesus Christ and Mythology*, pp. 37–8.
4. Hume, op. cit., p. 115 note. Further references to this work will be given in the text under the prefix '*HU*'.
5. Lecky, *History of the Rise and Influence of the Spirit of Rationalism in Europe* (London: Longmans, Green, 1865); reprinted (New York: Braziller, 1955) p. 101 (my italics). Cf. chap. 6 of this volume for a qualifying note on the intellectual milieu of the period which saw the emergence of this famous treatise.
6. Jaynes, *The Origin of Consciousness in the Breakdown of the Bicameral Mind* (Boston: Houghton Mifflin, 1976), fly-leaf summary.
7. Solzhenitsyn, *The Cancer Ward* trans. Rachel Frank (New York: Dial, 1968) p. 164.
8. Paul Dietl, 'On Miracles', *American Philosophical Quarterly*, Vol. 5, No. 2 (April 1968) pp. 130–4, p. 132.
9. Broad, 'Hume's Theory of the Credibility of Miracles', *Proceedings of the Aristotelian Society* (New Series) XVII (1916–17) pp. 77–94; reprinted in *Human Understanding: Studies in the Philosophy of David Hume*, A. Sesonske and N. Fleming (eds) (Belmont: Wadsworth, 1965) pp. 86–98, p. 86.
10. Odegard, 'Miracles and Good Evidence', *Religious Studies*, Vol. 18 (1982) pp. 37–46, p. 38.
11. The archetypal statement of this claim, in its eighteenth century form, is given by William Paley in his *A View of the Evidences of Christianity* (1794) and *Natural Theology* (1802).
12. Lewis, *Miracles* (London/New York: Macmillan, 1947) p. 124.
13. Broad, op. cit., p. 94.
14. Penelhem, *Hume* (London: Macmillan, 1975) p. 178.

Chapter 3:   MIRACLES AND NATURAL NECESSITY

1. Huxley, *Science and Christian Tradition: Essays* (London: Macmillan, 1894) p. 133.
2. Lewis, op. cit., p. 124.
3. Flew, *God and Philosophy* (London: Hutchinson, 1966) p. 149. A theological formulation of, what might be taken as, the same argument is given by Tillich: 'Miracles cannot be interpreted in terms of a supernatural interference in natural processes. If such an interpretation were true, the manifestation of the ground of being would destroy the structure of being; God would be split within himself, as religious dualism has asserted.' *Systematic Theology* (London: Nisbet, 1964) 3 vols., I, p. 129.
4. Huxley, op. cit., p. 133.
5. McKinnon, *American Philosophical Quarterly*, Vol. 4, No. 4 (1967) pp. 308–14.

6. Cf. R. F. Holland, 'The Miraculous', *American Philosophical Quarterly*, Vol. 2, No. 1 (1965) pp. 43–51, p. 46.
7. Robinson, 'Miracles', *Ratio*, Vol. ix, No. 2 (1967) pp. 155–66, p. 159. The position is one that is endorsed by Malcolm Diamond, 'Miracles', *Religious Studies* Vol. 9 (1973) pp. 307–24.
8. Cf. in this connexion the words of John Maynard (later, Lord) Keynes after reading through the masses of Newton's private papers following their being opened to public scrutiny in 1936: 'Newton was not the first of the age of reason. He was the last of the magicians. He looked on the whole universe and all that there is in it as a *riddle*, as a secret which could be read by applying pure thought to certain evidence, certain mystic clues which God had laid about the world to allow a sort of philosopher's treasure hunt to the esoteric brotherhood. He believed that these clues were to be found partly in the evidence of the heavens and in the constitution of elements (and that is what gives the false suggestion of his being an experimental natural philosopher), but also partly in certain papers and traditions handed down by the brethren in an unbroken chain back to the original cryptic revelation in Babylonia. He regarded the universe as a cryptogram set by the Almighty.' Quoted by B. J. T. Dobbs, *The Foundations of Newton's Alchemy* (Cambridge: Cambridge University Press, 1975) pp. 13–14. Cf. chap. 11 in this volume.
9. Holland, op. cit., p. 48. Similar views are expressed by Richard Swinburne, *The Concept of a Miracle* (London: Macmillan, 1970) p. 27; and by Margaret Boden 'Miracles and Scientific Explanation', *Ratio*, Vol. xi, No. 2 (1969) pp. 137–44, p. 140.
10. Smart, 'Miracles and David Hume', *Philosophers and Religious Truth* (London: SCM, 1964) pp. 26–56, pp. 39–41.
11. Swinburne, op. cit., p. 26.
12. Nowell-Smith, 'Miracles', *New Essays in Philosophical Theology*, ed. A. Flew and A. McIntyre (London: SCM, 1955) pp. 243–53. The essay was originally published in the *Hibbert Journal*, Vol. xlviii (1950) pp. 354–60.
13. Swinburne, op. cit., p. 53.

Chapter 4: MIRACLES AND MIND

1. Odegard, op. cit., p. 41.
2. Lewis, op. cit., p. 58.
3. Broad, op. cit., p. 96.
4. Smart, op. cit., pp. 47–8.
5. Lewis, op. cit., p. 59.
6. Lewis, ibid., pp. 56–7.
7. Broad, op. cit., p. 90.
8. Dietl, op. cit., p. 132.
9. Dietl, ibid., p. 132.
10. Boden, op. cit., p. 140.
11. Broad, 'The Relevance of Psychical Research to Philosophy', *Religion, Philosophy and Psychical Research: Selected Essays* (London: Rout-

ledge, Kegan Paul, 1953) pp. 7–26. Cf. also, Broad, *Lectures on Psychical Research, incorporating the Perrott Lectures given at Cambridge University in 1959 and 1960* (London: Routledge, Kegan Paul, 1962) pp. 3–4.

12. Broad, 'Hume's Theory of the Credibility of Miracles', op. cit., p. 96.
13. Jones, *Sigmund Freud: Life and Work* (London: Hogarth, 1953) 2 vols., I, p. 45.

Chapter 5: MIRACLES AS A MODE OF THE SUPER-NORMAL

1. Bultmann, *Jesus Christ and Mythology*, p. 15.
2. Broad, 'Hume's Theory of the Credibility of Miracles', op. cit., p. 96.
3. Schniewind, 'A Reply to Bultmann' (1943), *Kerygma and Myth*, I, pp. 45–101, p. 51 (my interpolations).
4. Thielicke, 'The Restatement of New Testament Mythology', *Kerygma and Myth*, I, pp. 138–74, pp. 174, 173.
5. Landrum, 'What a Miracle Really Is', *Religious Studies* Vol. 12 (1976), pp. 49–57, pp. 52–3.
6. F. L. Cross (ed.) (Oxford: Oxford University Press, 1957) p. 920.
7. Cf. Aquinas, *Summa Theologica*, I, 110, 4.
8. Lecky, op. cit., pp. xix–xx.
9. Swinburne, op. cit., pp. 8–9 (my italics).
10. Schopenhauer, 'Versuch über das Geistersehn und was damit zusammenhängt', *Parerga und Paralipomena* (1851), *Sämtliche Werke* (Wiesbaden: Brokhaus, 1960) V, pp. 239–329: trans. E. F. J. Payne, 'Essay on Spirit Seeing and everything connected therewith' *Parerga and Paralipomena* (Oxford: Clarendon, 1974) 2 vols., I, pp. 227–309, p. 266.

Chapter 6: SUPER-NORMALITY AS A MODE OF THE REAL

1. Lecky, op. cit., pp. 27, 161, 162.
2. Cf., in this connexion, three works of especial relevance which, together, contain an extensive bibliography relating to the matters in hand – Henri F. Ellenberger, *The Discovery of the Unconscious: The History and Evolution of Dynamic Psychiatry* (New York: Basic Books, 1970); Alan Gauld, *The Founders of Psychical Research* (London: Routledge, Kegan Paul, 1968); and R. Lawrence Moore, *In Search of White Crows: Spiritualism, Parapsychology and American Culture* (New York: Oxford University Press, 1977).
3. *Proceedings of the Society for Psychical Research* (July, 1882), I (1883), pp. 3–4 (my italics). *Proceedings* of the Society have been issued since the foregoing date and a *Journal* from February 1884. See below.
4. The last 'witch', as may be mentioned, had not yet been burned in Europe – an event which, as far as is known, took place in 1782 at Glarus, Switzerland, with Anne Göldi the benighted victim.
5. Gassner, he fully conceded, also possessed this manipulative power, but without knowing its true nature.
6. Cf. in the foregoing regard – Mesmer, *Mémoire sur la découverte du*

magnétisme animal (Paris: Didot, 1779).

7.   Podmore, *From Mesmer to Christian Science: A Short History of Mental Healing* (London: Methuen, 1909); reprinted (New York: University Books, 1963) p. xix.

8.   Darnton, *Mesmerism and the End of the Enlightenment in France* (Cambridge, Mass.: Harvard University Press, 1968) p. 10.

9.   Darnton, ibid., pp. 10–11.

10. Cf. Puységur, *Mémoires pour servir à l'histoire et à l'établissement du magnétisme animal* (1784); 2nd edn (Paris: Cellot, 1809).

11. Questions relating to the accuracy of such diagnoses, and whether they represent anything more than what is already known in the patient's waking state (or, perhaps, by the 'magnetizer'), though of great intrinsic interest, may be put aside as being peripheral to the immediate discussion.

12. Cf. Puységur, *Du magnétisme animal, considéré dans ses rapports avec diverses branches de la physique générale* (Paris: Desenne, 1807).

13. Ellenberger, op. cit., p. 158.

14. Bertrand's essay, more accurately, arrived too late for consideration by the Academy. Cf. Bertrand, *Traité du somnambulisme et des différentes modifications qu'il présente* (Paris: Dentu, 1823); and (Général) Noizet, *Mémoire sur le somnambulisme et le magnétisme animal* (Paris: Plon, 1854). See below.

15. Cf. also, the testimony to the 'magnetized' Hauffe holding forth in the purest High German, a form of speech which contrasted sharply with the roughness of her natural Swabian dialect, as well as frequently resorting to a language which neither her clinical observer nor his attendant friends could understand, but, which she was able to 'translate' for them. See below.

16. Kerner, *Die Seherin von Prevorst. Eröffnungen über das innere Leben und über das Hineinragen einer Geisterwelt in die unsere* (Stuttgart/Tübingen: Cotta, 1829) 2 vols.; translated by Mrs. Crane, *The Seeress of Prevorst, being revelations concerning the inner-life of man, and the inner-diffusion of a world of spirits in the world we inhabit* (New York: Harper, 1845).

17. Passing mention may be made of the fact that 'magnetic' healing was, also, introduced very early into the prosperous French slave-colony of Saint Domingue by Puységur's second brother, Antoine Hyacinthe, Count de Chastenet (1752–1809), a naval officer, who had himself initially aroused the former to an interest in mesmerism; and further, that it was here avidly taken up, not only by the white population, but, by the slaves themselves. The point leads to an interesting anthropological speculation regarding the *voodo* practices for which the territory, under the name of Haiti, has come to be notorious. In short, that these practices, and particularly those relating to healing, are not exclusively African in origin, as is generally taken for granted, but, to a substantial degree, have a European, *mesmeric*, root.

18. Of the foregoing, two, in particular, are especially worthy of mention. First, Phineas Parkhurst Quimby (1802–66), one of whose patients was Mary Eddy Baker (1821–1910), the founder of Christian

Science. Secondly, Andrew Jackson Davis (1826–1910), the 'Pough-keepsie Seer', an ill-educated youth of few prepossessions, whose vast rhapsodic cosmology, *The Principles of Nature* (publicly dictated while in the 'magnetic' state) went through nearly thirty editions in just as many years. Davis ('by and through'), *The Principles of Nature, Her Divine Revelations, and a Voice to Mankind* (New York: Lyon and Fishbough, 1847). In this regard, too, mention may be made of the documented testimony to the 'magnetized' Davis dictating in Hebrew, Arabic and Sanskrit. Cf. Moore, op. cit., p. 11.

19. Elliotson, *Numerous Cases of Surgical Operations Without Pain in the Mesmeric State* (Philadelphia: Lea and Blanchard, 1843); and Esdaile, *Mesmerism in India and its Practical Application in Surgery and Medicine* (London: Longman, Brown, Green and Longmans, 1846). The two works are reprinted in *Significant Contributions to the History of Psychology*, Series A, ed. Daniel N. Robinson, Vol. x (Washington D.C.; University Publications of America, 1977). As with Braid, Elliotson was led to an interest in mesmerism through a demonstration by a visiting Frenchman. Esdaile, working in the less restrictive environment of India, was directly influenced by Elliotson's writings.

20. Cf. John Hughes Bennett, *The Mesmeric Mania of 1851, with a Physiological Explanation of the Phenomena Produced* (Edinburgh: Sutherland and Knox, 1851). The account, written on the spot and at the time, is all the more interesting for its outright rejection of any form of supernaturalism. With any degree of open-mindedness, it may be taken as having an interesting bearing on the conclusion of a recent writer, Roger Thompson, in his scholarly appraisal of the events at Salem: 'What-on earth-had happened? Why had a whole colony for a period of six months taken leave of its senses? . . . The only safe and honest answer . . . is that, in the last resort, we just do not know . . . It is arguable that the rationalist tradition which has dominated western thought since the eighteenth century has excluded a whole world of paranormal or psychic phenomena from our cognisance. Perhaps there were perceptions and experiences available to our distant forefathers which now elude us.' *The Witches of Salem* (London: Folio, 1982) pp. 183, 188.

21. Schopenhauer, op. cit., p. 268.

22. Schopenhauer, ibid., p. 270.

23. Moore, op. cit., p. 4.

24. Cf. Wallace, *Miracles and Modern Spiritualism* (London/Glasgow, 1875); 2nd edn (London: Trubner, 1886).

25. Gauld, op. cit., p. 140.

26. Cf. E. E. Lewis, *A Report of the Mysterious Noises heard in the House of Mr. John D. Fox, in Hydesville, Arcadia, Wayne County* (Canadaigua: E. E. Lewis, 1848). The book/pamphlet is one containing statements by the Fox family together with the depositions of thirteen other witnesses which were taken at the time and collated by Lewis, a local printer. It is not without interest that, more than half a century

later, in 1904, the skeleton of a man was actually found in the 'Fox house' following the collapse of a cellar wall. Reports of the discovery were prominently carried in the *Rochester Democrat and Chronicle* for 23 November 1904, and the *Boston Journal* for the same day. As a vivid prologue to the foregoing, one is reminded of the circumstances described by Pliny the Younger in his letter (Epistle XXII) to Licinius Sura; trans. Betty Radice, *Pliny: Letters and Panagyricus* (Cambridge, Mass.: Harvard University Press, 1969) 2 vols., I, pp. 543–9, p. 547.

27. Moore, op. cit., p. 3.
28. Parker, *Life and Correspondence of Theodore Parker*, ed John Weiss (New York: Appleton, 1864) 2 vols., I, p. 428. The remarks are in the form of rough notes meant for sermons.
29. Parker, ibid., p. 428.
30. Moore, op. cit., pp. 15–6.
31. Gauld, op. cit., p. 214.
32. Gauld, ibid., pp. 215–6. Cf. the biography of Home by his wife – Mme. D. D. Home, *D. D. Home: His Life and Mission* (London: Trubner, 1888). The original sources of the work are now in the archives of the Society for Psychical Research. Cf., also, Quin (W. T. W.), 4th Earl of Dunraven, *Experiences in Spiritualism with Mr. D. D. Home*, (London: Thomas Scott, 1869); reprinted with an introduction by Sir Oliver Lodge (London: Society for Psychical Research, 1924) For a contemporary appraisal of the significance of Home, see Elizabeth Jenkins, *The Shadow and the Light: A Defence of Daniel Dunglas Home the Medium* (London: Hamish Hamilton, 1982).
33. Gauld, ibid., p. 214.
34. Crookes, 'Notes of an Enquiry into the Phenomena called Spiritual' (January 1874); 'Experimental Investigation of a New Force' (July 1971); and 'Some Further Experiments on Psychic Force' (October 1871). The three articles were later incorporated by Crookes into his book *Researches in the Phenomena of Spiritualism* (London: Burns, 1874). They are reprinted, as part of the latter, in R. G. Medhurst/ K. M. Goldney/M. R. Barrington, *Crookes and the Spirit World: A Collection of writings by or concerning the work of Sir William Crookes, O.M., F.R.S., in the field of psychical research* (London: Souvenir, 1972).
35. Cf. Wallace, *My Life: A Record of Event and Opinions* (London: Chapman and Hall, 1905) 2 vols., II, pp. 286–7. Of further interest in this regard is his wider remark on the significance of Home: 'When we consider that Home's *séances* almost always took place in private houses at which he was a guest, and with people absolutely above suspicion of collusion with an impostor, and also in daytime or in a fully illuminated room, it will be admitted that no form of legerdemain will explain what occurred.' Ibid., p. 287.
36. Crookes, 'Some Further Experiments on Psychic Force'; reprinted Medhurst/Goldney/Barrington, op. cit., pp. 36–7.
37. Crookes, *'Psychic Force and Modern Spiritualism': A Reply to the "Quarterly Review"'* (December 1871); reprinted Medhurst/Goldney/

Barrington, ibid., pp. 61–92, p. 61. See chap. 7 in this volume.

38. Crookes, *Presidential Address to the British Association for the Advancement of Science, 1898*, pp. 34–5.

39. The article from which these words are taken, 'On Space of Four Dimensions', later came to constitute the first chapter of a book by Zöllner on his experiments with Slade – *Die transcendentale Physik und die sogenannte Philosophie* (Leipzig, 1879); trans. C. C. Massey *Transcendental Physics* (London: Harrison, 1880). References are given to the pages of this latter.

40. Zöllner, op. cit., p. 18.

41. Zöllner, ibid., xlv.

42. Zöllner, ibid., pp. xlv, xlviii.

43. It must be added that the virtually contemporaneous discovery of both ether and nitrous oxide anaesthesia was certainly a contributory factor to this lack of interest. At the same time, there is no disguising the, by any standard, abysmal primitiveness in the art and practice of medicine which went with the orthodoxy of the period – as is to be seen in the reminiscence of Sir Frederick Treves regarding the London Hospital in the 1850s where, as he recalls, all the wounds in a ward would be washed with the same sponge from the same bowl of water. *The Elephant Man and other Reminiscences* (London: Cassel, 1923) p. 57.

44. It may be added that, in 1843, Elliotson founded the journal *Zoist* of which he remained editor until its demise in 1856. At the time, it was the only vehicle for the dissemination of the results of 'magnetic' therapy and was, throughout its existence, the target of virulent attack by the official medical organ, *The Lancet*. Of passing interest, too, is the fact that Elliotson, a prominent opponent of spiritualistic claims, became a convert to the movement following 'sittings' with Home in the mid-1860s.

45. Charcot, 'Sur les divers états déterminés par l'hypnotisation chez les hystériques', *Comptes-Rendus hebdomadaires des séances de l'Académie des Sciences*, XCIV (1882), I, 403–5.

46. Richet, 'Du somnambulisme provoqué', *Journal de l'Anatomie et de la Physiologie normales et pathologiques de l'homme et des animaux*, II (1875), pp. 348–77. In anticipation of later reference to Richet, it is worth mention that, besides being among the select band of those who, in the 1880s, brought about the establishment of *psychology* as an independent discipline, he was, also, in 1913, to become a Nobel Prizewinner for research relating to the foundation of *immunology*. Reference may be made, too, to the famous work which Richet published towards the end of his life on the subject of the *psychical* – *Notre sixième sense* (Paris: Montaigne, 1928); trans. Fred Rothwell, *Our Sixth Sense* (London: Rider, 1929).

47. Heidenhain, *Der sog thierische Magnetismus: Physiologische Beobachtungen* (Leipzig: Breitkopf and Härtel, 1880); trans. by L. C. Wooldridge, *Hypnotism or Animal Magnetism* (London: Paul, 1880), with a Preface by George Romanes, p. 47. The work, as may be added, reached a wide audience in both Germany and England, with the

English translation being sponsored by Ludwig of the 'Helmholtz' School. In this regard, too, mention may be made of the fact that, in his Preface, Romanes warns against the over-simplicity of Heidenhain's claims though, at the same time, praising him for bringing the provocativeness of the phenomenon to scientific attention. Further, the propagandist conclusion drawn by Heidenhain in bringing the work to a close: '*Can it be called reasonable, when an agitation, arising from good principles, but ignorant of the nature and aims of science, seeks to wrest from physiology the most essential aid to its advance... Vivisection?*' Ibid., p. 48 (Heidenhain's italics).

48.   The point, indeed, is one that is reflected in the slightly earlier claim of Heidenhain that '*the hypnotic state is nothing more than an artificially produced catalepsy*'. Ibid., p. 25.

49.   A vital factor in this debacle is to be seen in the fact that, unlike his opponents at Nancy, Charcot never induced the hypnotic state himself but relegated this task to his assistants. See below.

50.   Cf. Charcot, 'Leçons sur les maladies du système nerveux', *Oeuvres complètes* (Paris: Progrès Médical, 1890), Vol. III, pp. 299–359.

51.   Bernheim, *De la suggestion dans l'état hypnotique et dans l'état de veille* (Paris: Doins, 1884).

52.   Bernheim, *De la suggestion et de ses applications à la thérapeutique* (Paris: Doins, 1886).

53.   The work also received an early English translation by Christian A. Herter, under the somewhat anomalous title of *Suggestive Therapeutics* (New York: Putnam, 1888).

54.   Bernheim, op. cit.,; translated by Herter under the revised title *Hypnotism and Suggestion in Psychotherapy* (New York: University Books, 1964) p. 90.

55.   Bernheim, ibid., pp. 90–1.

56.   Bernheim, ibid., p. 183.

57.   For these and other biographical details see Liébeault, *Pour constater la réalité du magnétisme. Confession d'un hypnotiseur. Extériorisation de la force neurique ou fluide magnétique.* (Paris: Libraire du magnétisme, n.d.).

58.   Liébeault, *Du sommeil et des états analogues, considérés surtout au point de vue de l'action du moral sur le physique* (Paris: Masson, 1866).

59.   Liébeault, *Le sommeil provoqué et les états analogues* (Paris: Doin, 1889).

60.   Cf. The claim of Noizet that it was he who, in 1819, converted Bertrand to the *mental* theory of the effect.

61.   The point is one that has been classically developed by Pierre Janet (1859–1947) in his famous *Les médications psychologiques* (Paris: Alcan, 1919).

62.   Bernheim, op. cit.; trans. by Herter, p. 28.

63.   Bernheim, ibid., p. 28.

64.   Bernheim, ibid., pp. 206–7.

65.   Bernheim, ibid., pp. 207, 209 (my italics).

66.   Bernheim, ibid., p. 72.

67.   Cf. Charcot's own intimation of this latter possibility in his development away from the field of *neuro-physiology* to the position of his

very last work – where, in testifying that he had seen patients go to Lourdes and return healed he speculates that the 'mechanism' of such cures might ultimately be found in an increased knowledge of the phenomenon of *faith*-healing. 'La foi qui guérit, *Archives de Neurologie* XXV (1893), pp. 72–87.

68. Dessoir, Max, *Bibliographie des modernen Hypnotismus* (Berlin: Dünker, 1888). The work specifically excludes popular articles from magazines and newspapers, as, also, reference to novels, stories and plays on the subject.

69. James, 'What Psychical Research has Accomplished', *The Will to Believe and Other Essays in Popular Philosophy* (New York: Longmans, Green, 1897) pp. 299–327, p. 302.

70. Marcuse, *Hypnosis: Fact and Fiction* (London: Pelican, 1959) p. 19. Cf. also Nicholas P. Spanes and Theodore X. Barber, 'Towards a Convergence in Hypnosis Research', *American Psychologist*, Vol. 29, No. 7 (July 1974), pp. 500–11.

71. Schopenhauer, op. cit., p. 268.

Chapter 7: THE SYSTEMATIC INVESTIGATION OF THE SUPER-NORMAL

1. Hall, Trevor H. *The Spiritualists* (London: Duckworth, 1962).

2. Carpenter, 'Spiritualism and its Recent Converts', *Quarterly Review*, (October 1871).

3. Crookes, 'Psychic Force and Modern Spiritualism: A reply to the "Quarterly Review"' (December 1871); later reprinted by Crookes, together with associated correspondence, in his *Researches in the Phenomena of Spiritualism*, Medhurst/Goldney/Barrington, op. cit., pp. 61–105.

4. Crookes – Medhurst/Goldney/Barrington, ibid., p. 79. So inaccurate, indeed, were the details of Carpenter's diatribe that, in the words of a recent writer, they could only be excused 'because he had erred in orthodoxy's service'. Brian Inglis, *Natural and Supernatural: A History of the Paranormal from Earliest Times to 1914* (London: Hodder and Stoughton, 1978); reprinted (London: Sphere Books, 1979) p. 293.

5. Clifford, 'On the Nature of Things-in-Themselves', *Lectures and Essays*, ed L. Stephen and F. Pollock (London: Macmillan, 1879) 2 vols., II, pp. 71–88, p. 78. The essay, which subsequently became widely known, originally appeared as an article in *Mind* (Old Series), January 1878, a year before the author's early death.

6. James, *The Boston Daily Advertiser*, 10 March 1869, quoted in *William James on Psychical Research*, ed Gardner Murphy and Robert O. Ballou (London: Chatto and Windus, 1960) p. 21. The passage is taken from a review by James of Epes Sargent's *Planchette: The Despair of Science* (Boston: Roberts, 1869). It was written, as may be mentioned, some sixteen years before the beginning of James' serious interest in the psychical. See below.

7. Sidgwick's best known philosophical work, his famous *The Methods of Ethics*, was published in 1874 (London: Macmillan).

8. Cf. the fact that the names of Sidgwick, Myers, Gurney, Leaf and the two Balfours are specifically given by one authority as among a short list of the most outstanding Cambridge intellectuals of the 1870s – D. H. Newsome, *Godliness and Good Learning* (London: Murray, 1961) pp. 27, 219. Rayleigh, Professor of Experimental Physics at Cambridge (from 1884), was later to become an original member of the Order of Merit as well as Nobel Prizewinner for physics in 1904. Passing mention may be made, too, of the fact that Clifford was also a Fellow of Trinity before going to take up the Chair of Applied Mathematics at University College, London, in 1870. See above.

9. Of these later members, especial mention may be made of Mrs. Eleanor Sidgwick (see below), Richard Hodgson (1855–1905), a later arrival at Cambridge, Frank Podmore (1856–1910), an Oxford man (see above), and, more latterly, Alice Johnson (1860–1940) of Cambridge, a protégé of Mrs. Sidgwick. See below.

10. With this union, Sidgwick, who was already brother-in-law to a future Archbishop of Canterbury through the marriage of his sister to E. W. Benson, was also made brother-in-law to a future Prime Minister, Arthur Balfour.

11. Gauld, op. cit., p. 116.

12. Gauld, ibid., p. 139.

13. Sidgwick himself held the post for nine out of the first eighteen years of the Society's existence and, in this respect, as Gauld notes, 'was thus able to exercise over it a degree of control very unusual in the President of a learned Society'. Ibid., p. 139.

14. Moses (London: London Psychological Press, 1883). The work – which originally dates from the early 1870s and which went through many editions – was published by Moses, a graduate of Oxford, under the pseudonym 'M. A. Oxon.' Its popularity and relative literary merit has made it, as Gauld comments, 'the Bible of British Spiritualism, or at least the leading piece of patristic literature'. Ibid., p. 78.

15. The paper, whose theme aroused widespread popular interest at the time, was accepted by the Anthropological sub-section of the Association on the casting vote of its Chairman, Wallace. It was later published by the Society for Psychical Research – 'On some Phenomena Associated with Abnormal Conditions of Mind', *Proceedings S.P.R.* I (1882–3), pp. 238–44.

16. Gauld, ibid., p. 79. The claims, which date from 1872, were the outcome of Moses' participation, with two of his close friends, in a 'home (spiritualistic) circle', a practice widely popular at the time and which, in the event (and according to the testimony), soon came to yield dramatic *physical*, as well as *mental*, effects.

17. Gauld, ibid., pp. 78–9.

18. Broad, 'Henry Sidgwick and Psychical Research', *Religion, Philosophy and Psychical Research*, pp. 86–115, p. 87.

19. Broad, ibid., p. 87.

20. Broad, ibid., pp. 89–90.

21. Broad, ibid., p. 90.
22. Cf. the same vital interest as expressed by James. Thus, in writing a few years before his own active involvement in, and, later, massive contribution to, *psychical* research: 'Are the much despised "Spiritualism" and the "Society for Psychical Research" to be the chosen instruments for a new era of faith? It would surely be strange if they were; but if they are not, I see no other agency that can do the work.' Letter to Thomas Davidson dated 30 March 1884 – *The Letters of William James*, edited by (his son) Henry James (Boston: Atlantic Monthly Press, 1920) 2 vols., I, p. 237.
23. Gauld, ibid., p. 89.
24. Myers, *Fragments of Inner Life* (private printing, 1893); reprinted (London: Society for Psychical Research, 1961) p. 12.
25. Myers, 'In Memory of Henry Sidgwick', *Proceedings S.P.R.* XV (1900–1) pp. 452–62, p. 454.
26. Cf. the magnitude of this conception as indicated by Broad in the fact that, only a century earlier, so great a figure as Kant, after himself being among the very first to address the idea of the *psychical* in his *Dreams of a Spirit Seer* (1766), had come to the conclusion that this must, forever, remain an 'Idea of Reason'; and with this, a matter of (*rational*) *faith*, as opposed to *knowledge*. 'Immanuel Kant and Psychical Research', *Religion, Philosophy and Psychical Research*, pp. 116–55, p. 147.
27. Sidgwick, *Proceedings S.P.R.*, I (1882–3), pp. 7–12, p. 8. Cf. in this regard, the earlier plea of the young James.
28. Sidgwick, ibid., p. 12.
29. Cf. with regard to this latter – Hodgson, 'An Account of Personal Investigations in India and Discussion of the Authorship of the "Koot Hoomi" Letters', *Proceedings S.P.R.*, III (1885), pp. 207–380. The terms of Hodgson's report, as may be added, remain, to this day, the subject of uncompromising rejection by theosophists.
30. Podmore, *Modern Spiritualism: A History and Criticism* (London: Methuen, 1902) 2 vols., I, p. 228.
31. It is worth mention that the names of Home and Moses conspicuously fall outside the main terms of this generalization.
32. Cf., Gauld, op. cit., pp. 223–45 for a full synopsis and comprehensive bibliography of the circumstances surrounding these events.
33. James, *Proceedings S.P.R.*, XII (1896–7) pp. 2–10, p. 6.
34. Gauld, op. cit., p. 313. The references to the two cited works are, respectively: Gurney, with Myers and Podmore – (London: Society for Psychical Research, 1886) 2 vols.; and Myers (posthumously) – (London: Longmans, Green, 1903) 2 vols.
35. James, 'Frederic Myers' Services to Psychology', *Memories and Studies* (New York: Longmans, Green, 1911) pp. 145–70, p. 170.
36. Huxley, A., in a Foreword to a new (abridged) edition of Myers' *Human Personality* (New York: University Books, 1961) pp. 7–8. Myers' influence, it may be added, is reflected, most directly, in James' classic *The Varieties of Religious Experience: A Study in Human Nature* (London: Longmans, 1902).

37. For present purposes, the term may be taken as embracing the closely related idea of *clairvoyance*. To this extent, the more specialized problems associated with the third main category of the *mentalistic*, that is *precognition*, may be deliberately set aside as lying beyond the scope of the present discussion.

38. Gauld, 'Early Experiments in Thought-Transference Published by the S.P.R.', op. cit., Appendix 'A', pp. 356–60.

39. James, 'What Psychical Research has Accomplished', op. cit., p. 310. A list of Gurney's principal papers on hypnotism is given by Gauld, op. cit., p. 159.

40. Gauld, ibid., p. 153.

41. Gurney/Myers *Proceedings S.P.R.*, I (1882–3), pp. 116–55, p. 118.

42. Gauld, op. cit., p. 160.

43. Cf. in this regard, Gurney's earlier, and still important, work in the philosophy of music – *The Power of Sound* (London: Smith and Elder, 1880).

44. *Proceedings S.P.R.*, X (1894), pp. 25–422. The present details are taken from the pages of this report.

45. Gauld, op. cit., p. 184. Cf. the suggestion of Broad, in his Perrott Lectures, given at Cambridge in 1959–60, that 'such a census should be repeated at the present time ... with all the refinements which recent experience in taking Gallup polls would suggest'. *Lectures on Psychical Research* p. 112.

46. Gauld, op. cit., p. 251.

47. These and other details are taken mainly from the biography of Mrs. Piper written by her daughter – Alta L. Piper, *The Life and Work of Mrs. Piper*, with an introduction by Sir Oliver Lodge (London: Kegan Paul, Trench and Trubner, 1929). See also M. Sage, *Madame Piper et la Société anglo-americaine pour les recherches psychique. Préface de Camille Flammarion* (Paris: Lemarie, 1902) – abridged English version by N. Robertson, *Mrs. Piper and the Society for Psychical Research*, with a Preface by Sir Oliver Lodge (London: Johnson, 1903).

48. In what follows, the exclusive concern will be with the bare epistemological significance of Mrs. Piper's mediumship, leaving aside entirely the multi-faceted (and intrinsically fascinating) psychological issues arising in this connexion.

49. James, 'Report of the Committee on Mediumistic Phenomena', *Proceedings of the American Society for Psychical Research*, I (1886–9), pp. 102 ff. – reprinted in Murphy/Ballou, *William James on Psychical Research*, pp. 95–100. The substance of the paper was republished in the *Proceedings of the Society for Psychical Research* as part of the wider report on Mrs. Piper's mediumship – 'A Record of Observations of Certain Phenomena of Trance', *Proceedings*, VI (1889–90), pp. 651–9, reprinted Murphy/Ballou, op. cit., pp. 102–10. See below. The paper, it may be added, was read to the Society, in the absence of James himself, by his brother, Henry.

50. James, *Proceedings*, op. cit., pp. 658–9, reprinted Murphy/Ballou, op. cit., p. 100.

51. Hodgson, 'A Record of Observations of Certain Phenomena of

Trance', *Proceedings S.P.R.*, VIII (1892), pp. 1–167.

52.   Cf. Lodge/Myers/Leaf, 'A Record of Observations of Certain Phenomena of Trance', *Proceedings S.P.R.*, VI (1889–90), pp. 436–650.

53.   Hodgson, 'A Further Record of Observations of Certain Phenomena of Trance', *Proceedings S.P.R.*, XIII (1897–8), pp. 284–582. In this connexion, mention may be made, also, of two further papers on the challenge of Mrs. Piper's mediumship by other prominent members of the American branch of the Society – (Professor) W. R. Newbold, 'A Further Record of Observations of Certain Phenomena of Trance, Pt. II', *Proceedings S.P.R.*, XIV (1898–9), pp. 6–49; and (Professor) J. H. Hyslop, 'A Further Record of Observations of Certain Trance Phenomena', *Proceedings S.P.R.*, XVI (1901) pp. 1–649. Of interest, too, is the wider public attention received by these studies as indicated by the meeting and debate of the Medico-Legal Society of New York in 1902 – edited by Clark Bell, *Spiritism, Hypnotism and Telepathy as involved in the case of Mrs. Leonora Piper* (New York: Medical-Legal Journal, 1902).

54.   James, 'What Psychical Research has Accomplished', op. cit., p. 314.

55.   Gauld, op. cit., p. 274.

56.   Broad – in his Foreword to *Swan on a Black Sea; A Study in Automatic Writing* ('The Cummins–Willett Scripts'), Geraldine Cummins, ed. Signe Toksvig (London: Routledge, Kegan Paul, 1965) pp. vii–lii, pp. vii–viii. It may be added that what Broad says here relates, not only to the evidence outlined above, but, also, to that obtained in later years through other mediums who followed Mrs. Piper in working for the Society under conditions of control. Cf. Broad's appraisal of the significance of three of the most famous of these figures, Mrs. Leonard, Mrs. 'Willett' (Mrs. Coombe-Tennant) and Mrs. Warren Elliott in his *Lectures on Psychical Research*, chaps. XI–XIII.

57.   In putting aside any further pursuit of the work of the Sidgwick group, it is worth noting that, at the time of his death, in 1905, Hodgson was planning a third paper on Mrs. Piper's mediumship; and that, thereafter, was to play a significant part in the above-mentioned 'Cross-Correspondences'. In this connexion, too, mention may be made of the *tour de force* of Mrs. Sidgwick's massive (657 page) paper on Mrs. Piper which appeared in 1915 – *Proceedings S.P.R.*, XXVIII. Cf. also, the earlier paper of Podmore, the group's most severe sceptic, in supporting the super-normality of Mrs. Piper's mediumship – 'Discussion of the Trance-Phenomena of Mrs. Piper' *Proceedings S.P.R.*, XIV (1898–9) pp. 50–78.

58.   Broad, 'Henry Sidgwick and Psychical Research', op. cit., p. 115.

59.   Cf. the success of Rhine's first book on the subject, *New Frontiers of the Mind* (New York/Toronto: Farrer and Rinehart, 1937); and, later (London: Pelican, 1950).

60.   Hardy, *The Living Stream: A Restatement of Evolution Theory and its Relation to the Spirit of Man* (London: Collins, 1965) p. 253. Cf. his words written fifteen years earlier in his Presidential Address to the Zoology Section of the British Association for the Advancement of Science: 'If telepathy has been established, as I believe it has, then

such a revolutionary discovery should make us keep our minds to the possibility that there may be much more in living things and their evolution than our science has hitherto led us to expect.' *The Advancement of Science*, Vol. VI, No. 21 (1949), pp. 213–23, p. 223.

61. Nowell-Smith, op. cit., p. 243.

Chapter 8: SUPER-NORMALITY AS A MODE OF THE PRESENT

1. Taylor, *Superminds* (London: Macmillan, 1975). Cf. also, Taylor, *Nature*, 254 (April 1975) pp. 472–3.
2. Hasted, *The Metal-Benders* (London: Routledge, Kegan Paul, 1981).
3. Taylor, *Superminds*, p. 158. Cf. also, in anticipation of later discussion, his further remark: 'The refusal to take Geller seriously is not confined to scientists. The mass media are full of stories about Geller being exposed or of some chemicals or conjurors able to achieve the same effects.' Ibid., p. 158.
4. Hasted, op. cit., p. 3. This work, in particular, will receive prominence in the course of what is to follow. References will, henceforth be given in the text under the prefix '*MB*'.
5. Quoted by Hasted (*MB* 13) from, Uri Geller, *My Story* (New York: Praeger, 1975).
6. Randi, James, *The Magic of Uri Geller* (Buffalo: Prometheus, 1975); later republished (with certain additions) under the title *The Truth about Uri Geller: One of the most eye-opening exposes* [sic] *of the decade about psychic claims and magic!* (Buffalo: Prometheus, 1982).
7. Randi, ibid., p.5.
8. Randi, ibid., p. 117. See below.
9. Taylor, *Superminds*, pp. 80, 81.
10. Taylor, *Science and the Supernatural* (London: Panther, 1980).
11. Randi, *The Truth about Uri Geller*, p. 2.
12. Inglis, *The Hidden Power* (London: Cape, 1986) p. 179.
13. Cf. also, in this connexion, Hasted/Bohm/E. W. Bastin/B. O'Reagan, *Nature*, 254 (April 1975) pp. 470–2. See below for a note on Hasted's use of latchkeys in his experiments.
14. Cf. also, in particular, the earliest of these reports – edited by C. Panati, *The Geller Papers: Scientific Observations on the Paranormal Powers of Uri Geller* (Boston: Houghton Mifflin, 1976).
15. The point made here by Hasted reflects, as he makes plain, an admission of Randi himself. (Cf. *MB* 14, 258.)
16. To which he adds, in reiterating a further theme of the preceding discussion: 'The lack of such a theory has led to the observations themselves being discredited, and indeed there are various social and psychological pressures which reinforce this discredit. It is an interesting example of the thesis that scientific observations are often judged by social criteria' (*MB* 1). See chap. 9 in this volume.
17. Cf. also, in this connexion – Hasted, 'An Experimental Study of the Validity of the Metal Bending Phenomena', *Journal of the Society For Psychical Research*, Vol. 48, No. 770 (December 1976) pp. 365–83.

18. Hasted's use of *latchkeys* in the present regard is to be explained, partly in terms of experimental standardization, and partly, as he makes plain, in those of a previously acquired technical expertise in the handling of their tensile properties. (Cf. *MB* 8–9). With this, too, there is a further consideration which, though relating more especially to the 'touching' mode of the phenomenon, is also worthy of note, namely: 'Many spoons are so weak that anyone with moderately strong hands might bend them. But latchkeys . . . are much tougher, and I know few people who can bend them with one hand pressed against a hard surface' (*MB* 10).

19. There is, also, the point, as he makes it, that the use of ferromagnetic metals must be avoided since 'spontaneous relaxation of domains might cause signals due to the Barkhausen effect' (*MB* 52).

20. Cf. further, his remarks that 'I have since successfully exposed the sensors to other subjects in other countries' (*MB* 52) and that 'at the time of writing, ten other groups of workers have successfully used essentially the same equipment as ours [with] their reporting of signals [constituting] an important confirmation of our findings' (*MB* 56).

21. Hasted, *Journal of the Society for Psychical Research*, Vol. 49, No. 773 (September 1977) pp. 583–91, p. 583. The subject, it may be added, had previously figured prominently in experiments with Taylor; and, in the latter's book, is identified as a sixteen-year-old boy rating even 'as highly as Geller himself' in some of his abilities. Taylor, *Superminds*, p. 159.

22. Hasted, op. cit., p. 583. Cf. in supplementation of earlier remarks, Hasted's *rationale* for the subject being engaged in, for example, the activity of aircraft modelling: 'A most important lesson which is taught to the metal-bender by use of the strain gauge detector is the avoidance of over-concentration; he must learn "sudden inattention" if he wants results . . . The strongest events often take place, it appears, when the subject relaxes directly after concentration. He must learn to be patient and not to "concentrate on concentration"' (*MB* 54–5). Similar reasons are cited by Hasted for conducting his main experiments in the familiar circumstances of the subjects' own homes. (Cf. *MB* 23). See below.

23. Broad, *Lectures on Psychical Research*, p. 6

Chapter 9: THE CHALLENGE OF THE SUPER-NORMAL

1. Bultmann, *Kerygma and Myth*, p. 21.
2. Bultmann, *Jesus Christ and Mythology*, p. 47.
3. Gunkel, *Die Wirkungen des Heiligen Geistes* (Göttingen: Vandenhoeck and Ruprecht, 1888).
4. Bultmann, *Jesus Christ and Mythology*, pp. 47–8.
5. Bultmann, *Kerygma and Myth*, p. 121.
6. Cf. in this regard, the insight of the English commentator to the *kerygma* debate'. Thus, (Austin) Farrer: 'It may be that the real first step of Dr. Bultmann's whole plea is the exhortation to embrace

existentialism or drown, and that everything else is a mere corollary to that.' Ibid., p. 221.

7. Schopenhauer, 'Essay on Spirit Seeing and everything connected therewith', op. cit., pp. 264–5. Further references to this work will be given in the body of the text under the prefix '*SS*'.

8. Cf. in this connexion – though with no further pursuit of the matter – Schopenhauer's additional claim that, not only Kant's *two world* view, but, also, his own philosophy of *will* is to be seen as deriving support from the fact of 'magnetic'/mesmeric effects. Cf. ibid., 267, 301.

9. Schopenhauer, *Die Welt als Wille und Vorstellung* (Leipzig: Brockhaus, 1819) 2nd edn., 1844. Translated by E. F. J. Payne. (New York: Dover, 1958) 2 vols; I, p. xxiii (my italics).

Chapter 10: THE DEMISE OF SCIENTIFIC MATERIALISM

1. Schopenhauer, 'Essay on Spirit Seeing and everything connected therewith', op. cit., p. 229.

2. Schopenhauer, ibid., p. 300.

3. It is, of course, this aspect which, as resting on the *atomism* of Democritus, was later to constitute the inspiration behind the, still living, tradition associated with the name of Epicurus. The reader may be left with the thought of the strength of this strain in its relation to the, previously considered, views of Bultmann and Robinson.

4. Whittaker, *A History of the Theories of the Aether and Electricity* (London: Nelson, 1910) revised and enlarged 1951; reprinted (New York: Harper, 1960) 2 vols., I, pp. 12–13. Cf. also, the point, as made by Whittaker, of the influence of Democritus, through Gassendi, on Robert Boyle (1626–91), and, hence, on the future course of *chemistry*. Ibid., I, p. 293. See below.

5. Newton, *Opticks* (1704) Bk. III, Pt. 1; (New York: Dover, 1952) p. 400.

6. Cf. Laplace, *Oeuvres Complètes de Laplace* (Paris: Gautier Villars, 1878–1912) Vol. viii, p. 144.

7. Mach, *Die Mechanick in ihrer Entwickelung: Historisch-Kritisch Dargestellt* (Leipzig: Brockhaus, 1883); trans. T. J. McCormack, *The Science of Mechanics: A Critical and Historical Account of its Development* (Chicago: Open Court, 1893) 6th edn., 1960, pp. 588–9 (my final italics).

8. Maxwell, 'Molecules', *Nature*, Vol. VIII (1873); reprinted in *The Scientific Papers of James Clerk Maxwell*, ed. W. D. Niven (Cambridge: Cambridge University Press, 1890) 2 vols., II, pp. 361–77, esp. pp. 361, 376, 377.

9. Maxwell, ibid., p. 377.

10. Bohm, *Causality and Chance in Modern Physics* (London: Routledge, Kegan Paul, 1959–84) p. 39.

11. Bohr, 'Discussions with Einstein on Epistemological Problems in Atomic Physics', *Atomic Physics and Human Knowledge* (New York/London: Wiley, 1958) pp. 32–66, p. 34.

12. See below.

13. Eddington, *The Nature of the Physical World* (Cambridge: Cambridge University Press, 1929) pp. 1, 2.

14. Eddington, ibid., pp. xii, xiii.

15. Whittaker, op. cit., II, p. 51 (my italics).

16. Eddington, *The Philosophy of Physical Science* (Cambridge: Cambridge University Press, 1939) pp. 108–9 (my final italics).

17. Born, *Moderne Physik* (1933); trans. John Dougall, *Atomic Physics* (London/Glasgow: Blackie, 1935); 7th edn. (New York: Hafner, 1957) p. 99.

18. Heisenberg, *Across the Frontiers*; trans. Peter Heath (New York/London: Harper and Row, 1974) p. 114.

19. Bohr, op. cit., p. 60 (my italics).

20. Heisenberg, 'Fresh Fields', *Physics and Beyond: Encounters and Conversations*, trans. Arnold J. Pomerans, (New York/London: Harper and Row, 1971) pp. 70–81, pp. 80–1.

21. Heisenberg, ibid., p. 81.

22. Einstein/Podolsky/Rosen, *Physical Review* 47 (1935) pp. 777–80.

23. Einstein/Podolsky/Rosen, op. cit., p. 777.

24. Einstein/Podolsky/Rosen, ibid., p. 780. Cf. the rider to 'EPR' that this is not the case on the 'Copenhagen Interpretation' where, as it is held, the reality of one of the correlates must be denied: 'On this point of view, since either one or the other, but not both simultaneously, of the quantities P and Q can be predicted, they are not simultaneously real.' Ibid., p. 780.

25. Bohr, 'Quantum Mechanics and Physical Reality', *Nature* 136 (1935) p. 65; and, more fully – 'Can Quantum-Mechanical Description of Physical Reality be considered Complete?' *Physical Review*, 48 (1935), pp. 696–702.

26. Bell, *Physics*, 1 (1965) pp. 195–200.

27. Bohm, David, *Quantum Theory* (Englewood Cliffs: Prentice-Hall, 1951); chap. 22, sections 15–19 – 'The Paradox of Einstein, Rosen and Podolsky', pp. 611–23. For present, non-technical, purposes, the experiment may be seen as turning on the conception of *pairs* of discrete 'particles'/*photons* which, as produced *simultaneously* from a *singleton* state, move freely away from each other in opposite directions.

28. Cf. Aspect/Phillipe Grangier/Gérard Roger, 'Experimental Realization of Einstein–Podolsky–Rosen–Bohm *Gedankenexperiment:* A New Violation of Bell's Inequalities', *Physical Review Letters* Vol. 49, No. 2 (July 1982) pp. 91–4; and Aspect/Jean Dalibard/Roger, 'Experimental Test of Bell's Inequalities Using Time-Varying Analyzers', ibid., Vol. 49, No. 25 (December 1982) pp. 1804–7.

29. Cf. in this regard – Paul Davies, *God and the New Physics* (London/Melbourne: Dent, 1983); reprinted (London: Pelican, 1984).

30. Wheeler, 'Beyond the End of Time', C. Misner/K. S. Thorne/Wheeler, *Gravitation* (San Francisco: Freeman, 1973) pp. 1196–1217, p. 1217. The chapter/paper constitutes the substance of Wheeler's noted Marchon and Nuffield lectures given respectively at the Universities of Newcastle-upon-Tyne and Cambridge in May and July 1971.

31. Wheeler, ibid., p. 1217. Cf. further, his remark: 'Are we destined to return to the great concept of Leibniz of "pre-established harmony" ("Leibniz logic loop"), before we can make the next great advance?' Ibid., p. 1217. The point is one which will be the subject of further comment as well as (implicit) answer in the following chapter.
32. Clauser/Shimony, 'Bell's Theorem, experimental tests and implications', *Reports on Progress in Physics* Vol. 41 (1978) pp. 1881–1927. The paper, as may be noted, appeared before the conducting of the vital Aspect experiments.
33. Clauser/Shimony, ibid., p. 1881.
34. Clauser/Shimony, ibid., p. 1921.
35. Cf. Rae, Alastair I. M., *Quantum Physics: Illusions or Reality* (Cambridge: Cambridge University Press, 1986); as, also, Rae, 'Extrasensory quantum physics', *New Scientist* Vol. 112, No. 1536 (November 1986) pp. 36–9.

Chapter 11: PHYSICAL REALITY AND PHILOSOPHICAL IDEALITY

1. Schrödinger, *Mind and Matter* (Cambridge: Cambridge University Press, 1958) pp. 37–8.
2. Cf. in this regard, the vital comment of Schrödinger that 'consciousness is never experienced in the plural, only in the singular', op. cit., p. 55. See below.
3. Cf. the fact that the term is to be found neither in the Authorized Version of the Bible, nor in the works of Shakespeare.
4. What may be noted, too, is the ambivalence of the Cartesian position in this respect. For, despite the fact, for example, of Descartes' *personal* commitment to the *divine* origin of (some, at least) *dreams*, his definition of *mind* in terms of *consciousness/ awareness* is also open to implicative construction as an attack on the earlier tradition. See below.
5. Schopenhauer, *The World as Will and Representations*, op. cit., Vol. 1, p. 3.
6. Clifford, 'The Philosophy of the Pure Sciences', op. cit., I, pp. 254–340, p. 288.
7. References are given to the section numbers of the main body of the *Treatise*.
8. Russell, *History of Western Philosophy* (London: Allen and Unwin, 1946) p. 673.
9. On a point of accuracy, the latter originally appeared in 1748 as *Philosophical Essays concerning the Human Understanding* with the revised and present title being given in 1758.
10. Hume, *Treatise*, Bk. 1, Pt. II, Sect. VI (my italics).
11. Hume, *Enquiry*, II, 17. With necessary simplification, as well as freedom, the synopsis which follows is given to the fuller, if less aggressively pungent, argument of the *Treatise*.
12. Hume, *Treatise*, Bk. 1, Pt. 1, Sect. IV.
13. Hume, *Treatise*, Bk. 1, Pt. 111, Sect. V.

14. Hume, *Treatise*, Bk. 1, Pt. III, Sect. VI (Hume's main italics).
15. Cf. the anomaly of this conclusion in its relation to the virulence of Hume's rejection of the possibility of the *miraculous*. See Chapter 2 in this volume.
16. Hume, letter dated 8 June 1776 to his friend and publisher, William Strahan, just a few months before his death. Ed J. Y. T. Greig, *The Letters of David Hume* (Oxford: Clarendon, 1932) 2 vols. II, p. 322.
17. Hume, 'My Own Life' (April 1776); ed Greig, ibid., I, pp. 1–7, p. 2.
18. Kant, *Prolegomena zu einer jeden künftigen Metaphysik die als Wissenschaft wird auftreten können* (1783), *Schriften* (Ak. Ed.) IV, pp. 253–383; trans. Lewis White Beck, *Prolegomena to Any Future Metaphysics* (Indianapolis/New York: Bobbs-Merrill, 1951) p. 6. See below.
19. The remark is that of John Ker of Kersland, a leader of the Scottish Cameronians, who arrived in Hanover on the day of Leibniz's death. Cf. R. Latta, *Leibniz: The Monadology and other Philosophical Writings*, translated and introduced by Latta, Introduction, pp. 1–211, p. 16.
20. Leibniz, *Essais de Théodicée sur la Bonté de Dieu, la Liberté de l'Homme et l'Origine du Mal* (Amsterdam, 1710). The work, of course, is that which, in a later context, was so remorselessly lampooned by Voltaire in his *Candide*.
21. Leibniz/Clarke – *A Collection of Papers which passed between the late Learned Mr. Leibniz and Dr. Clarke in the years of 1715 and 1716 related to the Principles of Natural Philosophy and Religion* (London, 1717).
22. Cf. in this regard, Newton's idea of *space* as 'God's *sensorium*' – 'Is not infinite *space* the *sensory* of a Being incorporeal, living, intelligent, omnipresent?' *Opticks*, Query 28; op. cit., p. cxiv (my italics).
23. Alexander, H. G. – editor, *The Leibniz–Clarke Correspondence* (Manchester: Manchester University Press, 1956) Preface, p. vii.
24. Cf. Aristotle, *Physics*, IV. 2, 209.
25. Leibniz, 'Monadologie', *Opera Philosophica*, ed J. E. Erdmann, (Berlin, 1840).
26. Broad, *Leibniz: An Introduction* (Cambridge: Cambridge University Press, 1975), ed. C. Lewy, p. 88.
27. This, too, as may be mentioned, is an argument, which tradition has as going back to Zeno.
28. Leibniz, 'Monadologie' (3); trans. Leroy E. Loemker, *Leibniz: Philosophical Papers and Letters* (Chicago: Chicago University Press, 1956) pp. 643–52, p. 643.
29. Leibniz, ibid., (17); trans. Loemker, op. cit., p. 644. See below.
30. Leibniz, ibid., (63); trans. Loemker, ibid, p. 649.
31. Leibniz, ibid., (61); trans. Loemker, ibid, p. 649.
32. Cf. once more, the anomaly of the point that, despite the depth of Hume's *personal* antipathy towards the idea of the *miraculous* his *metaphysical* position is one which – like that of Berkeley, and unlike that of Leibniz – allows a full accommodation of such (putative) events. See above.
33. Cf. in particular, A. J. Ayer, *Language, Truth and Logic* (London: Gollancz, 1936). See below.
34. See above ch. 10 in this volume.

35.　Cf. in this regard, the words of Arthur Koestler: 'Newton was a crank theologian like Kepler, and like Kepler addicted to chronology; he dated the Creation from 4004 BC after Bishop Usher and held that the tenth horn of the fourth beast of the Apocalypse represented the Roman Church.' *The Sleepwalkers* (London: Hutchinson, 1959) p. 526. See above, Chapter 3, note 8.

36.　Cf. the famous proclamation of Einstein that 'God does not throw dice'. See ch. 10 in this volume. It is not without interest, too, to note the intimate interrelation between this primitive (*religious*) image and the 'classical' *scientific* ideal of eventually attaining an *exhaustive* understanding – a 'God's eye' view, as it were – of physical reality.

37.　Whyte, *Roger Joseph Boscovich, S.J., F.R.S. (1711–1787): Studies of His Life and Work on the 250th Anniversary of his Birth* – ed Whyte, (London: Allen and Unwin, 1961) pp. 106, 118, 119.

38.　Kant's own main effort in this direction is contained in his *Metaphysische Anfangsgründe der Naturwissenschaft/Metaphysical Foundations of Natural Science* (1786), a work which appeared between the two editions of the *Critique of Pure Reason* and which was the outcome of ideas originally sketched by him in 1765. They are ideas, too, on which he was working at the time of his death. See below.

39.　Boscovich himself, as may be mentioned, never uses the term 'atom'. Notwithstanding, there is still the caution of Whyte: 'However brilliant Boscovich's arguments and penetrating his insight into the task of a theory of fundamental structure, the *Theoria* often evokes a sense of unreality and uncertainty, even where the arguments are still formally valid. The reason for that is that it is not clear whether Boscovich's *puncta* ... can be identified in *physical* systems.' Op. cit., p. 111 (my final italic).

40.　Whyte, *The Unconscious Before Freud* (New York: Basic Books, 1960) p. 8.

41.　Whyte, ibid., pp. 8–9 (my italics).

42.　Whyte, ibid., p. 63.

43.　Whyte, ibid., pp. 27–8, 60, 86 (my final italics).

44.　Whyte, ibid., p. 66. Platner, as may be added, held the Chair of Medicine and Physiology at Leipzig during the latter decades of the century and was a prominent figure in the intellectual life of Germany during the period.

45.　The terms of this controversy have been carried into the present century, with the division between Freud's exclusively *causal* approach to the *unconscious*, and the outlook of Jung, with its insistence, also, on appeal to wider, *vitalistic*, considerations. It is a debate, too, which, *mutatis mutandis*, may be seen as anticipating the epistemological difficulties surrounding *quantum* theory.

46.　Kant, *Anthropologie in pragmatischer Hinsicht abgefasst* (1798), *Schriften* (Ak. Ed.) VII, pp. 117–333; trans. M. J. Gregor, *Anthropology from a Pragmatic Point of View* (Hague: Nijhoff, 1974) p. 135. The work itself is to be seen as Kant's manual for a highly popular course of lectures which, starting in the mid-1960s, he gave at Königsberg for some thirty years.

47.　The work, for current purposes, may be taken as deriving its fame from the scale of its (*speculative*) extension of Lockean (*empirical/causal*) psychology to the non-observable sphere of (*unconscious*) mind. Cf. too, Whyte's assessment of the significance of Herder in the present regard: 'The validity of Herder's outlook is remarkable, as far as we can judge it today. He hints at many important aspects of unconscious mental processes: their demonic and frightening power; their importance as the source of human nobility, of the unifying imagination, of poetry, and of dreams; their roots in childhood experience; their role in cognition; their greater accessibility in dreams, in passion, and in illness; and the opportunity they offer for therapy.' *The Unconscious Before Freud*, p. 117.

48. Leibniz, *Nouveaux Essais sur l'Entendement humain* (Amsterdam/Leipzig, 1765).

49. F. McEachran, *The Life and Philosophy of J. G. Herder* (Oxford: Clarendon, 1939) p. 23.

50. The abbreviation may be taken, henceforth, as relating exclusively to the *Kritik der reinen Vernunft/Critique of Pure Reason* (1781, 1787), *Schriften* (Ak, Ed.) III, IV.

51. Leibniz, *Nouveaux Essais*; translated and edited by P. Remnant and J. Bennett, (Cambridge: Cambridge University Press, 1981) p. 54.

52. Leibniz, ibid., p. 48.

53. Leibniz, ibid., p. 52 (my italics).

54. References to the work will be given in the body of the text to the translation by Norman Kemp Smith – (London: Macmillan, 1933). The pagination will be that of the Berlin Academy Edition with the letters 'A' and 'B' relating respectively, and following convention, to the first and second editions.

55. Kant, *Prolegomena*; translated by Beck, op. cit., p. 8.

56. They may be listed: (i) 'The world has a beginning in time, and is also limited as regards space . . .'/'The world has no beginning, and no limits in space . . .' (A426–7 B454–5); (ii) 'Every composite substance in the world is made up of simple parts . . .'/'No composite thing in the world is made up of simple parts . . .' (A434–5 B462–3); (iii) 'Causality in accordance with laws of nature is not the only causality . . .'/'There is no freedom; everything in the world takes place solely in accordance with the laws of nature . . .' (A444–5 B472–3); (iv) 'There belongs to the world a being that is absolutely necessary . . .'/'An absolutely necessary being nowhere exists . . .' (A452–3 B480–1). They are divided by Kant under the heads of (a) the *mathematical* and (b) the *dynamical*, with (i) and (ii) falling under (a) and (iii) and (iv) under (b). The immediate discussion may be seen as relating to Kant's chronologically prior pre-occupation with (a), with the wider problems of (b), though resting on (a), being taken as of later determination.

57. Kant, letter to Garve dated 21 September 1798, *Schriften* (Ak. Ed.) XII, pp. 257–8; trans. Arnulf Zweig, *Kant: Philosophical Correspondence, 1759–99* (Chicago: Chicago University Press, 1967) p. 252 (my italics).

58. See above note 56.

59. Kant, loose fragment (undated), *Schriften* (Ak. Ed.) XVIII, fr. 5037, p. 69 (my translation). By way of consolidation, there may be reference to the words of Herman-J. de Vleerschauwer: 'Kant found the true Leibnizian epistemology [as opposed to its Wolffian interpretation] in the *Nouveaux Essais* brought to light [for him] in 1767. This discovery of Leibniz becomes very important from this time on.' *L'Évolution de la pensée Kantienne* (1939); trans. A. R. C. Duncan, *The Development of Kantian Thought* (Edinburgh: Nelson, 1962).

60. Kant, *De Mundi Sensibilis atque Intelligibilis Forma et Principiis* (1770), *Schriften* (Ak. Ed.) II, pp. 385, 419; translated and introduced by G. B. Kerford and D. E. Walford, *Kant: Selected Pre-Critical Writings and Correspondence with Beck* (Manchester: Manchester University Press, 1968) pp. 47–92.

61. Beattie, *Essay on the Nature and Immutability of Truth* (1770). Cf. Kant's castigation of this writer, as an adherent of the Scottish school of 'Common-sense' Philosophy. Thus, in the *Prolegomena*: 'I should think that Hume might fairly have laid as much claim to common sense as Beattie, and, in addition, to a critical reason (such as the latter did not possess)'. Trans. Beck, op. cit., p. 7.

62. Kant's first-hand acquaintance with the *Treatise*, as may be added, did not come until the early 1790s with the first German translation of this work.

63. Kant, letter to Marcus Herz dated 21 February 1772, *Schriften* (Ak. Ed.) X, pp. 129–30; trans. Zweig, op. cit., p. 73.

64. Smith, *A Commentary to Kant's 'Critique of Pure Reason'* (London: Macmillan, 1923) p. xxix.

65. Cf. the reflection of this latter division in the previously mentioned *antinomies*. The ground of this relation may be set aside as being beyond the bounds of the present concern.

66. Cf. in this regard, the words of Kant in a fragmentary note: 'Tetens investigated the concepts of human reason merely subjectively (human nature), but I investigated them objectively. The former analysis is empirical, the latter transcendental'; and, again, more ironically: 'I concerned myself not with the evolution of concepts like Tetens (actions through which concepts are generated), nor with the analysis of them, like Lambert, but merely with their objective validity. I am no rival to these men'. *Schriften* (Ak. Ed.) XVIII, frs. 4901, 4900, p. 23 (my translations).

67. Cf. the same point as expressed earlier in his *Anthropology*: 'People who study the soul usually take the terms *inner sense* and *apperception* as synonymous despite the fact that "inner sense" should be reserved for a psychological (applied) consciousness and "apperception" for a logical (pure) consciousness'. Trans. Gregor, op. cit., p. 142. For a more detailed discussion of the issues raised here, see T. C. Williams, *The Unity of Kant's 'Critique of Pure Reason': Experience, Language and Knowledge* (Lewiston/Queenston: Mellen, 1987).

68. Schrödinger, *What is Life? The Physical Aspects of the Living Cell* (Cambridge: Cambridge University Press, 1945) p. 31.

69. The passage is not to be taken as endorsing the figment, as propagated, most notably, by Ayer, through the fame of his *Language, Truth and Logic*, of a failure by Kant to appreciate the importance of *compound*, for example, *hypothetical* and *disjunctive*, propositions. It is, rather, to underscore his full and early recognition that the basic/constituent elements of these are to be seen as *categorical* in form. Cf. in this regard: 'I have never been able to accept the interpretation which logicians give of judgement in general. It is, they declare, the representation of a relation between two concepts. I do not here dispute with them as to what is defective in this interpretation – that in any case it applies only to *categorical*, not to hypothetical and disjunctive judgements (the two latter containing a relation not of concepts but of judgements), an oversight from which many troublesome consequences have followed' (B 141).

70. The special problems associated with *algebra*, as, also, more recent advances in the field, may for present purposes be taken as derivative from the ontologically, as well as chronologically, prior conditions of *arithmetic* and (Euclidean) *geometry*.

71. This is not, of course, to say that such (mathematical) *intuitions/ relations* cannot, also, be *empirically* demonstrated, as, for instance, on paper. It is merely to emphasize the ontological primacy of the former.

72. The conclusion is one that is entirely consonant with the previously noted thesis that, for Kant, *all* knowledge is to be taken as arising from *experience*. See below.

73. Cf. more fully: 'Consequently, mathematics is the only science that has definitions. For the object which it thinks it exhibits *a priori* in intuition, and this object certainly cannot contain either more or less than the concept, since it is through the definition that the concept of the object is given – and given originally, that is without its being necessary to derive the definition from any other source' (A729–30 B757–8).

74. Cf.: 'Before we can analyse our representations, the representations must themselves be given, and therefore as regards *content* no concepts can first arise by way of analysis' (A77 B103). See below.

75. Cf. Kant's remark that *philosophical* knowledge rests on 'acroamatic (discursive) proofs [that is, "proofs" which] *may be conducted by the agency of words alone.*' (A735 B763. My final italics). There may be note, too, though without pursuing the matter, that, on the Kantian view, *ethical* propositions are, also, to be seen as falling under the present head.

76. Cf.: 'Mathematics and physics, the two sciences in which reason yields theoretical knowledge, have to determine their objects *a priori*, the former doing so quite purely, *the latter having to reckon, at least, partially, with sources of knowledge other than reason*' (Bx. My main italics).

77. For a more detailed discussion of the issues raised here, see Williams, op. cit.

78. Cf. the main divisions of the *Prolegomena* which are themselves

headed by precisely these three questions.

79. The tenets embraced under the *logical positivist* so-called *principle of significance* may be briefly summarized. Thus – (a) that the only *real/valid/true* propositions are those falling under the bare terms of its own (Humean) formulation of the *analytic-synthetic* distinction; (b) that all other subject-predicate assertions, for example, and most particularly, those relating to *religion/ethics/metaphysics*, are to be regarded as no more than mere *'pseudo*-propositions'; and (c) that it is only (a), as opposed to (b), which are to be viewed as having any *meaning/significance*. To this extent, the overriding contentions of the outlook may be laid for inspection. On the one hand, there is the claim (x) that the entire realm of the (*ampliative*) *meaningful* is reducible, in the last resort, to statements which are *scientific* in the sense of being *empirical/probablistic* in nature. On the other hand, (y) that the 'seeming' propositions of *religion/ethics/metaphysics* are to be relegated to the status of, what, in the extreme, must be taken as, expressions of exclusively *physiological/psychological* determination, for example need, hope, approval, aversion and so on. See below.

80. The same must also be said of the much quoted counter-instance to *Euclidean* geometry of Einstein's conception of the shortest distance between two points in *astro-physical* space being 'the curved path followed by a *light* "particle"/"ray"'. This, of course, for Kant, would be a mode of *discursive* knowledge, as opposed to *pure intuition*.

81. Kant, *Schriften*, XXI, XXII. Cf. in particular, Convolutes X, XI and XII under the head of 'Transition from the Metaphysical Foundations of Natural Science to Physics' in XXII.

82. Kant, ibid., XXII, p. 411 (my translation). Cf. in this connexion, Kant's rudimentary anticipation of, what may be conceived as, a *unified* (electro-magnetic) *spectrum*: 'Are they stuffs, or merely powers, i.e. modified "stuff"?'. Ibid., p. 411 (my translation).

83. Cf. letter from Kant to J. H. Lambert dated 31 December 1765, *Schriften*, X, p. 56; trans. Zweig, op. cit., p. 49.

84. Kant, *Schriften*, XXII, Convolutes X, XI and XII.

85. Kant, letter dated 21 September 1798, op. cit., p. 256; trans. Zweig, op. cit., p. 251.

86. Cf. in this regard, the glorious exaggeration of Alfred North Whitehead in his Gifford Lectures for 1927–8: 'The safest general characterization of the European philosophical tradition is that it consists of a series of footnotes to Plato.' *Process and Reality: An Essay in Cosmology* (London: Macmillan, 1929) p. 63.

87. The latter terminology is to be seen as embracing the former in the context of Kant's (methodological) assimilation of the *physical* to the *perceptual/mentalistic*.

Chapter 12: KNOWLEDGE, SUPER-NORMALITY AND FAITH

1. Schopenhauer, *The World as Will and Representation*, trans. Payne, op. cit., II, p. 3.

2. Schopenhauer, ibid., II, pp. 3–4.

3. Schrödinger, *Mind and Matter*, p. 40.

4. Schrödinger, ibid., p. 40. The original reference from Jung is *Eranos Jahrbuch* (1946), p. 398.

5. Cf. in the former regard, two books, in particular, Fritjof Capra, *The Tao of Physics: An Examination of the Parallels between Modern Physics and Eastern Mysticism* (Boulder: Shambhala, 1975) and Gary Zukav, *The Dancing Wu Li Masters: An Overview of the New Physics* (New York: Morrow, 1979).

6. Cf. the (Newtonian) basis of this position as portrayed by Koestler: 'It is only by bringing into the open the inherent implications of Newtonian gravity, that one is able to realize the enormous courage – or sleepwalker's assurance – that was needed to use it as the basic concept of cosmology. In one of the most reckless and sweeping generalizations in the history of thought, Newton filled the entire space of the universe with interlocking forces of attraction, issuing from all particles of matter, across the boundless abysses of darkness.' Op. cit., p. 504.

7. Koestler, ibid., p. 535. Cf. the significance of what Koestler says here in its relation to the *philosophical* outlook of Stephen W. Hawking in his recent and best selling work *A Brief History of Time: From the Big Bang to Black Holes* (New York/London: Bantam, 1988).

8. See chap. 2 in this volume.

9. Schopenhauer, 'Essay on Spirit Seeing and everything connected therewith', trans. Payne op. cit., pp. 226, 302. Cf. the development of this idea by Gustav Fechner, *Elemente der Psychophysik* (Leipzig: 1860) 2 vols., II, pp. 526–30; and by William James, *Human Immortality: Two Supposed Objections to the Doctrine* (London: Watt, 1898). Cf. also, Jung, *Naturerklärung und Psyche* (Zurich: Rascher, 1952), trans. R. F. C. Hull, *Synchronicity: An Acausal Connecting Principle* (London: Routledge, Kegan Paul, 1972).

10. Schopenhauer, 'Essay on Spirit Seeing and everything connected therewith', op. cit., p. 268 (my italics).

11. The *incomprehensibility* of the doctrine is, on the view in hand, to be seen as a necessary feature of its connotation.

12. Cf. Kant's *philosophical/theological* development of these views in his *Die Religion innerhalb der Grenzen der blossen Vernunft* (1793), *Schriften* (Ak. Ed.) VI, pp. 1–292; trans. with an introduction by Theodore M. Greene and Hoyt H. Hudson, *Religion within the Limits of Reason Alone* (Chicago: Open Court, 1934).

13. Jenkins, Easter Sunday 1989, Tyne-Tees television programme 'Inner Sense'.

14. Perry, London, 20 February 1982, p. 8; reprinted, Perry, *Psychic Studies: A Christian View* (London: Aquarian Press, 1984) pp. 26–8. Cf. the situation as described by Schopenhauer just over a century and a quarter ago, in the instance with regard to the Roman Church: 'On the 4th August, 1856, the Roman Inquisition issued a circular to all the bishops, in which it called upon them in the name of the Church to use their utmost influence against the practice of Animal Magnetism. The reasons for this are given with striking want of

lucidity and great vagueness, and even here are not unmixed with falsehood. This circular is published in the "Turin Journal" of December, 1856, and again in the French "Univers" and reprinted from this in the "Journal des Débats" of January 3rd, 1857.' *Über den Willen in der Natur* (Frankfurt, 1836), expanded 3rd edn. 1867; trans. (Mme.) Karl Hillebrand, *On the Fourfold Root of the Principle of Sufficient Reason and The Will in Nature* (London: Bell, 1889), revised and reprinted 1891, pp. 215–380, p. 358 note.

15. Perry, ibid.
16. Perry, ibid.
17. Perry, ibid., Francis Underhill (Bishop), Chairman, 'Report to the Archbishop of Canterbury: Archbishop's Committee on Spiritualism' (1939), first published in *The Christian Parapsychologist*, Vol. 3, No. 2 (March 1979) pp. 40–73. Cf. the assessment of the terms and circumstances of the Report by Perry, 'Lang, Underhill and the 1939 Report', ibid., Vol. 3, No. 3 (June 1979) pp. 83–6. Cf. also Angus Haddow, 'The Churches and Psychical Research: A review of some twentieth-century official documents', ibid., Vol. 3, No. 9 (December 1980) pp. 291–303.
18. Perry, ibid., 'The Church of Scotland: Report of the Working Party on Parapsychology' (May 1976).
19. As a prime instance of the perniciousness/divisiveness of the doctrine, there may be mention of the recent and highly publicized pronouncement by Pope John-Paul II (August 1989) that, because of 'Israel's infidelity to God', this same Being, through Christ (and the Roman Church), came to make a *new* 'Covenant' with human kind for the working-out of his *Will*. The point is all the more worth making since, far from being the facile statement of an errant mind, it is one which goes to the very heart of the view in hand.
20. Cf. the consideration, as already delineated, that it is Bultmann's blurring of this distinction which, among other things, leads him in the direction of his later extravagance.
21. Cf. the conception as it is encapsulated in the major religions of the East. With this, too, is the fact of it being, also, a far from negligible strain within the stream of Christianity itself. Philosophically, as may be added, it is an idea which, again, may be traced, at least, to Plato.
22. Whyte, *The Unconscious Before Freud*, pp. 9–10. Cf. as given earlier, the same idea as expressed by Tillich. See above chap. 1 in this volume.

Bibliography

Works referred to in the text are given below. The full range of indebtedness is, of course, much wider than this.

Aquinas, Thomas, *Summa Theologica*.

Aristotle, *Physics*.

Aspect, Alain, Grangier, Phillipe, Roger, Gérard, 'Experimental Realization of Einstein–Podolsky–Rosen–Bohm, *Gedankenexperiment*: A New Violation of Bell's Inequalities', *Physical Review Letters*, Vol. 49, No. 2 (July 1982) pp. 91–4.

Aspect, Alain, Dalibard, Jean, Roger, Gérard, 'Experimental Test of Bell's Inequalities Using Time-Varying Analyzers', *Physical Review Letters*, Vol. 49, No. 25 (December 1982) pp. 1804–7.

Ayer, A. J., *Language, Truth and Logic* (London: Gollancz, 1936).

Barrett, William F., 'On Some Phenomena Associated with Abnormal Conditions of Mind', *Proceedings of the Society for Psychical Research*, I (1882–3) pp. 238–44.

Beattie, James, *Essay on the Nature and Immutability of Truth* (1770).

Bell, Clark, editor, *Spiritism, Hypnotism and Telepathy as involved in the case of Mrs. Leonora Piper* (New York: Medico-Legal Journal, 1902).

Bell, John S., 'On the Einstein–Podolsky–Rosen Paradox', *Physics* I (1965) pp. 195–200.

Bennett, John Hughes, *The Mesmeric Mania of 1851, with a Physiological Explanation of the Phenomena Produced* (Edinburgh: Sutherland and Knox, 1851).

Berkeley, George, *A Treatise Concerning the Principles of Human Nature* (1710).

Berkeley, George, *Three Dialogues between Hylas and Philonous* (1713).

Bernheim, Hippolyte, *De la suggestion dans l'état hypnotique et dans l'état de veille* (Paris: Doin, 1884).

Bernheim, Hippolyte, *De la suggestion et de ses applications à la thérapeutique* (Paris: Doins, 1886); trans. Christian A. Herter, under the title *Suggestive Therapeutics* (New York: Putnam, 1888); reprinted under the revised title *Hypnotism and Suggestion in Psychotherapy* (New York: University Books, 1964).

Bertrand, Alexandre, *Traité du somnambulisme et des différentes modifications qu'il présente* (Paris: Dentu, 1823).

Boden, Margaret, 'Miracles and Scientific Explanation', *Ratio*, Vol. xi, No. 2 (1969) pp. 137–44.

Bohm, David, 'The Paradox of Einstein, Rosen and Podolsky'; chap. 22, Sects. 15–19 of *Quantum Theory* (Englewood Cliffs: Prentice Hall, 1951) pp. 611–23.

Bohm, David, *Causality and Chance in Modern Physics* (London: Routledge, Kegan Paul, 1959/84).

Bohr, Niels, 'Quantum Mechanics and Physical Reality', *Nature*, 136 (1935) p. 65.

Bohr, Niels, 'Can Quantum–Mechanical Description of Physical Reality be Considered Complete?', *Physical Review*, 48 (1935) pp. 696–702.

Bohr, Niels, 'Discussions with Einstein on Epistemological Problems in Atomic Physics', *Atomic Physics and Human Knowledge* (New York/ London: Wiley, 1958) pp. 32–66.

Bonhoeffer, Dietrich, *Widerstand und Ergebung: Briefe und Aufzeichnungen aus der Haft*; trans. R.-Fuller, P. Clark, and others, *Letters and Papers from Prison*, enlarged edition, edited by E. Bethge (London: SCM, 1971).

Born, Max, *Moderne Physik* (1933), trans. J. Dougall, *Atomic Physics* (London/Glasgow: Blackie, 1935), 7th edn. (New York: Hafner, 1957).

Boscovich, Roger Joseph, *Theoria Philosophiæ Naturalis* (Venice, 1758).

Broad, C. D., 'Hume's Theory of the Credibility of Miracles', *Proceedings of the Aristotelian Society*, New Series XVII (1916–17) pp. 77–94; reprinted in A. Sesonske and N. Fleming (eds) *Human Understanding: Studies in the Philosophy of David Hume* (Belmont: Wadsworth, 1965) pp. 86–98.

Broad, C. D., 'Henry Sidgwick and Psychical Research', *Religion, Philosophy and Psychical Research: Selected Essays* (London: Routledge, Kegan Paul, 1953) pp. 86–115.

Broad, C. D., 'Immanuel Kant and Psychical Research', *Religion, Philosophy and Psychical Research: Selected Essays* (London: Routledge, Kegan Paul, 1953) pp. 116–55.

Broad, C. D., 'The Relevance of Psychical Research to Philosophy', *Religion, Philosophy and Psychical Research: Selected Essays* (London: Routledge, Kegan Paul, 1953) pp. 7–26.

Broad, C. D., *Lectures on Psychical Research, incorporating the Perrott Lectures given in Cambridge University in 1959 and 1960* (London: Routledge, Kegan Paul, 1962).

Broad, C. D., Foreword to *Swan on a Black Sea: A Study in Automatic Writing* ('The Cummins–Willett Scripts') (ed.) Signe Toksvig, (London: Routledge, Kegan Paul, 1963) pp. vii–lii.

Broad, C. D., *Leibniz: An Introduction*, edited by C. Lewy (Cambridge: Cambridge University Press, 1975).

Bultmann, Rudolf, and others, *Kerygma und Mythos: Ein Theologisches Gespräch*, edited by H. W. Bartsch (Hamburg: Reich, 1947), 2 vols., I, pp. 15–48, trans. R. H. Fuller, *Kerygma and Myth: A Theological Debate* (SPCK, London, 1953), 2 vols., I, pp. 1–44.

Bultmann, *Jesus Christ and Mythology* (New York: Scribner, 1958).

Bultmann, Rudolf and Jaspers, Karl, *Myth and Christianity: An Inquiry into the Possibility of Religion without Myth* (New York: Noonday, 1958).

Capra, Fritjof, *The Tao of Physics: An Examination of the Parallels between Modern Physics and Eastern Mysticism* (Boulder: Shambhala, 1975).

Carpenter, W. B., 'Spiritualism and its Modern Converts', *Quarterly Review* (October 1871).

Charcot, Jean-Martin, 'Sur les divers états nerveux déterminés par l'hypnotisation chez les hystériques', *Comptes-Rendus hebdomadaires des séances de l'Académie des Sciences*, XCIV (1882), I, pp. 403–5.

Charcot, Jean-Martin, 'Leçons sur les maladies du système nerveux', *Oeuvres Complètes* (Paris: Progrès Médical, 1890), III, pp. 299–359.

Charcot, Jean-Martin, 'La foi qui quérit', *Archives de Neurologie* XXV (1893) pp. 72–87.

Church of England – Underhill, Francis (Bishop), Chairman, 'Report to the Archbishop of Canterbury: Archbishop's Committee on Spiritualism' (1939); first published in *The Christian Parapsychologist*, Vol. 3, No. 2 (March 1979), pp. 40–73.

Church of Scotland – 'Report of the Working Party on Parapsychology' (May 1976).

Clauser, John and Shimony, Abner, 'Bell's Theorem; experimental tests and implications', *Reports on Progress in Physics*, Vol. 41 (1978) pp. 1881–1927.

Clifford, W. K., 'The Philosophy of the Pure Sciences', *Lectures and Essays*, ed L. Stephen and F. Pollock (London: Macmillan, 1879), 2 vols., I, pp. 254–340.

Clifford, W. K., 'On the Nature of Things-in-Themselves', *Lectures and Essays*; edited by L. Stephen and F. Pollock (London: Macmillan, 1879), 2 vols., II, pp. 71–88.

Crookes, William, 'Experimental Investigation of a New Force', *Quarterly Journal of Science* (July 1871); later incorporated by Crookes into his book *Researches in the Phenomena of Spiritualism* (London: Burns, 1874).

Crookes, William, 'Some Further Experiments on Psychic Force', *Quarterly Journal of Science* (October 1871); later incorporated by Crookes into his book *Researches in the Phenomena of Spiritualism* (London: Burns, 1874).

Crookes, William, *Psychic Force and Modern Spiritualism: A Reply to the 'Quarterly Review'* – special pamphlet; reprinted in R. G. Medhurst, K. M. Goldney and M. R. Barrington, *Crookes and the Spirit World; a collection of writings by or concerning the work of Sir William Crookes, O.M., F.R.S. in the field of psychical research* (London: Souvenir, 1972) pp. 61–92.

Crookes, William, 'Notes of an Enquiry into the Phenomena called Spiritual', *Quarterly Journal of Science* (January 1874); later incorporated by Crookes into his book *Researches in the Phenomena of Spiritualism* (London: Burns, 1874).

Crookes, William, *Researches in the Phenomena of Spiritualism* (London: Burns, 1874).

Crookes, William, *Presidential Address to the British Association for the Advancement of Science, 1898*.

Cross, F. L., ed. *Oxford Dictionary of the Christian Church* (Oxford: Oxford University Press, 1957).

Darnton, Robert, *Mesmerism and the End of the Enlightenment in France* (Cambridge, Mass.: Harvard University Press, 1968).

Davies, Paul, *God and the New Physics* (London/Melbourne: Dent, 1983); reprinted (London: Pelican, 1984).

Davis, Andrew Jackson ('by and through'), *The Principles of Nature, Her Divine Revelations, and a Voice to Mankind* (New York: Lyon and Fishbough, 1847).

Descartes, René, *Discours de la méthode/Discourse on Method* (1637).

Descartes, René, *Meditationes de Prima Philosophia/Meditations on First Philosophy* (1641).

Dessoir, Max, *Bibliographie des modernum Hypnotismus* (Berlin: Düncker, 1888).

Diamond, Malcolm, 'Miracles', *Religious Studies*, Vol. 9 (1973) pp. 307–24.

Dietl, Paul, 'On Miracles', *American Philosophical Quarterly*, Vol. 5, No. 2 (April 1968) pp. 130–4.

Dobbs, B. J. T., *The Foundations of Newton's Alchemy* (Cambridge: Cambridge University Press, 1975).

Eddington, Arthur, *The Nature of the Physical World* (Cambridge: Cambridge University Press, 1929).

Eddington, Arthur, *The Philosophy of Physical Science* (Cambridge: Cambridge University Press, 1939).

Einstein, Albert, Podolsky, Boris, Rosen, Nathan, 'Can Quantum-Mechanical Description of Physical Reality be Considered Complete?' *Physical Review*, 47 (1935) pp. 777–80.

Ellenberger, Henri F., *The Discovery of the Unconscious: The History and Evolution of Dynamic Psychiatry* (New York: Basic Books, 1970).

Elliotson, John, *Numerous Cases of Surgical Operations Without Pain in the Mesmeric State* (Philadelphia: Lee and Blanchard, 1843); reprinted in *Significant Contributions to the History of Psychology*, Series 'A', ed Daniel N. Robinson, Vol. X (Washington, D.C.: University Publications of America, 1977).

Esdaile, James, *Mesmerism in India and its Practical Application in Surgery and Medicine* (London: Longman, Brown, Green and Longmans, 1846); reprinted in *Significant Contributions to the History of Psychology*, Series 'A', edited by Daniel N. Robinson, Vol. X (Washington, D.C.: University Publications of America, 1977).

Farrer, Austin, 'The *Kerygma* Debate – An English Appreciation', Rudolf Bultmann, and others, *Kerygma and Myth* (London: SPCK, 1953) I, pp. 212–22.

Fechner, Gustav Theodor, *Elemente der Psychophysik* (Leipzig, 1860), II.

Flew, Antony, *God and Philosophy* (London: Hutchinson, 1966).

Frankfort, H. and Frankfort, H. A., *Before Philosophy* (London: Pelican, 1949); originally published as *The Intellectual Adventure of Ancient Man* (Chicago: Chicago University Press, 1946).

Freud, Sigmund, *Die Zukunft Einer Illusion* (Leipzig/Vienna/Zurich, 1927); trans. W. D. Robson-Scott, *The Future of An Illusion* (London: Hogarth, 1928).

Gauld, Alan, *The Founders of Psychical Research* (London: Routledge, Kegan Paul, 1968).

Geller, Uri, *My Story* (New York: Praeger, 1975).

Gunkel, Hermann, *Die Wirkungen des Heiligen Geistes* (Göttingen: Vandenhoeck and Ruprecht, 1888).

Gurney, Edmund, *The Power of Sound* (London: Smith and Elder, 1880).

Gurney, Edmund and Myers, Frederic W. H., '[First] Report of the Literary Committee', *Proceedings of the Society for Psychical Research*, I (1882–3) pp. 116–55.

Gurney, Edmund, with Myers, F. W. H. and Podmore, F. *Phantasms of the Living* (London: Society for Psychical Research, 1886), 2 vols.

Haddow, Angus, 'The Churches and Psychical Research: A Review of some twentieth century official documents', *The Christian Parapsychologist*, Vol. 3, No. 9 (December 1980), pp. 291–303.

Hall, Trevor H., *The Spiritualists* (London: Duckworth, 1962).

Hardy, Alister, Presidential Address, Zoology Section, British Association for the Advancement of Science, *The Advancement of Science*, Vol. VI, No. 21 (1949), pp. 213–23.

Hardy, Alister, *The Living Stream: A Restatement of Evolution Theory and its Relation to the Spirit of Man* (London: Collins, 1965).

Hasted, John, Bohm, David, Bastin, E. W., O'Reagan, B., *Nature* 254 (April 1975) pp. 470–2.

Hasted, John, 'An Experimental Study of the Validity of the Metal Bending Phenomena', *Journal of the Society for Psychical Research*, Vol. 48, No. 770 (December 1976) pp. 365–83.

Hasted, John, 'Physical Aspects of Paranormal Metal Bending' *Journal of the Society for Psychical Research*, Vol. 49, No. 773 (September 1977) pp. 583–91.

Hasted, John, *The Metal-Benders* (London: Routledge, Kegan Paul, 1981).

Hawking, Stephen W., *A Brief History of Time: From the Big Bang to Black Holes* (New York/London: Bantam, 1988).

Heidenhain, Rudolf, *Der sog thierische Magnetismus: Physiologische Beobachtungen* (Leipzig: Breitkopf and Härtel, 1880); trans. L. C. Woolridge *Hypnotism or Animal Magnetism* (London: Paul, 1880), with a Preface by George Romanes.

Heisenberg, Werner, 'Fresh Fields', *Physics and Beyond: Encounters and Conversations*; trans. Arnold J. Pomerans, (New York/London: Harper and Row, 1971) pp. 70–81.

Heisenberg, Werner, *Across the Frontiers*; trans. Peter Heath, (New York/London: Harper and Row, 1974).

Hodgson, Richard, 'An Account of Personal Investigations in India and Discussion of the Authorship of the "Koot Hoomi" Letters', *Proceedings of the Society for Psychical Research*, III (1885) pp. 207–380.

Hodgson, Richard, 'A Record of Observations of Certain Phenomena of Trance', *Proceedings of the Society for Psychical Research*, VIII (1892) pp. 1–167.

Hodgson, Richard, 'A Further Record of Observations of Certain Phenomena of Trance'. *Proceedings of the Society for Psychical Research*, XIII (1897–8) pp. 284–582.

Holland, R. F., 'The Miraculous', *American Philosophical Quarterly*, Vol. 2, No. 1 (1965) pp. 43–51.

Home, Daniel Dunglas, Mme., *D. D. Home: His Life and Mission* (London: Trubner, 1888).

Hume, David, *A Treatise of Human Nature* (1739).

Hume, David, *An Enquiry concerning the Human Understanding* (1748), ed L. A. Selby-Bigge, *Enquiries concerning Human Understanding and concerning the Principles of Morals* (Oxford: Clarendon, 1902) 3rd edn 1975.

Hume, David, *The Letters of David Hume*; edited by J. Y. T Greig (Oxford: Clarendon, 1932), 2 vols.

Huxley, T. H., *Science and Christian Tradition: Essays* (London: Macmillan, 1894).

Hyslop, J. H., 'A Further Record of Observations of Certain Trance Phenomena', *Proceedings of the Society for Psychical Research*, XVI (1901) pp. 1–649.

Inglis, Brian, *Natural and Supernatural* (London: Hodder and Stoughton, 1978); reprinted (London: Sphere Books, 1979).

Inglis, Brian, *The Hidden Power* (London: Cape, 1986).

James, William, *William James on Psychical Research*, ed Gardner Murphy, and Robert O. Ballou (London: Chatto and Windus, 1960).

James, William, 'Report of the Committee on Mediumistic Phenomena', *Proceedings of the American Society for Psychical Research* I (1886–9); reprinted under the title 'A Record of Observations of Certain Phenomena of Trance', *Proceedings of the Society for Psychical Research* VI (1889–90) pp. 651–9.

James, William, Presidential Address to the Society for Psychical Research, *Proceedings of the Society for Psychical Research*, XII (1896–7) pp. 2–10.

James, William, 'What Psychical Research has Accomplished', *The Will to Believe and Other Essays in Popular Philosophy* (New York: Longmans, Green, 1897) pp. 299–327.

James, William, *Human Immortality: Two Supposed Objections to the Doctrine* (London: Watt, 1898).

James, William, *The Varieties of Religious Experience: A Study in Human Nature* (London: Longmans, 1902).

James, William, 'Frederic Myers' Services to Psychology', *Memories and Studies*, (New York: Longmans, Green, 1911) pp. 145–70.

James, William, *The Letters of William James*, ed (his son) Henry James (Boston: Atlantic Monthly Press, 1920) 2 vols., I.

Janet, Pierre, *Les médications psychologiques* (Paris: Alcan, 1919).

Jaynes, Julian, *The Origin of Consciousness in the Breakdown of the Bicameral Mind* (Boston: Houghton Mifflin, 1976).

Jenkins, Elizabeth, *The Shadow and the Light: A Defence of Daniel Dunglas Home the Medium* (London: Hamish Hamilton, 1982).

Jones, Ernest, *Sigmund Freud: Life and Work* (London: Hogarth, 1953), 2 vols., I.

Jung, Carl, *Naturerklärung und Psyche* (Zurich: Rascher, 1952); trans. R. F. C. Hull, *Synchronicity: An Acausal Connecting Principle* (London: Routledge, Kegan Paul, 1972).

Kant, Immanuel, *Traüme eines Geistersehers erläutert durch Traüme der Metaphysik* (1766) *Schriften* (Ak. Ed.), II pp. 315–73; trans. Emanuel F. Goerwitz, edited and notes by Frank Sewell, *Dreams of a Spirit Seer* (London: Swan, Sonnenschein, 1890).

Kant, Immanuel, *De Mundi Sensibilis atque Intelligibilis Forma et Principiis* (1770), *Schriften* (Ak. Ed.), II pp. 385–419; trans. and introduced G. B. Kerford, and D. E. Walford, 'On the Form and Principles of the Sensible and Intelligible World', *Kant: Selected Pre-Critical Writings and Correspond-*

ence with Beck (Manchester: Manchester University Press, 1968) pp. 47–92.

Kant, Immanuel, *Kritik der reinen Vernunft* (1781, 1787), *Schriften* (Ak. Ed.), III, IV; trans. Norman Kemp Smith, *Immanuel Kant's 'Critique of Pure Reason'* (London: Macmillan, 1929).

Kant, Immanuel, *Prolegomena zu einer jeden künftigen Metaphysik die als Wissenschaft wird auftreten können* (1783), *Schriften* (Ak. Ed.), IV, pp. 253–383; trans. and introduced by Lewis White Beck, *Prolegomena to any Future Metaphysics* (Indianapolis/New York: Bobbs-Merrill, 1951).

Kant, Immanuel, *Metaphysische Anfangsgründe der Naturwissenschaft* (1786), *Schriften* (Ak. Ed.), IV, pp. 445–563; trans. and introduced by J. Ellington, *Metaphysical Foundations of Natural Science* (Indianapolis/New York: Bobbs-Merrill, 1970).

Kant, Immanuel, *Die Religion innerhalb der Grenzen der blossen Vernunft* (1793), *Schriften* (Ak. Ed.) VI, pp. 1–292, trans. with an introduction and notes by Theodore M. Greene and Hoyt H. Hudson *Religion within the Limits of Reason Alone* (Chicago: Open Court, 1934).

Kant, Immanuel, *Anthropologie in pragmatischer Hinsicht abgefasst* (1798), *Schriften* (Ak. Ed.) VII, pp. 117–333; trans. and introduced by M. J. Gregor, *Anthropology from a Pragmatic Point of View* (Hague: Nijhoff, 1974)

Kant, Immanuel, *Lose Blätter, Schriften* (Ak. Ed.) XVIII.

Kant, Immanuel, *Opus Postumum, Schriften* (Ak. Ed.) XXII.

Kant, Immanuel, *Kant: Philosophical Correspondence, 1759–99*; trans. and ed Zweig, Arnulf (Chicago: Chicago University Press, 1967).

Kerner, Julius, *Die Seherin von Prevorst: Eröffnungen über das innere Leben und über das Hineinragen einer Geisterwelt in die unsere* (Stuttgart/Tübingen, Cotta, 1829), 2 vols.; trans. Mrs. Crane, *The Seeress of Prevorst, being revelations concerning the inner-life of man, and the inter-diffusion of a world of spirits in the world we inhabit* (New York: Harper, 1845).

Koestler, Arthur, *The Sleepwalkers* (London: Hutchinson, 1959).

Landrum, George, 'What a Miracle Really Is', *Religious Studies* 12 (1976) pp. 49–57.

Laplace, Pierre, de, *Oeuvres Complètes de Laplace* (Paris: Gautier Villars, 1878–1912), Vol. viii.

Latta, R., *Leibniz: The Monadology and Other Philosophical Writings*, trans. and introduced by Latta, Introduction, pp. 1–211.

Lecky, W. E. H., *History of the Rise and Influence of the Spirit of Rationalism in Europe* (London: Longmans, Green, 1865); reprinted (New York: Braziller, 1955).

Leibniz, Gottfried W., *Essais de Théodicée sur la Bonté de Dieu, la Liberté de l'Homme et l'Origine du Mal* (Amsterdam, 1710).

Leibniz, Gottfried W./Clarke, Samuel. *The Leibniz Clarke Correspondence* (1717); edited and with a Preface by H. G. Alexander (Manchester: Manchester University Press, 1956).

Leibniz, Gottfried W., *Nouveaux Essais sur l'entendement humain* (Leipzig, 1765); trans. P. Remnant and J. Bennett, *New Essays on Human Understanding* (Cambridge: Cambridge University Press, 1981).

Leibniz, Gottfried W., 'Monadologie'/'Monadology' (1840); trans. Leroy E.

Loemker, *Leibniz: Philosophical Papers and Letters* (Chicago: Chicago University Press, 1956), pp. 643–52.

Lewis, C. S., *Miracles* (London/New York: Macmillan, 1947).

Lewis, E. E., *A Report of the Mysterious Noises heard in the House of Mr. John D. Fox, in Hydesville, Arcadia, Wayne County* (Canadaigua: E. E. Lewis, 1848).

Liébeault, Ambroise, *Pour constater la réalité du magnétisme. Confession d'un hypnotiseur. Extériorisation de la force neurique ou fluide magnétique* (Paris: Libraire du Magnétisme, n.d.).

Liébeault, Ambroise, *Du sommeil et des états analogues, considérés surtout au point de vue de l'action du moral sur le physique* (Paris: Masson, 1866).

Liébeault, Ambroise, *Le sommeil provoqué et les états analogues* (Paris: Doin, 1889).

Locke, John, *Essay Concerning Human Understanding* (1690).

Lodge, Oliver/Myers, F. W. H./Leaf, W. 'A Record of Observations of Certain Phenomena of Trance', *Proceedings of the Society for Psychical Research*, VI (1889–90) pp. 436–650.

Mach, Ernst, *Die Mechanick in ihrer Entwickelung Historisch-Kritische Dargestellt* (Leipzig: Brockhaus, 1883); trans. T. J. McCormack, *The Science of Mechanics: A Critical and Historical Account of its Development* (Chicago: Open Court, 1893), 6th edn., 1960.

Marcuse, F. L., *Hypnosis: Fact and Fiction* (London: Pelican, 1959).

Maxwell, James Clerk, 'Molecules', *Nature*, VIII (1873); reprinted in *The Scientific Papers of James Clerk Maxwell*, edited by W. D. Niven (Cambridge: Cambridge University Press, 1890), 2 vols., II.

McEachran, F., *The Life and Philosophy of J. G. Herder* (Oxford: Clarendon, 1939).

McKinnon, Alastair, '"Miracles" and "Paradox"', *American Philosophical Quarterly*, Vol. 4, No. 4 (1967) pp. 308–14.

Medhurst, R. G./Goldney, K. M./Barrington, M. R., *Crookes and the Spirit World: A collection of writings by or concerning the work of Sir William Crookes, O.M., F.R.S., in the field of psychical research* (London: Souvenir, 1972).

Mesmer, Franz Anton, *Mémoire sur la découverte du magnétisme animal* (Paris: Didot, 1779).

Moore, R. Lawrence, *In Search of White Crows: Spiritualism, Parapsychology and American Culture* (New York: Oxford University Press, 1977).

Moses, William Stainton ('M.A. Oxon.'), *Spirit Teachings* (London: London Psychological Press, 1883).

Myers, Frederic W. H., *Fragments of Inner Life* (Private printing, 1893); reprinted (London: Society for Psychical Research, 1961).

Myers, Frederic W. H., 'In Memory of Henry Sidgwick', *Proceedings of the Society for Psychical Research*, XV (1900–1) pp. 452–62.

Myers, Frederic W. H., *Human Personality and its Survival of Bodily Death* (London: Longmans, Green, 1903), 2 vols.; abridged version with a Foreword by Aldous Huxley (New York: University Books, 1961).

Newbold, W. R., 'A Further Record of Observations of Certain Phenomena of Trance, Pt. II', *Proceedings of the Society for Psychical Research*, XIV (1898–9) pp. 6–49.

Newsome, D. H., *Godliness and Good Learning* (London: Murray, 1961).

Newton, Isaac, *Opticks* (1704) – (New York: Dover, 1952).

Noizet, François, *Mémoire sur le somnambulisme et le magnétisme animal* (Paris: Plon, 1854).

Nowell-Smith, Patrick, 'Miracles', *Hibbert Journal*, xlviii (1950) pp. 354–60; reprinted in *New Essays in Philosophical Theology*, ed A. Flew and A. McIntyre (London: SCM, 1955) pp. 243–53.

Odegard, Douglas, 'Miracles and Good Evidence', *Religious Studies*, Vol. 18 (1982) pp. 37–46.

Paley, William, *A View of the Evidences of Christianity* (1794).

Paley, William, *Natural Theology* (1802).

Panati, C. (ed.), *The Geller Papers: Scientific Observations on the Paranormal Powers of Uri Geller* (Boston: Houghton Mifflin, 1976).

Parker, Theodore, *Life and Correspondence of Theodore Parker*; ed John Weiss (New York: Appleton, 1864), 2 vols, I.

Penelhum, Terence, *Hume* (London: Macmillan, 1975).

Perry, Michael, 'The psychic and the spiritual', *The Times* (London, 20 February 1982) p. 8; reprinted in Michael Perry, *Psychic Studies: A Christian View* (London: Aquarian Press, 1984) pp. 26–8.

Perry, Michael, 'Lang, Underhill and the 1939 Report', ed Michael Perry *The Christian Parapsychologist*, Vol. 3, No. 3 (June 1979) pp. 83–6.

Piper, Alta, L., *The Life and Work of Mrs. Piper* (London: Kegan Paul, Trench and Trubner, 1929), with an introduction by Sir Oliver Lodge.

Plato, *The Republic*.

Plato, *Timaeus*.

Pliny, the Younger, *Letters and Panegyricus* 2 vols., I; trans. Betty Radice (Cambridge, Mass.: Harvard University Press, 1969).

Podmore, Frank, 'Discussion of the Trance-Phenomena of Mrs. Piper', *Proceedings of the Society for Psychical Research* XIV (1898–9) pp. 50–78.

Podmore, Frank, *From Mesmer to Christian Science: A Short History of Mental Healing* (London: Methuen, 1909); reprinted (New York: University Books, 1963).

Podmore, Frank, *Modern Spiritualism: A History and Criticism* (London: Methuen, 1902) 2 vols., I.

Puységur, Armand-Marie-Jacques de Chastenet, Marquis de, *Mémoires pour servir à l'histoire et à l'établissement du magnétisme animal* (1784), 2nd edn (Paris: Cellot, 1809).

Puységur, Armand-Marie-Jacques de Chastenet, Marquis de, *Du magnétisme animal, considéré dans ses rapports avec diverses branches de la physique générale* (Paris: Desenne, 1807).

Quin, (W.T.W.), 4th Earl of Dunraven, *Experiences in Spiritualism with Mr. D. D. Home* (London: Thomas Scott, 1869); reprinted with an introduction by Sir Oliver Lodge (London: Society for Psychical Research, 1924).

Rae, Alastair I. M., *Quantum physics: illusion or reality* (Cambridge: Cambridge University Press, 1986).

Rae, Alastair I. M., 'Extrasensory quantum physics', *New Scientist*, Vol. 112, No. 1536 (November 1986), pp. 36–9.

Randi, James, *The Magic of Uri Geller* (Buffalo: Prometheus, 1975); reprinted as *The Truth about Uri Geller: One of the most eye-opening exposes* [sic] *of the decade about psychic claims and magic* (Buffalo: Prometheus, 1982).

Rhine, J. B., *New Frontiers of the Mind* (New York/Toronto: Farrar and Rinehart, 1937); reprinted (London: Pelican, 1950).

Richet, Charles, 'Du somnambulisme provoqué' *Journal de l'Anatomie et de la Physiologie normales et pathologiques de l'homme et des animaux*, II (1875) pp. 348–77.

Richet, Charles, *Notre sixième sense* (Paris: Montaigne, 1928); translated by Fred Rothwell, *Our Sixth Sense* (London: Rider, 1929).

Robinson, Guy, 'Miracles', *Ratio*, Vol. ix, No. 2 (1967) pp. 155–66.

Robinson, John A. T., *Honest to God* (London: SCM, 1963).

Robinson, John A. T., 'The Debate Continues', *The Honest to God Debate: Some Reactions to the book 'Honest to God' with a new chapter by its author, John A. T. Robinson*, ed D. L. Edwards (London: SCM, 1963) pp. 232–75.

Russell, Bertrand, *History of Western Philosophy* (London: Allen and Unwin, 1946).

Sage, M., *Madame Piper et la Société anglo-americaine pour les recherches psychiques* (Paris: Lemarie, 1902), préface de Camille Flammarion; abridged English version by N. Robertson, *Mrs. Piper and the Society for Psychical Research* (London: Johnson, 1903) with a Preface by Sir Oliver Lodge.

Schniewind, Julius, 'A Reply to Bultmann' (1943), *Kerygma and Myth* (London: SCM, 1953), I, pp. 45–101.

Schopenhauer, Arthur, *Die Welt als Wille und Vorstellung* (Leipzig: Brockhaus, 1819), 2nd edn. 1844; trans. E. F. J. Payne, *The World as Will and Representation* (New York: Dover, 1958), 2 vols.

Schopenhauer, Arthur, *Über den Willen in der Natur* (Frankfurt, 1836), expanded 3rd edn. 1867; trans. (Mme) Karl Hillebrand, *On the Fourfold Root of the Principle of Sufficient Reason and the Will in Nature* (London: Bell, 1889), revised and reprinted 1891, pp. 215–380.

Schopenhauer, Arthur, 'Versuch über das Geistersehn und was damit zusammenhängt', *Parerga und Paralipomena* (1851), *Sämtliche Werke* (Wiesbaden: Brokhaus, 1960), V, pp. 239–329; trans. E. F. J. Payne, 'Essay on Spirit Seeing and everything connected therewith', *Parerga and Paralipomena* (Oxford: Clarendon, 1974) 2 Vols., I, pp. 227–309.

Schrödinger, Erwin, *What is Life? The Physical Aspects of the Living Cell* (Cambridge: Cambridge University Press, 1945).

Schrödinger, Erwin, *Mind and Matter* (Cambridge: Cambridge University Press, 1958).

Sidgwick, Eleanor (Mrs)/Johnson, Alice, 'Report on the Census of Hallucinations', *Proceedings of the Society for Psychical Research* X (1894) pp. 25–422.

Sidgwick, Eleanor (Mrs.), 'Discussion of the Trance Phenomena of Mrs. Piper', *Proceedings of the Society for Psychical Research*, XXVIII (1915) pp. 1–657.

Sidgwick, Henry, *The Methods of Ethics* (London: Macmillan, 1874).

Sidgwick, Henry (with others), *Proceedings of the Society for Psychical Research* (July, 1882), I (1883) pp. 3–4.

Sidgwick, Henry, Presidential Address to the (newly formed) Society for Psychical Research, *Proceedings of the Society for Psychical Research*, I (1882–3) pp. 7–12.

Smart, Ninian, 'Miracles and David Hume', *Philosophers and Religious Truth* (London: SCM, 1964) pp. 25–56.

Smith, Norman Kemp, *A Commentary to Kant's 'Critique of Pure Reason'* (London: Macmillan, 1923).

Solzhenitsyn, Aleksander, *The Cancer Ward*; trans. Rebecca Frank, (New York: Dial, 1968).

Spanes, Nicholas P./Barber, Theodore X., 'Towards a Convergence in Hypnosis Research', *American Psychologist*, Vol. 29, No. 7 (July, 1974) pp. 500–11.

Swinburne, Richard, *The Concept of a Miracle* (London: Macmillan, 1970).

Taylor, John, *Nature* 254 (April 1975) pp. 472–3.

Taylor, John, *Superminds: An Enquiry into the Paranormal* (London: Macmillan, 1975).

Taylor, John, *Science and the Supernatural* (London: Panther, 1980).

Tetens, N. N., *Philosophische Versuche* (1777).

Thielicke, Helmut, 'The Restatement of New Testament Mythology', *Kerygma and Myth* (London: SCM, 1953), I, pp. 138–74.

Thompson, Roger, *The Witches of Salem* (London: Folio, 1982).

Tillich, Paul, *The Shaking of the Foundations* (New York: Scribner, 1948).

Tillich, Paul, *Systematic Theology* (London: Nisbet, 1964), 3 vols., I.

Treves, Frederick, *The Elephant Man and other Reminiscences* (London: Cassel, 1923).

Vleeschauwer, Herman-J, de, *L'Évolution de la pensée Kantienne* (1939); trans. A. R. C. Duncan, *The Development of Kantian Thought* (Edinburgh: Nelson, 1962).

Wallace, Alfred Russel, *Miracles and Modern Spiritualism* (London/Glasgow, 1875); 2nd edn. (London: Trubner, 1886); reprinted (New York: Arno, 1975).

Wallace, Alfred Russel, *My Life: A Record of Events and Opinions* (London: Chapman and Hall, 1905), 2 vols., II.

Wheeler, John Archibald, 'Beyond the End of Time', C. Misner/K. S. Thorne/Wheeler, *Gravitation* (San Francisco: Freeman, 1973), pp. 1196–1217.

Whitehead, Alfred North, *Process and Reality: An Essay in Cosmology* (London: Macmillan, 1929).

Whittaker, Edmund, *A History of the Theories of the Aether and Electricity* (London: Nelson, 1910) revised and enlarged, 1951; reprinted (New York: Harper, 1960), 2 vols.

Whyte, L. L., *The Unconscious Before Freud* (New York: Basic Books, 1960).

Whyte, L. L., editor and main contributor, *Roger Joseph Boscovich, S.J., F.R.S., 1711–1787; Studies of His life and Work on the 250th Anniversary of his Birth* (London: Allen and Unwin, 1961).

Williams, T. C., *The Unity of Kant's 'Critique of Pure Reason': Experience, Language and Knowledge* (Lewiston/Queenston: Mellen, 1987).

Zöllner, J. C. Friedrich, 'On Space of Four Dimensions', *Quarterly Journal of*

Science (April 1878), later reprinted by Zöllner as the first chapter of his *Die transcendentale Physik.*

Zöllner, J. C. Friedrich, *Die transcendentale Physik und die sogenannte Philosophie* (Leipzig, 1879); trans. C. C. Massey, *Transcendental Physics* (London: Harrison, 1880).

Zukav, Gary, *The Dancing Wu Li Masters: An Overview of the New Physics* (New York: Morrow, 1979).

Index